T0225678

AUTOMATED PHYSICAL DATABASE DESIGN and TUNING

EMERGING DIRECTIONS IN DATABASE SYSTEMS AND APPLICATIONS

Series Editor
Sham Navathe
Professor
Georgia Institute of Technology
College of Computing
Atlanta, Georgia, U.S.A.

Automated Physical Database Design and Tuning, Nicolas Bruno
Patterns of Data Modeling, Michael Blaha

Forthcoming Publications

Advanced Data Management, Edward Omiecinski
Bioinformatics Database Systems, Jason T.L. Wang and Katherine G. Herbert

AUTOMATED PHYSICAL DATABASE DESIGN and TUNING

NICOLAS BRUNO

CRC Press
Taylor & Francis Group
Boca Raton   London   New York

CRC Press is an imprint of the
Taylor & Francis Group, an **informa** business

CRC Press
Taylor & Francis Group
6000 Broken Sound Parkway NW, Suite 300
Boca Raton, FL 33487-2742

First issued in paperback 2017

© 2011 by Taylor and Francis Group, LLC
CRC Press is an imprint of Taylor & Francis Group, an Informa business

No claim to original U.S. Government works

ISBN 13: 978-1-138-11406-7 (pbk)
ISBN 13: 978-1-4398-1567-0 (hbk)

Visit the Taylor & Francis Web site at
http://www.taylorandfrancis.com

and the CRC Press Web site at
http://www.crcpress.com

To Pia, Tomas, and Lucas

Contents

Preface

Relational database systems have evolved significantly since their inception over 30 years ago. New applications are now more complex than ever, and tuning a production system for performance has become a critical yet time-consuming activity. Due to the increasing complexity in both application workloads and query engines, even experienced database administrators (or DBAs) cannot fully understand the ramifications of tuning decisions throughout the whole system. As a consequence, the industry began providing automated tuning tools that systematically explore the space of alternatives and guide DBAs. A critical element of such tuning is physical database design, because the choice of physical structures—such as indexes—has a significant impact on the performance of the database system. In this book we present a detailed overview of the fundamental ideas and algorithms to automatically recommend changes to the physical design of a database system.

Book Organization

The book is divided into three parts. In the first part (Chapters 1 to 3) we introduce the necessary technical background to better understand the remaining chapters. Specifically, in Chapter 1 we briefly introduce SQL, the most widely used language to query database systems, and the space of execution plans that can be used to answer SQL queries. In Chapter 2 we give an overview of query optimization (which translates SQL queries into efficient execution plans) and argue that the choice of access paths (e.g., indexes) is crucial for performance. In Chapter 3 we formally introduce the physical design problem, show that it is algorithmically difficult to solve, and review initial research in the literature.

In the second part (Chapters 4 to 7) we extensively discuss automated physical design techniques. Specifically, we cover the fundamental research ideas in the last 15 years that resulted in a new generation of tuning tools. To simplify the presentation we exclusively focus on indexes (but we lift this restriction in Chapters 8 and 9). We organize the discussion into the search space of alternatives (Chapter 4), the necessity of a cost model to compare such alternatives (Chapter 5), and different mechanisms to traverse and enumerate the search space (Chapter 6). We finally discuss practical aspects in real-world tuning tools (Chapter 7).

In the third part (Chapters 8 to 12) we explore new advances in the area of automated physical design. In Chapters 8 and 9 we generalize previous approaches to other physical structures, such as materialized views, partitioning, and multidimensional clustering. In Chapter 10 we analyze different workload models for new types of applications. In Chapter 11 we generalize the optimizing function of current physical design tools to cope with other application scenarios. Finally, in Chapter 12 we discuss some open-ended challenges in the area of physical database design.

Scope

We believe that this book would be a good addition to the repertoire of database professionals in both academia and industry. Database faculty and students will find valuable insights on well-established principles and cutting-edge research results in the area of automated physical design. The book will also help experienced DBAs to gain a deeper understanding on how automated tuning tools work in database installations and the different challenges and opportunities that will be involved in designing next-generation tuning tools.

Acknowledgments

Large portions of this book originated from research papers conceived in the DMX group at Microsoft Research in collaboration with Surajit Chaudhuri (the ACM, IEEE, and VLDB organizations gave permissions to reuse and adapt previously published material in this book). Many thanks to Sanjay Agrawal, Arvind Arasu, Surajit Chaudhuri, César Galindo-Legaria, Raghav Kaushik, Christian König, Alan Lazzarich, Vivek Narasayya, Ravi Ramamurthy, and Manoj Syamala for giving very useful feedback that improved many aspects of the book presentation.

Part I

Background

Chapter 1

Declarative Query Processing in Relational Database Systems

A common approach to classify programming languages is around *paradigms*, broadly defined as fundamental styles of computer programming. A traditional classification distinguishes between imperative languages (in which we specify *how* to obtain results) and declarative languages (in which we specify *what* we want without detailing *how* to reach the answer).* In this chapter we contrast these two approaches and motivate the declarative capabilities of Structured Query Language (SQL), the most prevalent query language in relational database systems. We then briefly review how SQL queries are evaluated in modern systems and how, in turn, query processing is influenced by the availability of database indexes. As a consequence, the set of available indexes, or the *physical design* of a database, is a very important aspect for performance tuning. We next motivate the physical database design problem and note that, unless done automatically, it conflicts with the goal of a declarative language. In fact, understanding which are the right indexes for a given query (or set of queries) forces us to think about *how* queries would be evaluated. Any effective step toward a solution to the physical design problem not only would make application development more declarative but also would decrease the total cost of ownership of database installations.

1.1 An Exercise in Imperative Programming

Suppose that we have two arrays of integers, R and S, and we need to compute the number of times that some element in R matches some element in S, including duplicates (let us denote this functionality by countMatches). The

---

*This distinction has been recently blurred by advances in programming languages. We now have declarative dialects in imperative languages (e.g., LInQ dialects in the Microsoft .NET framework) and procedural extensions to declarative languages.

C# code fragment below illustrates how we could use `countMatches` to count matching pairs of elements:

```
int[] R = new int[] { 1, 2, 3, 4, 4, 5 };
int[] S = new int[] { 2, 2, 4, 4, 4, 4, 6, 8 };
int result = countMatches(R, S); // result should be 10
```

A simple and efficient implementation of `countMatches`, called `count-Matches1`, is shown in Figure 1.1. This function exhaustively enumerates all possible pairs of elements from arrays R and S and accumulates in variable c the total number of matches. The complexity of `countMatches1` is $\mathcal{O}(N^2)$, where $N = \max(|R|, |S|)$. Note also that `countMatches1` does not require additional memory (other than the return variable) to compute the result.

If we can use additional memory, `countMatches1` can be improved by creating a hash table of distinct values from R (along with their multiplicities) and probing this hash table for each element in S. The algorithm `countMatches2` in Figure 1.1 illustrates this approach. The complexity of `countMatches2` is $\mathcal{O}(N)$, where $N = \max(|R|, |S|)$. Except for very small inputs (where the overhead of maintaining the hash table becomes noticeable) `countMatches2` would generally outperform `countMatches1`. Furthermore, it seems that we cannot do much better than `countMatches2`.

In certain situations, however, we may outperform `countMatches2` by exploiting certain characteristics of the input arrays. Suppose, for instance, that both R and S are sorted. In that situation, we can use the alternative function `countMatches3` in Figure 1.1. The idea in `countMatches3` is to synchronously traverse both ordered arrays and skip elements from one array that are guaranteed not to match any element in the other (this procedure leverages the fact that both arrays are sorted). Once we locate a match, we compute the multiplicity of the value in both arrays and update the total count. The complexity of `countMatches3` is $\mathcal{O}(N)$, where $N = \max(|R|, |S|)$, the same as that of `countMatches2`. In practice, however, `countMatches3` is faster than `countMatches2` because it does not require allocating memory and maintaining hash tables.

Interestingly enough, if at least one array is sorted, we can use a different approach that computes the result without necessarily examining all the elements in both arrays. Suppose that S is sorted. We can then traverse each element r in R and locate, using binary search, the smallest position in S with an element greater than or equal to r. Then, we traverse matching elements in S (if any) and accumulate the results. The algorithm `countMatches4` in Figure 1.1 illustrates this approach. The complexity of `countMatches4` is $\mathcal{O}(|R| \cdot \log |S|)$. Depending on the actual sizes of R and S, `countMatches4` can be the fastest, slowest, or anything in between compared with the alternative approaches.

We have so far described several possible algorithms to calculate our desired answer and have shown that the choice of the most effective algorithm

```
int countMatches1 (int[] R, int[] S) {
    int c = 0;
    foreach (int r in R)
        foreach (int s in S)
            if (r == s) c++;
    return c;
}

int countMatches2 (int[] R, int[] S) {
    Dictionary<int, int> ht = new Dictionary<int,int>();
    foreach (int r in R)
        if (ht.ContainsKey(r)) ht[r]++;
        else ht.Add(r, 1);
    int c = 0;
    foreach (int s in S)
        if (ht.ContainsKey(s)) c += ht[s];
    return c;
}

int countMatches3 (int[] R, int[] S) {
    int c = 0;
    int pR = 0, pS = 0;
    while (pR < R.Length && pS < S.Length)
        if (R[pR] < S[pS]) pR++;
        else if (R[pR] > S[pS]) pS++;
        else { // R[pR]==S[pS]
            int cR = 1, cS = 1;
            while (pR + cR < R.Length && R[pR] == R[pR + cR]) cR++;
            while (pS + cS < S.Length && S[pS] == S[pS + cS]) cS++;
            c += cR * cS;
            pR += cR;
            pS += cS;
        }
    return c;
}

int countMatches4 (int[] R, int[] S) {
    int c = 0;
    foreach (int r in R) {
        int pS = getSmallestPositionGE(S, r);
        while (pS < S.Length && S[pS] == r) {
            c++;
            pS++;
        }
    }
    return c;
}
```

FIGURE 1.1 Different implementations of function countMatches.

depends on properties of both data (e.g., size and order) and the environment (e.g., available memory). If we were to design a generic and robust approach to calculate our answer, we would need to implement a high-level decision procedure to pick which variant to use for each call. This procedure should be able to estimate the expected running time of each alternative and avoid using inapplicable algorithms (e.g., the hash-based approach `countMatches2` when there is no available memory). The implementation of `countMatches` would therefore be as follows:

```
int countMatches(int[] R, int[] S,
        bool isRsorted, bool isSsorted, bool hasEnoughMemory) {
    // 1- estimate the cost of each alternative, discarding
       inapplicable ones
    // 2- invoke the alternative that is expected to be the
       most efficient
}
```

We have now designed a very efficient, generic, and robust framework to compute the number of matches among elements of two arrays. While it is not straightforward, the generic algorithm can potentially take advantage of the physical layout of data, the availability of additional memory, and the relative sizes of the input arrays. We can even claim that it introduces some (very limited) "declarative" flavor into the language. If we repeat this exercise for several other common operations, we would obtain a library that allows us to manipulate and query arrays in different ways, by specifying what we want rather than exactly how to obtain the answer.

A key problem with this approach, however, is the lack of flexibility and composability, which appears even for the simple scenarios discussed next. Suppose that we want to change the definition of `countMatches` so that it considers that `r` in R and `s` in S match whenever $|r-s| \leq 100$. In this case, we would need to revise all algorithms and perhaps even to discard those that make assumptions that no longer hold (e.g., the hash-based alternative in `countMatches2` can handle only equality matches). We could, in principle, keep extending `countMatches` so that it progressively (1) considers arbitrary types for R and S elements by using templates or generics, (2) abstracts the matching function so that it can be specified as a parameter from the outside, and (3) implements other alternatives that leverage special cases for performance. As we see next, we will quickly run into severe limitations even in this relatively simple scenario.

Suppose now that we want to compute matching pairs with a value greater than, say, 500. In this case, we could preprocess the input arrays eliminating all values smaller than or equal to 500 and use the resulting arrays as inputs to the `countMatches` algorithm. However, we would already be specifying one concrete way of obtaining results (first filter, then count matches). Alternatively, if just a few elements are greater than 500, we could "push" the filter *inside* `countMatches` itself and therefore avoid the initial filtering step. If elements in `S` are sorted, we could use a modified version of `countMatches4` that skips over elements in `R` that are greater than 500 and employs binary search only on the remaining (very few) elements to compute our result without reading `S` completely. Implementing such complex strategies generically is far from simple, since in our example filtering and `countMatches` interact with and have to be aware of each other (it gets progressively more difficult as our repertoire of routines grows). Imagine if our task is to obtain triplets of matching values among three tables by reusing or extending `countMatches`! In general, for each routine to be fully composable while still retaining declarative capabilities, we need to create some sort of meta-environment to reason with each routine both separately and in conjunction with others (clearly not a straightforward task). In effect, this is precisely the feature set that the declarative query processing capabilities of the `SQL` provide.

1.2   SQL: Declarative Query Processing

Structured Query Language is a declarative language designed for querying and updating data in relational database management systems (DBMSs). The data model in `SQL` is simple. All information in a database is structured in tables, which are defined as multisets of rows (rows are also called tuples). Each row, in turn, contains one value for each typed column in the table. Suppose that we want to model information about employees working in departments. We could then use two tables, shown in Figure 1.2. In the figure, each row in table `Emp` represents one employee and contains the employee's ID (column `EId`), name, title, and salary as well as the ID of the department the employee works in (`DId`) and the ID of the employee's manager (`MId`). In turn, each row in table `Dept` represents a department and contains the department ID (`DId`), a description, the city where the department is located, and its yearly budget. We represent the relationship of an employee working in a department by matching `DId` values in the `Emp` and `Dept` tables.

`SQL` queries take tables as inputs and return tables as outputs and can therefore be easily composable. The generic form of a `SQL` query is as follows:

```
SELECT     expressions
FROM       relational inputs
WHERE      predicate
GROUP BY   columns
HAVING     predicate
ORDER BY   columns
```

The `FROM` clause defines the query data sources, which can be either database tables or nested `SQL` queries themselves. By definition, the combined

EId	Name	Title	Salary	DId	MId
25	Mary	Engineer	90K	100	23
40	John	Writer	65K	100	5
21	Peter	Accountant	70K	101	3
...	...	...	...	...	...

Table Emp

DId	Description	City	Budget
100	R&D	Seattle	10M
101	Finance	New York	1M
102	Sales	Seattle	1M
...	...	...	...

Table Dept

FIGURE 1.2   Tables modeling employees and departments.

data source of a SQL query is the Cartesian product of each multiset referenced in the FROM clause. The predicate in the WHERE clause serves as a filter to restrict the set of tuples in the combined data source. The SELECT clause reshapes the tuples that satisfy the WHERE clause, by selecting a subset of their columns and optionally specifying expressions obtained by manipulating such columns (e.g., 1.1 * Salary). The GROUP BY clause, when present, specifies that the tuples in the combined data source must be separated in groups, where each group agrees on the values of the GROUP BY columns. If a GROUP BY clause is present, the expressions in the SELECT clause can be defined only over either the GROUP BY columns or aggregate values (e.g., SUM or AVG) of other columns. In this way, each group of tuples with the same GROUP BY column values is transformed into a representative tuple in the result. A HAVING clause can be present only if there is a GROUP BY clause and specifies a predicate to restrict the groups that are considered in the output (since it refers to groups of tuples, the predicate can use either GROUP BY columns or other column aggregates). Finally, the ORDER BY clause specifies an order of the results and can be used only in the outermost query block (i.e., there cannot be ORDER BY clauses in subqueries).

The canonical way of evaluating a SQL query can be summarized in the following seven steps (note, however, that this "recipe" is almost never used to actually evaluate SQL queries, as there are significantly more efficient alternatives):

1. Evaluate each nested relational input in the FROM clause that is not already a table.

2. Generate the Cartesian product of all tables in the FROM clause.

3. Evaluate the predicate in the WHERE clause over each row in the Cartesian product, eliminating rows that do not satisfy the predicate.

4. Group the remaining tuples, where each group has the same values for all columns in the GROUP BY clause.

5. Obtain a row for each group, which consists of evaluating the expressions in the SELECT clause (including aggregates).

6. Evaluate the predicate in the HAVING clause on each representative row, eliminating those that do not satisfy the predicate.

7. Sort the tuples by the columns in the ORDER BY clause.

To illustrate the expressive power of the SELECT SQL statement, consider again tables Emp and Dept in Figure 1.2, and suppose that we want to obtain a list of all departments in Seattle, sorted by their budget. We can then use the following query:

```
SELECT Dept.DId
FROM Dept
WHERE Dept.City = 'Seattle'
ORDER BY Dept.Budget
```

Suppose now that we want to obtain the names of all employees in departments with over $10 million in budget. We can then issue any of the following three SQL queries:

```
Q1 =   SELECT Name
       FROM Emp, Dept
       WHERE Emp.DId = Dept.DId AND Dept.Budget > 10M


Q2 =   SELECT Name
       FROM Emp, ( SELECT Dept.DId FROM Dept
                   WHERE Dept.Budget > 10M ) as LargeD
       WHERE Emp.DId = LargeD.DId


Q3 =   SELECT Name
       FROM Emp
       WHERE Emp.DId IN (SELECT Dept.DId FROM Dept
                         WHERE Dept.Budget > 10M )
```

Note that while Q1 is expressed using a single block, Q2 uses a nested subquery in the FROM clause. In turn, Q3 uses a nested subquery in the WHERE clause, leveraging the relational operator IN, which returns true if the left operand is present in a single-column table specified by the second relational operand. Note that all these queries are equivalent.

As a final example, suppose we want to obtain a list of all cities where more than 10 engineers, working in low-budget departments, earn more than their managers. The following SQL query calculates the result:

```
SELECT D.City
FROM Emp E, Emp M, Dept D
WHERE E.DId = D.DId AND E.Title='Engineer' AND D.Budget < 100K
      AND E.MId = M.EId AND E.Salary > M.Salary
GROUP BY D.City
HAVING count(*) > 10
```

This is quite a sophisticated query that would not be straightforward to implement efficiently in an imperative language. Moreover, note that in all the previous examples we have not given any specific procedure to reach the results but instead have specified what the result should be. Going back to the motivating example in Section 1.1, the algorithm countMatches can be expressed using the following simple SQL query*:

```
SELECT COUNT(R.s)
FROM R, S
WHERE R.r = S.s
```

In addition to being very concise, this query would be executed by a carefully chosen algorithm that takes into account characteristics of both data and the environment. Since the actual procedure to evaluate a query is abstracted out from the developer, extending countMatches to handle more complex scenarios is much easier than for the imperative examples of Section 1.1. As an example, suppose we want to count all matches greater than 500 from three tables R, S, and T. We could then use the following query variation, which is straightforward to write and would still be executed efficiently by the database engine:

```
SELECT COUNT(R.s)
FROM R, S, T
WHERE R.r = S.s and S.s = T.t and R.r > 500
```

1.2.1 Updating Data

SQL queries that select data are very common, but they cannot modify data stored in tables. For that purpose, SQL introduces data manipulation primitives, which can insert, delete, or update values in tables. As an example, to

---

*When there are aggregate expressions in the SELECT clause but no GROUP BY clause, the result implicitly considers all tuples in the result as belonging to the same group.

increase the salary of all employees based in Seattle by 10%, we can use the following UPDATE query:

```
UPDATE Emp
SET Salary = 1.1 * Salary
WHERE Emp.DId IN ( SELECT Dept.DId FROM Dept
                   WHERE Dept.City = 'Seattle' )
```

UPDATE queries are defined by the updated table, the set of assignment operations, and a predicate that constrains which rows in the table to actually modify. Similarly, DELETE queries are specified by a table and a predicate that identifies which rows to delete, and INSERT queries are specified by a table and either an explicit set of tuples or another SQL query that returns the tuples to insert.

1.3 Processing SQL Queries

We now briefly explain how SQL queries are actually evaluated in a database system. Our exposition is necessarily high level and omits many details and special cases. The objective of this section is to introduce the reader to concepts that are needed in later chapters—mostly by example—but it is by no means comprehensive. References at the end of this chapter provide many additional details.

In a database system, tables are stored on disk as a sequence of pages, which typically range from 4 KB to 64 KB in size. Tuples in a table are laid out in pages sequentially, using a variety of encodings that balance tuple size and processing efficiency. Each tuple in a table is given a record id (or RID for short), which identifies both the page that contains the tuple and the offset inside the page. Pages are the unit of input/output (I/O) transfer and can be cached in memory (in what is called a buffer pool).

The execution environment in a relational database system can be seen as a virtual machine. Modern query engines provide a layer of abstraction on top of several operating system services, such as memory management, I/O subsystems, and schedulers, and expose a runtime environment to efficiently evaluate SQL queries. A query optimizer (which is the subject of Chapter 2) takes an input SQL query and transforms it into a program to be executed (also called an *execution plan*) on this virtual machine. An execution plan is typically a tree of physical operators that precisely determine how a query is to be evaluated. Physical operators take sequences of tuples as inputs and produce an output sequence of tuples (the output of the root operator in the tree is the result of the query). Physical operators are usually designed using the iterator model, which allows operators to consume their inputs incrementally, without necessarily materializing intermediate results produced by other operators.

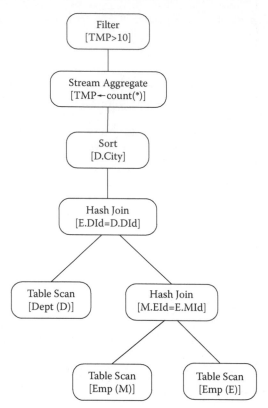

FIGURE 1.3   Execution plan for an SQL query.

To illustrate these concepts, consider again the query on page 10 that obtains a list of all cities where more than 10 engineers working in low-budget departments earn more than their managers. Figure 1.3 shows an execution plan for this query. Each node in the figure corresponds to a physical operator. At the bottom of the tree there are Scan operators, which read tuples from a given table and pass them up to the next operator in the plan. Additionally, Scan operators can filter tuples on the fly based on single-table predicates. The Scan operator on table Emp (alias E) filters all employees that are not engineers, while the Scan operator on table Emp (alias M) routes all employees to the next operator. These two Scan operators are inputs to a Hash Join operator, which matches every (engineer) employee with his or her corresponding manager (join operators simultaneously perform a Cartesian product and an intertable predicate and exist because this combined operation is very common). A Hash Join operator builds a hash table for each tuple in the right input (hashed by Emp.EId) and probes each tuple from the left input (hashing it by Emp.MId) against it (the procedure is similar to function countMatches2 in Figure 1.1 but additionally returns the matched tuples). As with Scan operators, Hash Join operators can apply residual predicates on the matched tuples before passing them to the next operator. Specifically, the `Hash Join` operator in the figure passes only matching tuples for which employees earn more than their managers. The result of this operator is a relation of all engineers who earn more than their managers. This intermediate result is input to the second `Hash Join` operator in the figure, which matches employees and the corresponding departments (the `Scan` operator over `Dept` (alias D) discards all departments with high budgets). This second `Hash Join` operator produces the list of all engineers who earn more than their managers and work in low-budget departments, along with their department information. This intermediate result is sorted by department cities (`Sort` operator) and passed to a `Stream Aggregate` operator, which counts the number of tuples in each group of consecutive tuples with the same department city (leveraging the sorted property enforced by the previous `Sort` operator). The output of the `Stream Aggregate` operator is a relation of pairs of cities and the number of engineers earning more than their managers working in a low-budget department in such cities. This intermediate result is then filtered by the final `Filter` operator, which discards the cities with counts smaller than or equal to 10, producing the desired answer.

We make some additional observations concerning execution plans and evaluation strategies for `SQL` queries. First, we note that there are several possible implementations of operators. For instance, `Hash Joins` are just one of many alternatives to process relational joins. Other operators can be applicable in some scenarios only (e.g., `Merge Joins` require that inputs are sorted by the join columns). Second, some operators pipeline intermediate results (e.g., `Scan` operators pass each tuple up to the next operator without first reading the whole table), while others need to buffer/materialize the whole input before producing tuples (e.g., the `Sort` operator). Third, operators are very sophisticated and go considerably beyond our simple functions in Figure 1.1. For instance, `Hash Joins` can adapt to skewed data, gracefully spill to disk if the input data are larger than the available memory, and leverage sophisticated optimizations (e.g., bitmap filters). Finally, a factor that usually makes a big difference in performance is the presence of relevant indexes, described next.

1.3.1 Database Indexes

Indexes are a very important feature in relational engines, which can drastically improve query processing performance. An index is defined over a sequence of columns of a table and results in an access path for obtaining tuples satisfying certain predicates. Consider an index defined over table `Emp` on column `EId`. We denote such index as `Emp(EId)`. The most popular implementation for indexes, which we use in this book, uses B^+-*trees*, which ensure efficient insertion, retrieval, and removal of records identified by a key. A B^+-tree is a dynamic, multilevel tree, where each node is associated with a range of values for the index columns, and represents all tuples in the index table that lie within such range. In a B^+-tree, in contrast to a B-tree, all records

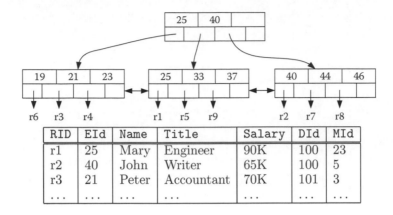

FIGURE 1.4 B$^+$-tree indexes in relational database systems.

are stored at the leaf level of the tree; only keys are stored in interior nodes. Internal nodes in a B$^+$-tree further divide the range in smaller subranges, which point to lower B$^+$-tree nodes, and leaf nodes in a B$^+$-tree point to actual tuples in the index table. Additionally, each leaf node in the B$^+$-tree has pointers to its siblings, which allows fast in-order tuple traversal.

Consider Figure 1.4, which graphically represents a small B$^+$-tree indexing column EId in table Emp (for presentation purposes, the index contains three or four entries in each node rather than the more commonly used value of hundreds of entries). The root node of the B$^+$-tree spans over all tuples in Emp and subdivides employees in three ranges: EId < 25, $25 \leq$ EId < 40, and $40 \leq$ EId. Each range is associated with a pointer to another B$^+$-tree node. Consider the left-most leaf node in the figure. It represents three tuples with EIds 19, 21, and 23. Associated with each value in this node there is a pointer to the corresponding tuple in the index table (the pointer is represented in the figure using r_i values and typically is implemented as the RID associated with each tuple in the table).

We next summarize several aspects that are relevant to our discussion, and at the end of the chapter we refer the reader to pointers for additional information.

Primary vs. secondary indexes. The index shown in Figure 1.4 is known as a *non-clustered* index, because it contains pointers to actual tuples in leaf nodes rather than the tuples themselves. In contrast, a *clustered* index contains the actual tuples in the leaf nodes, and thus it fully represents the index table. For that reason, database systems typically allow at most a single clustered index for each table. A table with no clustered index is stored as a sequence of unordered tuples, in what is called a *heap*.

Single- vs. multicolumn indexes. The example in Figure 1.4 is defined over a single column EId of table Emp. In general, indexes can be defined over multiple columns of the underlying table. In that case, internal nodes are defined on ranges of composite values from the index columns.

Querying indexes. Consider an index $I = T(c_1, c_2, \ldots, c_n)$. The two main querying operations we can perform over such an index are `Index Scans` and `Index Seeks`. Scanning an index locates the left-most leaf node in the B$^+$-tree and returns the values of the columns in the index *without* actually going to the heap or clustered index. Since non-clustered indexes are typically defined over a subset of the table columns, they are smaller than the corresponding table heap or clustered index. Therefore, `Index Scans` are good evaluation alternatives if the query requires only a subset of columns present in the index pages. The second operator, `Index Seek`, provides an efficient way to evaluate predicates of the form $c_1 = v_1$ (or, generally, $c_1 = v_1 \wedge \ldots \wedge c_k = v_k \wedge c_{k+1} \leq v_{k+1}$). We can evaluate this predicate efficiently by *seeking* the index, that is, traversing the tree from the root to the first tuple in a leaf node that satisfies all predicates (if there is such a tuple) and performing the analogous of an `Index Scan` as previously described from that point until the index leaf page where the predicate is no longer satisfied. Unlike binary search trees, B$^+$ trees have very high fan-out (typically in the order of hundreds), which reduces the number of I/O operations required to find an element in the tree. Thus, a height of at most five suffices for virtually all table sizes. Therefore, seeking an index can be done using a handful of I/Os, which is very efficient. Moreover, a large fraction of index internal nodes might already be resident in memory. If a query requires columns that are not part of the index definition, a subsequent lookup to the table heap or clustered index is required. In that case, the RID of each tuple is used to look up into the table heap (or an additional seek for the case of clustered indexes). Since tuples in heaps or clustered indexes are not necessarily laid out in the same order as tuples in secondary indexes, such lookup typically requires an additional disk I/O, which can quickly become expensive.

Updating indexes. Each time a tuple is modified, inserted, or deleted, all relevant indexes are updated as well. For inserts and deletes on a table, all indexes defined over such table are updated. For an update statement, only those indexes that are defined over an update column are modified. Thus, `INSERT/DELETE/UPDATE` statements are the main factor against wider index adoption (the second drawback being storage constraints). An update-intensive query workload may suffer performance degradation due to the presence of multiple indexes.

Key vs. included columns. Some database systems have the ability to differentiate index columns into *key columns* and *included columns*. The main difference between these two types of columns is that included columns are not part of B$^+$-tree internal nodes but are present in the leaf nodes. Therefore, we cannot use an index to evaluate predicates that involve its included columns, but we can obtain these columns without requiring a lookup over the clustered index or heap. We separate key and included columns in an index using a | sign. As an example, Emp(Salary | EId, DId) refers to an index on table Emp with key column Salary and included columns EId and DId.

1.3.1.1   Index-Based Query Processing

To better understand how indexes can be used in the context of query processing, consider again the SQL query whose execution plan we showed in Figure 1.3, and suppose that we create the following database indexes:

E1 = Emp(EId, Salary)

E2 = Emp(Title)

D1 = Dept(DId | Budget, City)

Figure 1.5 shows an execution plan for the query in the previous section that exploits such indexes. Index E2 is first used to seek employees who are engineers. For that purpose, the corresponding B^+-tree is traversed, and all such employees are passed upward in the execution plan. However, the tuples in E2 contain only the Title column (and the corresponding RID of the original tuple), so an additional lookup to the base table is performed (using an **Index Join** alternative). The result of this lookup contains all relevant columns for every employee that is an engineer. Next, a second **Index Join** operator is used to obtain the department of each employee. For each employee, we seek index D1 to locate the corresponding department. The second **Index Seek** operator using index D1 evaluates a residual predicate discarding all employees in departments with high budgets, which considerably reduces the number of employees. Then, a third **Index Join** operator finds the manager of each employee using index **Index Seeks** over D1 and discards employees who earn less than their managers. The result of this third join is the set of all employees in low-budget departments who earn more than their managers. From this point on, the plan behaves exactly like the alternative one in Figure 1.3.

As we have shown, indexes can be used to obtain new execution plans to evaluate queries. In addition to **Scan** operators to obtain base table tuples, we can leverage different index strategies to obtain the same result. Although the examples in this section are simple, there are alternatives that intersect or combine intermediate results produced by multiple indexes on the same table (see Section 2.1.2 for an example). Index-based plans may significantly improve query performance (e.g., the index-based plan in Figure 1.5 executed three times faster than the alternative plan in Figure 1.3 for the same query on a synthetic database). Of course, this is not always the case. As an example, if there are many engineers in table Emp, the alternative in Figure 1.5 would quickly become more expensive than that in Figure 1.3 due to a large number of table lookups in the first **Index Join** operator. Indexes also need

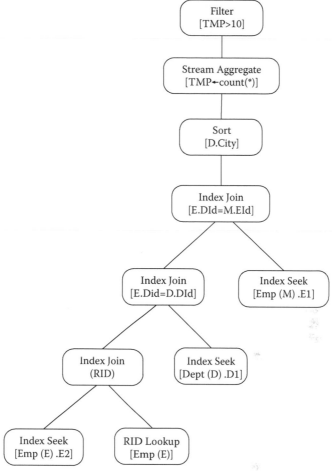

FIGURE 1.5   Index-based execution plan for a SQL query.

to be maintained for every update to their corresponding tables, and they use additional disk space to redundantly store database tuples. Finally, indexes that are very useful to a given query might degrade performance for other queries (e.g., updates).

For all these reasons, there has always been a great amount of interest in deciding, for a given query workload, what would be a reasonably good set of indexes to materialize in the database to maximize query processing performance. Database developers and administrators spend significant amounts of time not only writing SQL queries but also choosing indexes that enable efficient executions for such queries. Recall that SQL is a declarative language, and therefore developers should not worry about *how* queries are executed. What happens in practice, though, is that developers *guess* how queries would be executed* and, based on experience or trial-and-error procedures, come up with a set of indexes to materialize that would make the query execute in a specific—efficient—way. Of course, this procedure conflicts with the goal of a declarative language, because it forces an understanding, to a certain extent, of *how* queries would be executed under different index configurations. In this book we introduce the reader to several tools and techniques that attempt to assist and simplify the problem of selecting and tuning the set of physical structures (including indexes) in a database system.

1.4   Summary

- SQL is the most popular language to query and manipulate database systems and allows developers specify *what* to do rather than *how* to do it.

- Modern database systems are sophisticated and have a large repertoire of alternatives to evaluate input queries efficiently.

- Indexes are a very important database feature that can result in more efficient query plans, but they need to be maintained.

- Deciding which indexes to materialize for a given query workload, unless done automatically, represents a step back from declarative SQL.

1.5   Additional Reading

In this chapter we briefly introduced several concepts that are needed in the rest of the book, but we omitted lengthy discussions and details. The SQL language was originally proposed in 1974[1] and resulted in several standards describing all its aspects, the last one introduced in 2008.[6] One of the several database textbooks that extensively covers database management systems is *Database Management Systems* by Ramakrishnan and Gehrke,[7] and another one more focused on implementation is *Database System Implementation* by Garcia-Molina et al.[4] As for more specific references, Comer surveys B+-trees,[2] Graefe discusses query processing techniques in detail,[5] and Galindo-Legaria et al. analyze query processing for update statements.[3]

---

*Sometimes guesses are very accurate, but many times they reflect some poor or even mystical understanding on the innerworkings of database systems.

References

1. Donald D. Chamberlin and Raymond F. Boyce. SEQUEL: A structured English query language. In *Proceedings of the 1974 ACM SIGFIDET Workshop on Data Description, Access and Control*, 1974.

2. Douglas Comer. Ubiquitous B-tree. *ACM Computing Surveys*, 11, 1979.

3. César A. Galindo-Legaria, Stefano Stefani, and Florian Waas. Query processing for SQL updates. In *Proceedings of the ACM International Conference on Management of Data (SIGMOD)*, 2004.

4. Hector Garcia-Molina, Jeffrey D. Ullman, and Jennifer Widom. *Database System Implementation*. Prentice-Hall, 2000.

5. Goetz Graefe. Query evaluation techniques for large databases. *ACM Computing Surveys*, 25, 1993.

6. International Organization for Standarization. Information technology—Database languages—SQL—Part 1: Framework (SQL/ Framework). ISO/IEC 9075-1:2008. Accessible at http://www.iso.org/ iso/iso_catalogue/catalogue_tc/catalogue_detail.htm? csnumber=45498.

7. Raghu Ramakrishnan and Johannes Gehrke. *Database Management Systems*, 3rd ed. McGraw-Hill, 2002.

Chapter 2

Query Optimization in Relational Database Systems

As discussed in the previous chapter, database management systems (DBMSs) let users specify queries using high-level declarative languages such as SQL. Then, the DBMS determines the best way to evaluate the input query and to obtain the desired result. To answer a SQL query, a typical DBMS goes through a series of steps, illustrated in Figure 2.1:

1. The input query, treated as a string of characters, is *parsed* and transformed into an internal data structure (i.e., an algebraic tree). This step performs both syntactic and semantic checks over the input query, rejecting all invalid requests.

2. The algebraic tree is *optimized* and turned into an execution plan. A query execution plan indicates not only the operations required to evaluate the input query but also the order in which they are performed and the specific algorithms used at each step.

3. The execution plan is evaluated, and results are sent back to the user.

The *query optimizer* is the component in the DBMS that is responsible for finding an efficient *execution plan* to evaluate the input query. For that purpose, the query optimizer searches a large space of alternatives and chooses the one that is expected to be least expensive to evaluate.

Although implementation details vary among specific DBMSs, virtually all optimizers share the same high-level conceptual structure and conduct the search of execution plans in a cost-based manner. More specifically, optimizers assign each candidate plan its *estimated* cost and choose the plan with the least expected cost for execution. The estimated cost of a plan is defined as the expected amount of resources that the execution engine would require to evaluate such plan. Query optimization can therefore be viewed as a complex search problem defined by three interacting components, illustrated in Figure 2.2:

Search space: The search space characterizes the set of execution plans that would be considered by the optimizer. For instance, some optimizers consider only certain subsets of join trees or impose restrictions on the alternative ways to process subqueries.

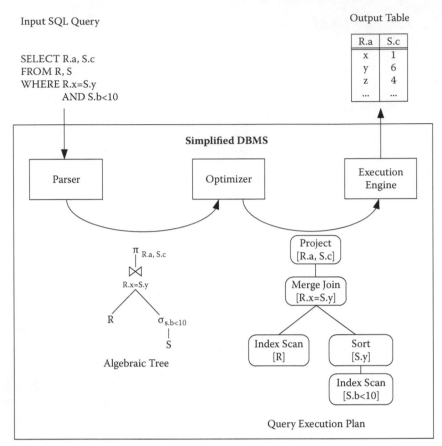

FIGURE 2.1　Executing SQL queries in a relational database system.

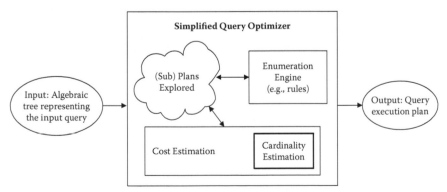

FIGURE 2.2　Simplified architecture of a database query optimizer.

Cost model: The cost model assigns a cost value to every point in the search space through estimation of the resources consumed by the plan. The quality of the plan returned by the optimizer is only as good as its cost model.

Enumeration strategy: The search space can be characterized without specifying a strategy to generate all candidate plans. The enumeration strategy serves this purpose, and its goal is to traverse all interesting plans in the search space efficiently (note that regions in the search space that are guaranteed to be suboptimal for an input query can be skipped by the enumeration strategy).

The task of an optimizer is nontrivial given the very large number of execution plans for an input query, the large variance in response time of the plans in the search space, and the difficulty of accurately estimating costs of plans. A desirable optimizer is one for which (1) the search space includes plans with low cost, (2) the cost model is accurate, and (3) the enumeration strategy is efficient. In this chapter we describe each of these aspects in detail.

2.1   Search Space

The search space of an optimizer depends on the set of physical operators supported by the database engine and the set of algebraic equivalences among execution subplans. Often, the main source of diversity within an optimizer arises from the supported set of equivalence-preserving algebraic transformations.

2.1.1   Operator Reordering

An important class of transformations exploits the commutativity property among operators. We next describe three examples of such transformations.

2.1.1.1   Join Reordering

Optimizers can restrict the allowed sequences of join operations to limit the search space and therefore improve optimization time. For example, certain optimizers allow only linear sequences of join operations and defer Cartesian products until after all joins are processed. However, since join operations are commutative and associative, the sequence of joins in an operator tree does not need to be linear. Specifically, a query joining relations R_1, R_2, R_3, and R_4 can be algebraically represented and evaluated as $(R_1 \bowtie R_2) \bowtie (R_3 \bowtie R_4)$, where the symbol $\bowtie$ represents the join operator. Such query trees are called bushy and typically require materializing intermediate relations. While bushy

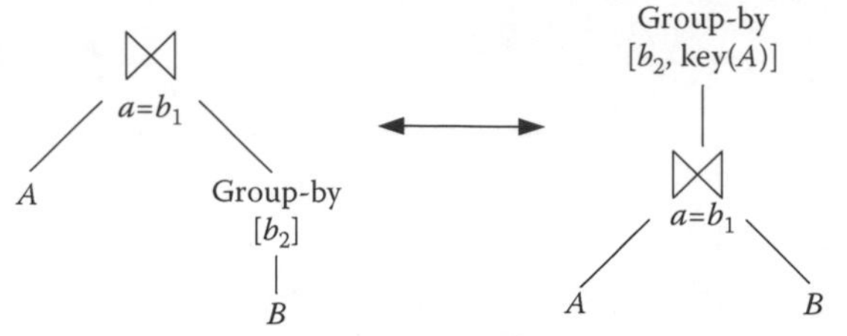

FIGURE 2.3 Reordering JOIN and GROUP BY clauses.

trees may result in a cheaper query plan, they considerably increase the cost of enumerating the search space. In general, most systems focus on linear join sequences and some restricted subsets of bushy join trees. Deferring Cartesian products may also miss opportunities in some decision support queries where a single big table joins with multiple small tables. Performing some Cartesian products among these small tables before joining them with the big table can result in a significant reduction in cost.

2.1.1.2 Group-By and Join Clauses

In the conceptual evaluation of a SQL query block, the processing of the join precedes that of the group-by (see Section 1.2). Similarly, a group-by clause in a subquery in the FROM clause is conceptually evaluated before the joins in the outer query block. Some algebraic transformations enable commuting group-by and join operators. The evaluation of a group-by operator can potentially result in a significant reduction in the number of tuples, since only one tuple is generated for every partition of the relation induced by the group-by. At the same time, joins might eliminate large portions of an input relation, resulting in fewer tuples to subsequently group. Therefore, in some cases we can significantly reduce the cost of a query by reordering join and group-by clauses.

As an example of such transformations, a group-by clause can be pulled up above a join, as long as (1) we add a key of the other join relational input to the set of grouping columns, and (2) the join predicate is not defined over an aggregated column (or the resulting join is not well formed). Figure 2.3 illustrates this transformation (note that b_2 must include b_1 so that the original join is well formed). Conversely, a group-by clause can be pushed below a join $R \bowtie S$ (down to S) whenever (1) the grouping columns include a key of R, (2) the columns from S in the join predicate are included in the grouping columns or derived from them via functional dependencies, and (3) aggregates are defined in terms of columns in S.

2.1.1.3 Outerjoins

One-sided outerjoins are asymmetric operators in SQL that preserve all of the tuples of one relation. For instance, a left outer join between tables R and

S (denoted $R \to S$) is similar to the join $R \bowtie S$ but additionally returns all rows in R that do not match any row in S (these additional tuples have NULL values in columns in S). Symmetric outerjoins preserve both the input relations. Unlike regular joins, a sequence of outerjoins and joins does not freely commute. However, the following algebraic equivalence allows pulling outerjoins above a block of joins:

$$R \bowtie (S \to T) \equiv (R \bowtie S) \to T$$

After outerjoins have been delayed in this manner, joins may be freely re-ordered. As with other transformations, there is no guarantee as to which alternative is better in all cases, and thus the use of this identity needs to be cost based.

2.1.2 Access Path Selection

Earlier query optimizers chose at most one index for accessing tuples of a table in a given query (see, for instance, the examples in Chapter 1). For queries with complex single-table predicates, more advanced strategies can manipulate multiple indexes simultaneously to efficiently obtain the qualifying tuples. Consider as an example a SQL query that returns all engineers who earn less than $50,000:

```
SELECT *
FROM Emp
WHERE Title = 'Engineer' AND Salary < 50000
```

and suppose that we have single-column indexes $E1 = Emp(Title)$ and $E2 = Emp(Salary)$. Traditionally, the alternative plans that the optimizer would consider for the query would be either (1) a table or clustered index scan filtering each tuple by both predicates, or (2) an index seek using either $E1$ or $E2$, followed by lookups to the primary index to obtain the remaining columns, followed by a filter on the predicate that was not evaluated by the index. By using both indexes simultaneously, we can sometimes obtain better execution plans. In this case, we could perform what is called an *index intersection* as follows:

1. Use index $E1$ to obtain all RIDs of tuples satisfying Title = 'Engineer' (each index contains, in addition to the index columns, the RID of each tuple).

2. Similarly, use index $E2$ to obtain all RIDs of tuples that satisfy Salary < 50000.

3. Intersect both lists of RIDs (this procedure is similar to a join).

4. Fetch the resulting records (which satisfy both predicates).

This alternative can greatly reduce execution times because (1) the individual indexes $E1$ and $E2$ are in general smaller than the clustered index, (2) the intersected list of RIDs can be much smaller than either of the original lists, and thus much fewer RID lookups are needed, and (3) if the predicates use equalities, specialized intersection algorithms can be used that return RIDs in order of the clustered index, which accelerates subsequent lookups.

In general, we can intersect several indexes to answer complex single-table predicates, although at some point the benefit from additional index intersections is outweighed by its cost. Additionally, there are analogous strategies to handle disjunctive predicates using RID unions, and negation predicates using RID differences or two seek operations (e.g., employees who are not engineers). Considering these alternatives certainly increases the search space considerably, so some optimizers use heuristics (similar to those for join reordering) to limit the number of such alternatives.

2.1.3   Query Decorrelation

Suppose that table `Dept` has a column `ContactId`, which corresponds to the employee, in table `Emp` that is the contact for each department in `Dept`. Consider the following `SQL` query that obtains the employees who are the contacts for the departments they work in (we add column `ContactId` to the schema of the `Dept` table):

```
SELECT Emp.Name
FROM Emp
WHERE Emp.DeptId IN ( SELECT Dept.DId
                      FROM Dept
                      WHERE Emp.EId = Dept.ContactId )
```

The traditional strategy to process this query would evaluate the inner subquery for each tuple of table `Emp` in the outer query block (this is sometimes called *tuple iteration semantics*). An obvious optimization applies when the inner subquery references no variables from the outer query block. In such cases, the inner query block can be evaluated only once. Instead, if the inner subquery mentions a variable from the outer query block, we say that the query blocks are *correlated*. For example, in the previous query, `Emp.EId` acts as the correlated variable in the inner query block. Much work in the literature has identified techniques to decorrelate (or *unnest*) such correlated nested queries by "flattening" them into a single-block alternative. For example, since `Dept.Did` is unique for each department, the nested query is equivalent to the following alternative that does not use subqueries:

```
SELECT E.Name
FROM Emp E, Dept D
WHERE E.DeptId = D.DeptId
   AND E.EmpId = D.ContactId
```

The complexity of the unnesting problem depends on the structure of the query (e.g., whether the nested subquery has aggregates). The simplest case, of which the previous query is an example, can be modeled with semijoins (which can be further transformed in regular joins if unique constraints are satisfied as in the given example). The problem is more complex when aggregates are present in the nested subquery, since unnesting requires pulling up the aggregation without violating the semantics of the nested query, which can be especially complex in the presence of duplicates and NULL values.

2.1.4 Other Transformations

There are several additional transformations that exploit special cases or common patterns, some of which we briefly discuss:

Partial preaggregation: In some scenarios, rather than fully pushing a group-by below a join, we can unfold a group-by clause into a local, more fine-grained group-by clause, which is pushed down the join, and a global group-by clause, which performs the final aggregation. Such staged computation may still be useful in reducing the join costs because of the data reduction effect of the local aggregate but requires the aggregate function to satisfy certain properties (e.g., distributivity).

Materialized views: Materialized views are results of views (i.e., queries) that are stored and used by the optimizer transparently. Given a set of materialized views and a query, the problem is to optimize the query while leveraging available materialized views as much as possible. This problem introduces the challenge of identifying potential reformulations of the query so that it can use one or more of the materialized views.

Common subexpressions: When intermediate results are defined multiple times in a query, there are opportunities for avoiding multiple identical computations. Several specialized techniques leverage this fact to produce efficient plans that spool and reuse common subexpressions.

Parallelism: When multiple processors are available, each operator in the query tree can be parallelized by partitioning the input among available processors and later combining results. Parallelism can reduce the overall time to process a query but also has overheads in the partitioning and merging stages.

2.2 Cost Model

As we discussed so far, there are many logically equivalent algebraic expressions associated to a given query and multiple ways to implement each of these expressions. Even if we ignore the computational complexity of enumerating the space of possibilities, there remains the question of deciding which of the operator trees consumes the least resources. Resources may be central processing unit (CPU) time, input/output (I/O) cost, memory, or a combination of these. Therefore, given a partial or full operator tree, being able to accurately and efficiently evaluate its cost is of fundamental importance. Cost estimation must be accurate (optimization is only as good as its cost estimates) and efficient (it is in the inner loop of query optimization). The basic framework for estimating costs is based on the following recursive approach:

1. Collect statistical summaries of stored data.
2. Given an operator in the execution plan and statistical summaries for each of its subplans, determine:
   a. Statistical summaries of the output
   b. Estimated cost of executing the operator

The procedure can be applied to an arbitrary tree to derive the costs of each operator. The estimated cost of a plan is then obtained by combining the costs of each of its operators. The resources needed to execute a query plan (and thus the plan cost) are a function of the sizes of the intermediate query results. Therefore, the cost estimation module heavily depends on cardinality estimates of subplans generated during optimization. The following example illustrates how sizes of intermediate results can significantly change the chosen plan.

Consider the following query template, where @C is a numeric parameter:

```
SELECT *
FROM R,S
WHERE R.x = S.y and R.a < @C
```

Figure 2.4 shows the execution plans produced by an optimizer when we instantiate @C with the values 20, 200, and 2,000. Although the three instantiated queries are syntactically very similar, the resulting optimal query plans are considerably different. For instance, in Figure 2.4a, the optimizer estimates that the number of tuples in *R* satisfying *R.a* < 20 is very small.

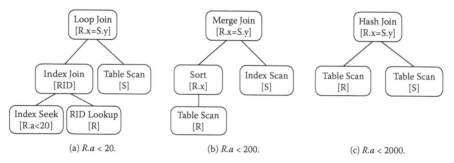

(a) *R.a* < 20.   (b) *R.a* < 200.   (c) *R.a* < 2000.

FIGURE 2.4   Query execution plans for various instances of a template query.

Consequently, using a nonclustered index over $R.a$, the resulting plan first re-trieves the RIDs of all tuples in R that satisfy $R.a < 20$. Then, using lookups against table R, it looks up the actual tuples that correspond to those RIDs. Finally, it performs a nested-loop join between the subset of tuples of R calcu-lated before, and table S, which is sequentially scanned. For the case @C=2000 in Figure 2.4c, the optimizer estimates that the number of tuples of R satisfy-ing $R.a < 2000$ is rather large. The resulting plan therefore scans both tables sequentially (discarding on the fly the tuples from R that do not satisfy the condition $R.a < 2000$) and then performs a hash join to obtain the result (in this scenario, the lookups of the previous plan would have been too numerous and therefore too expensive). Finally, Figure 2.4b shows yet another execution plan that is chosen when the number of tuples of R satisfying the predicate is neither too small nor too large. In this case, table S is scanned in increasing order of $S.y$ using a clustered index, and table R is first scanned sequentially (discarding invalid tuples on the fly as before) and then sorted by $R.x$. Finally, a merge join is performed on the two intermediate results.

The previous examples illustrate that the cardinality of intermediate results plays a fundamental role in the choice of execution plans. We next discuss how cardinality estimation is done in a query optimizer.

2.2.1   Statistical Summaries of Data

For every table, statistical information usually includes the number of tuples, the average size of each tuple, and other values, such as the number of physical pages used by the table or the number of distinct tuples in the table. Statis-tical information on table columns, if available, is helpful for estimating the cardinality of range or join predicates. A large body of work in the literature studies the representation of statistics on a given column or combination of columns. In most systems, information on the data distribution on a column is provided by histograms, since they can be built and maintained efficiently by using sampling techniques.

Histograms divide the values of a column (or set of columns) into a number of buckets and associate with each bucket some aggregated information. The number of buckets influences the accuracy of the histogram but also affects memory usage, since relevant histograms are loaded into memory during opti-mization. Both the particular procedure used to select bucket boundaries and the aggregated information associated with each bucket lead to different fam-ilies of histograms. An example is the family of equi-depth histograms, which divide the domain of a column in a table with n tuples among k buckets so that each range has approximately the same number of values n/k. Other histogram variants are equi-width, max-diff, and end-biased histograms, which are illus-trated in Figure 2.5. Although single-dimensional histograms are widely used, multidimensional histograms are relatively rare.

In addition to histograms, database systems maintain other statistics, such as the number of distinct values in a column (and sometimes certain combinations of columns), the fraction of NULL values in a column, and specialized statistics for nonnumeric data values.

2.2.2 Cardinality Estimation

Histograms provide a compressed representation of the underlying column distribution. When manipulating such compact data structures, we generally make a number of simplifying assumptions. For instance, we assume that the tuples represented in a bucket are distributed uniformly in the bucket domain.

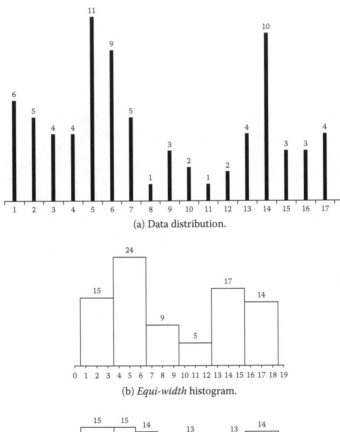

(a) Data distribution.

(b) *Equi-width* histogram.

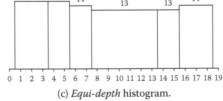

(c) *Equi-depth* histogram.

FIGURE 2.5 Histograms approximate the value distribution of columns in a database.

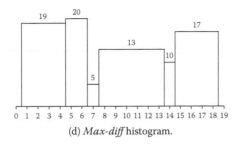

(d) *Max-diff* histogram.

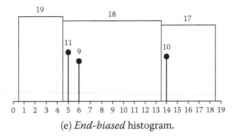

(e) *End-biased* histogram.

FIGURE 2.5   (Continued).

In absence of multidimensional statistics, we also assume that predicates in different columns are independent. Using these assumptions, there are simple procedures to estimate the number of output tuples for each operator. For instance, to estimate the cardinality of single-table range predicates we use interpolation over the histogram buckets. Join estimation requires that we combine information of two histograms, and involves aligning buckets and relying on simplifying assumptions on data distributions. Group-by queries leverage the number of distinct values, stored either globally at the column level or inside each histogram bucket.

2.3   Enumeration Strategy

An enumeration algorithm must pick an efficient execution plan for an input query by effectively exploring the search space. A software engineering consideration while designing an enumeration algorithm is to allow it to gracefully adapt to changes in the search space or cost model. Optimization architectures built with this paradigm are called *extensible optimizers*. Building an extensible optimize involves not just designing a better enumeration algorithm but also providing an infrastructure for evolution of the optimizer design. In this section we focus on three representative examples of such extensible optimizers. We first discuss System-R, an elegant approach that helped fuel much of the subsequent work in optimization. Then, we briefly review Starburst, an extensible prototype developed at IBM in the mid-nineties. Finally, we discuss in some detail Cascades/Volcano, a transformation-based enumeration algorithm that introduces several concepts that are used in subsequent chapters. Rather than providing a detailed description of all the features in these enumeration architectures, we give instead a high-level overview of the frameworks and focus on the specific components that are relevant to our discussion.

2.3.1 System-R

System-R was a seminal project that influenced much of the subsequent work in query optimization. We now present one of the fundamental algorithms introduced in System-R for the purpose of join enumeration. The join enumeration algorithm in System-R uses dynamic programming, and it assumes that the cost model satisfies the principle of optimality. Specifically, we assume that in order to obtain an optimal plan for a query consisting of k joins it suffices to consider only the optimal plans for query subexpressions that consist of fewer joins and to extend those plans with additional joins. In other words, the optimal plan is obtained by combining optimal subplans.

The dynamic programming algorithm, illustrated in Figure 2.6, views the input as a set of relations $\{R_1, \ldots, R_n\}$ to be joined and works in a bottom-up manner. We assume there is an associative array `bestPlan`, or each subset of tables $\mathcal{R}$, that returns the best calculated plan so far for $\mathcal{R}$. First, we generate plans for every table in the query (lines 1 and 2). Such access path selection is encapsulated in function `bestAccessPath` and consists of scans, seeks, or, optionally, more complex plans using index intersections and unions. Then, the dynamic programming algorithm performs $n - 1$ iterations in lines 3 to 8. At the end of the i-th iteration, we produce the optimal plans for all subexpressions that join i tables. Line 4 considers each subset $\mathcal{R}$ of i tables, and line 5 attempts to further partition each such subset into

```
JoinEnumeration ({R₁,...,Rₙ}:input tables)
1    foreach Rᵢ ∈ {R₁,...,Rₙ}
2       bestPlan({Rᵢ}) = bestAccessPath(Rᵢ)
3    for i = 2 to n
4       foreach R ⊂ {R₁,...,Rₙ} such that |R|=i
5          foreach R' ⊂ R such that R' ≠ ∅
6             candPlan = bestJoinAlternative(bestPlan(R'),
             bestPlan(R − R'))
7             if (cost(candPlan) < cost(bestPlan(R))
                // cost(NULL) = ∞
8                bestPlan(R) = candPlan
9    return bestPlan({R₁,...,Rₙ})
```

FIGURE 2.6 Dynamic programming algorithm to enumerate joins.

$\mathcal{R}'$ and $\mathcal{R} - \mathcal{R}'$. For each pair of table subsets, line 6 obtains the best plan that joins tables in $\mathcal{R}'$ and tables in $\mathcal{R} - \mathcal{R}'$. For that purpose, the procedure bestJoinAlternative tries different join implementations (e.g., hash-, merge-, and index-based joins). Note that the input to bestJoinAlternative is bestPlan($\mathcal{R}'$) and bestPlan($\mathcal{R} - \mathcal{R}'$), therefore leveraging the principle of optimality. Lines 7 and 8 update bestPlan for the current subset $\mathcal{R}$ based on the cost model (note that suboptimal plans are discarded and never considered again). Finally, line 9 returns the best plan for the whole set of tables, which corresponds to the optimal join reordering for the input query. We complement the description of the dynamic programming algorithm for join reordering with a couple of important refinements.

First, consider a query that represents the join among $\{R_1, R_2, R_3\}$ with the predicates $R_1.a = R_2.a = R_3.a$. Let us also assume that the cost of a hash-based join plan for $R_1 \bowtie R_2$ is smaller than that of a merge-based join alternative. In such a case, bestPlan($\{R_1, R_2\}$) would keep only the hash-based join alternative discarding the suboptimal merge-based join. However, note that if the merge-based join alternative is used in $R_1 \bowtie R_2$, the result of the join is sorted on columns $R_1.a$ and $R_2.a$. The sorted order may significantly reduce the cost of the subsequent join with R_3. Thus, pruning the merge join alternative for $R_1 \bowtie R_2$ can result in suboptimality of the global plan. The problem arises because the result of the merge join between R_1 and R_2 has an ordering of tuples in the output stream that is useful in a subsequent join. However, the hash-based join alternative, while cheaper locally, does not have such ordering. To address this problem, the dynamic programming algorithm is extended to keep in bestPlan an optimal plan for every choice of an "interesting" sort order. Two plans are then compared if they represent the same expression and have the same interesting order.

Second, note that the algorithm in Figure 2.6 enumerates all bushy plans (including those that perform early cartesian products). The algorithm can easily be adapted to enumerate through different search spaces by modifying line 5. For instance, if we want to consider only (left) linear join trees, line 5 should be changed to:

5	foreach $\mathcal{R}' \subset \mathcal{R}$ such that $|\mathcal{R}'| = 1$

Cartesian products can be avoided until all joins have been processed by further modifying line 5. Of course, the complexity of the algorithm and quality of resulting plans strongly depend on the search space that is enumerated.

2.3.2 Starburst

The Starburst project at IBM Almaden Research Center built an extensible relational DBMS. Query optimization in Starburst begins with a structural representation of the SQL query that is used throughout the optimization process. This representation is called the Query Graph Model (QGM). In the

QGM, a box represents a query block and labeled arcs between boxes represent table references across blocks. Each box contains information on the predicate structure and on the data stream order.

In the query rewrite phase of optimization, heuristic but sound rules are used to transform a QGM into another equivalent QGM. Rules are modeled as pairs of arbitrary functions. The first one checks the QGM for condition for applicability, and the second one enforces the transformation. A forward chaining rule engine governs the rules. Rules may be grouped in rule classes, and it is possible to tune the order of evaluation of rule classes to focus the search. Since any application of a rule results in a valid QGM, any set of rule applications guarantees query equivalence. The query rewrite phase does not have cost information available. This forces this module either to retain alternatives obtained through rule application or to use the rules in a heuristic way.

The second phase of query optimization is called plan optimization. In this phase, given a QGM, an execution plan is chosen. In Starburst, the physical operators (called LOLEPOPs) may be combined in a variety of ways to implement higher-level operators. Such combinations are expressed in a grammar-production-like language. The realization of a higher-level operation is expressed by its derivation in terms of the physical operators. In computing such derivations, comparable plans that represent the same physical and logical properties but have higher costs are pruned. Each plan has a relational description that corresponds to the algebraic expression it represents, an estimated cost, and physical properties (e.g., order). These properties are propagated as plans and are built bottom-up. Thus, with each physical operator, a function is associated that shows the effect of the physical operator on each of the aforementioned properties. The join enumerator in Starburst is similar to System-R's bottom-up enumeration scheme described in the previous section.

2.3.3   Volcano/Cascades

The Volcano/Cascades optimization framework was developed in the mid-nineties and used as the foundation for both academic and industrial query optimizers (e.g., Tandem's NonStop SQL and Microsoft SQL Server optimizers are based on this architecture). These optimizers work by manipulating *operators*, which are the building blocks of *operator trees* and are used to describe both the input declarative queries and the output execution plans. Consider the following simple SQL query:

```
SELECT *
FROM R, S, T
WHERE R.x = S.x AND S.y = T.y
```

Figure 2.7a shows a tree of logical operators that specify, in an almost one-to-one correspondence, the relational algebra representation of the query above. In turn, Figure 2.7c shows a tree of physical operators that corresponds

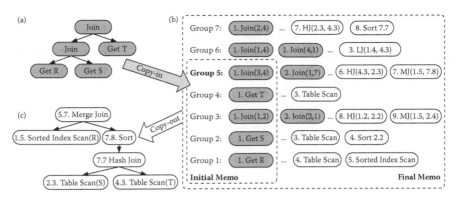

FIGURE 2.7 The MEMO structure in a Cascades optimizer. (Used with permission from Bruno, N. & Nehme, R. In *Proceedings of the ACM International Conference on Management of Data [SIGMOD]*, 2008.)

to an execution plan for the previous query. As we described earlier, the goal of the optimization process is to transform the original logical operator tree into an efficient physical operator tree. For that purpose, Cascades-based optimizers rely on two components: the MEMO data structure (which keeps track of the explored search space) and *optimization tasks* (which guide the search strategy). The following sections discuss these notions in more detail.

2.3.3.1 The Memo Data Structure

The MEMO data structure in Cascades provides a compact representation of the search space of plans. In addition to enabling memoization (a variant of dynamic programming), a MEMO provides detection of duplicate operator trees, cost management, and other supporting infrastructure needed during query optimization.

A MEMO consists of two key data structures, which we call *groups* and *groupExpressions*. A *group* represents all equivalent operator trees producing the same output. To reduce memory requirements, a *group* does not explicitly enumerate all its operator trees. Instead, it implicitly represents all the operator trees by using *groupExpressions*. A *groupExpression* is an operator having other *groups* (rather than other operators) as children. As an example, consider Figure 2.7b, which shows a MEMO for the simple query in the previous section (logical operators are shaded and physical operators use white background). In the figure, *group* 1 represents all equivalent expressions that return the contents of table *R*. Some operators in *group* 1 are logical (e.g., *Get R*), and some are physical (e.g., *Table Scan* and *Sorted Index Scan*, which read the contents of *R* from the primary index or from an existing secondary index, respectively). Likewise, *group* 3 contains all the equivalent expressions for *R* ⋈ *S*. Note that *groupExpression* 3.1 (i.e., *Join(1,2)*) represents all operator trees whose root is *Join*, first child belongs to *group* 1, and second child belongs to *group* 2. In this way, a MEMO compactly represents a potentially very large number of operator trees. Also note that the children of physical *groupExpressions* also point to the most efficient *groupExpression* in the corresponding *groups*. For instance, *groupExpression* 3.8 represents a hash join operator whose left-hand child is the second *groupExpression* in *group* 1 and whose right-hand child is the second *groupExpression* in *group* 2.

In addition to representing operator trees, the MEMO provides basic infrastructure for management of *groupExpression* properties. There are two kinds of properties. On one hand, *logical* properties are shared by all *groupExpressions* in a *group* and are therefore associated with the *group* itself. Examples of logical properties are the cardinality of a *group*, the tables over which the *group* operates, and the columns that are output by the *group*. On the other hand, *physical* properties are specific to physical *groupExpressions* and typically vary within a *group*. Examples of physical properties are the order of tuples in the result of a physical *groupExpression* (analogous to an interesting order in System-R) and the cost of the best execution plan rooted at a *groupExpression*.

2.3.3.2   Optimization Tasks

The enumeration algorithm in Cascades is divided into several *tasks*. Initially, the logical operator tree describing the input query is *copied into* the initial MEMO (see Figure 2.7b for an example). Then, the optimizer schedules the optimization of the *group* corresponding to the root of the original query tree (*group* 5 in the figure). This task in turn triggers the optimization of smaller and smaller operator subtrees and eventually returns the most efficient execution plan for the input query. This execution plan is *copied out* from the final MEMO and passed to the execution engine. Figure 2.8 shows the five types of tasks in a Cascades-based optimizer and the dependencies among them. We next describe each of these tasks in some detail.

OptimizeGroup: This task takes as inputs a *group* G, a cost-bound UB, and a set of *required physical properties* RP. It returns the most efficient execution plan (if one exists) that implements *group* G, costs no

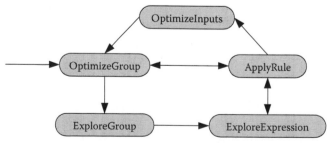

FIGURE 2.8   Optimization tasks in a Cascades optimizer.

more than UB, and satisfies the required properties RP. This task implements memoization by caching the best execution plan for a given set of required properties in the *winner circle* of the *group*. The winner circle of a group is an associative array that returns the best plan found so far for a given set of required properties. Subsequent calls to *OptimizeGroup* with the same required physical properties would return immediately with the best plan or a failure (depending on the value of UB). Optimizing a *group* involves exploring the *group* (see *ExploreGroup* task), and then applying all implementation rules (see *ApplyRule* task) to produce all the candidate physical operators that implement the logical counterparts in the *group*.

ExploreGroup: A *group* is explored by iteratively exploring each logical *groupExpression* in the *group* (see *ExploreExpr* task).

ExploreExpr: Exploring a logical *groupExpression* generates all logically equivalent alternatives of the input *groupExpression* by applying *exploration* rules (see *ApplyRule* task). This task also uses memoization to avoid repeated work. Consider a *join reordering* rule that transforms *groupExpression* G_1 into G_2. When eventually exploring G_2, it would not make sense to apply *join reordering* again, since we would obtain G_1 back. *ExploreExpr* uses a bitmap, called *pattern memory*, that keeps track of which transformation rules are valid and which ones should not be applied.

ApplyRule: In general, each rule is a pair of an antecedent expression (to match in the MEMO) and a consequent expression (to generate and introduce back in the MEMO). On one side, *exploration* rules transform logical operator trees into equivalent logical operator trees and can range from simple rules like join reordering to more complex ones like pushing aggregates below joins. An example of an exploration rule is the *join associativity* rule "JOIN(g_1, JOIN(g_2, g_3)) $\rightarrow$ JOIN(JOIN(g_1, g_2), g_3)."* On the other side, *implementation* rules transform logical operator trees into hybrid logical/physical trees by introducing physical operators into the MEMO. Implementation rules range from simple ones like transforming a logical join into a physical hash join to very complex ones that generate index strategies, discussed later. The *ApplyRule* task can be broken down into four components. First, all the bindings for the rule antecedent are identified and iterated over one by one (for complex rules, there can be different ways of matching the antecedent of the rule with operator trees in the current *group*). Second, the rule is applied to each binding generating one or more new expressions (for the previous rule, there is a single substitute per rule application, but in general there might

---

*This is a very simple exploration rule. More complex rules, especially implementation rules, have right sides that cannot be expressed as succinctly.

be more than one). Third, the resulting expressions obtained by applying the rules are integrated back into the MEMO, possibly creating new, unexplored *groups* (as an example, applying the join associativity rule to expression 5.1 in Figure 2.7b results in *groupExpression* 5.2, which points to a newly created *group* 7). Finally, each new *groupExpression* triggers follow-up tasks, which depend on its type. If it is a logical operator, the optimizer was exploring the *group* and thus an *ExploreExpr* task is scheduled for the new *groupExpression*. Otherwise, the expression inputs are optimized, and the cost of the physical plan is calculated (see *OptInputs* task).

OptInputs: This task optimizes the inputs of a given physical operator p and computes the best execution plan rooted at p. For each child p_i of p, it first calculates the required properties of p_i with respect to p and then schedules an *OptimizeGroup* task for the *group* of p_i. As an example, suppose that the root of the tree is a Merge Join operator. Since Merge Join expects the inputs ordered by the join column, the current task generates a required sort property for each of the inputs and optimizes the corresponding *groups* under this new optimization context. The *OptInputs* task also implements a cost-based pruning strategy. Whenever it detects that the lower bound of the expression that is being optimized is larger than the cost of an existing solution, it fails and returns no plan for that optimization goal.

As we can see, the five optimization tasks are nontrivial and depend on each other. For clarity of exposition, we now present a conceptually simplified version of the *OptimizeGroup* task that incorporates portions of the remaining tasks that are relevant in our context. Figure 2.9 shows the algorithm for *OptimizeGroup*, which takes as inputs a *group* G, required properties RP, and a cost upper-bound UB. *OptimizeGroup*(G,RP,UB) returns the most efficient physical *groupExpression* that satisfies RP and is under UB in cost (otherwise, it returns NULL). Initially, line 1 checks the *winner circle* for a previous call compatible with RP. If we find such plan, we return it (if its cost is below UB), or we return NULL otherwise. Otherwise, line 4 iterates over all enumerated physical *groupExpressions* in G (note that line 4 encapsulates *ExploreGroup*, *ExploreExpr*, and *ApplyRule*). For each such root *groupExpression* p, line 5 estimates the local cost of candP (i.e., without counting its inputs' costs). Then, line 8 calculates the input *group* and required properties for each of candP's inputs, and line 9 recursively calls *OptimizeGroup* to optimize them (note that the upper bound in the recursive call is decreased to UB - candP.cost). After each input is successfully optimized, lines 11 and 12 store the best implementation for each of candP's children and update its partial cost. If at any moment the current cost of candP becomes larger than UB, the candidate is discarded and the next one is considered (line 7). Otherwise, after candP is completely optimized, line 13 checks whether candP is the best plan found so

```
OptimizeGroup (G: group, RP: properties, UB: double)
return best groupExpression for G under UB cost satisfying RP
01  p = winnerCircle[G,RP]
02  if ( p is not NULL )
        if (p.cost < UB) return p
        else return NULL
03  bestP = NULL   // No precomputed solution, enumerate plans
04  foreach enumerated physical groupExpression candP
05      candP.cost = localCost( candP )
06      foreach input pᵢ of candP
07          if (candP.cost ≥ UB) continue to 4   // out of bound
08          Gᵢ = group of pᵢ
            RPᵢ = required properties for pᵢ
09          bestPᵢ= OptimizeGroup(Gᵢ, RPᵢ, UB-candP.cost)
10          if (bestPᵢ = NULL) continue to 4   // no solution
11          candP.bestChild[i] = bestPᵢ
12          candP.cost += bestPᵢ.cost
        // Have valid solution, update state
13      if (candP.cost < UB and candP satisfies RP)
            bestP = candP
            UB = candP.cost
14  winnerCircle[G,RP] = bestP
15  return bestP
```

FIGURE 2.9   Simplified algorithm for the *OptimizeGroup* task.

far. Finally, after all candidates are processed, line 14 adds the best plan to the winner circle for G and RP, and line 15 returns such plan.

2.3.3.3   The Rule Set

A crucial component in a Cascades-based optimizer is the rule set. In fact, the set of rules available to the optimizer is one of the determining factors in the quality of the resulting plans. In the rest of this section we discuss details on a small subset of implementation rules that deal with access path selection, since these will be relevant in subsequent chapters.

One of such rules transforms a logical expression consisting of a selection over a single table* into a physical plan that leverages available indexes (candidate plans include index scans, record id (RID) intersections, and lookups, among others). After binding the logical operator tree, this rule identifies the columns that occur in *sargable* predicates (i.e., predicates that can leverage index seeks), the columns that are part of a required sort property, and the

---

*The antecedent *groupExpression* is typically obtained by applying other rules (e.g., pushing selections under joins).

columns that are additionally referenced in nonsargable predicates or upward in the query tree. Then, it analyzes the available indexes and returns one or more candidate physical plans for the input subquery.

Consider the application of such a rule for a *groupExpression* that represents $\Pi_c(\sigma_{a=10}(R))$, and further suppose that column b is a required sort order. In this case, the rule identifies column a in a sargable predicate, column b as a required order, and column c as an additional column that is either output or referenced upward in the tree. This information allows the optimizer to identify the available indexes that might be helpful to implement an efficient subplan for the subquery. Suppose that an index on column a is available. The optimizer can then generate a physical operator tree that uses the index to retrieve all tuples satisfying $a=10$, looks up the remaining columns from a primary index, and finally sorts the resulting tuples in b order. If an index on columns (b, a, c) is also available, the optimizer might additionally generate an operator tree that scans the index in b order and filters on the fly the tuples that satisfy $a=10$. Depending on the selectivity of $a=10$, one alternative would be more efficient than the other, and eventually the optimizer would pick the one that results in the smallest execution cost.

Note that the same mechanism is used in another important rule that transforms logical joins in which the right child consists of a single-table expression into index-based join execution plans (which repeatedly access an index on the right child's table for each tuple produced by the left input). In this case, the same procedure is conducted but with respect to the inner table only, and the joined column in the table is considered as part of a sargable (equality) predicate. For instance, suppose that the logical subplan is $(\mathcal{Q} \bowtie_{\mathcal{Q}.x=T.y} T)$, where $\mathcal{Q}$ is a complex relational expression. Conceptually, the rule produces an index-based join plan and considers the right-hand side a single-table selection $\sigma_{T.y=?}(T)$ as before (where $T.y$ is a column in a sargable predicate with an unspecified constant value).

2.4   Summary

Query optimization in relational databases takes an input SQL query and produces an efficient execution plan to evaluate it. The optimization process can be seen as a complex search problem, defined by:

- The search space, which defines the set of plans that are considered by the optimizer
- The cost model, which provides a metric to compare alternative plans
- The enumeration algorithm, which is responsible for effectively traversing the search space of plans

2.5 Additional Reading

Query optimization has received considerable attention in the past 30 years, and there are many sources of information regarding every aspect of the problem. Chaudhuri summarizes many issues around query optimization discussed in this chapter.[2] For information on specific systems, we refer the readers to the seminal paper on System-R,[14] an overview of StarBurst,[10] and different references that discuss the Volcano/Cascades framework.[1,8,9] Several references explain in depth many issues that we covered only superficially, such as optimizing group-by queries,[4,15] queries with outer-joins,[6] plans that leverage multiple indexes for single-table predicates,[12] generic treatments of unnesting,[5,13] issues with materialized views,[3,7] and histograms and their use during cardinality estimation.[11]

References

1. Nicolas Bruno and Rimma Nehme. Configuration-parametric query optimization for physical design tuning. In *Proceedings of the ACM International Conference on Management of Data (SIGMOD)*, 2008.

2. Surajit Chaudhuri. An overview of query optimization in relational systems. In *Proceedings of the ACM Symposium on Principles of Database Systems (PODS)*, 1998.

3. Surajit Chaudhuri, Ravi Krishnamurthy, Spyros Potamianos, and Kyuseok Shim. Optimizing queries with materialized views. In *Proceedings of the International Conference on Data Engineering (ICDE)*, 1995.

4. Surajit Chaudhuri and Kyuseok Shim. An overview of cost-based optimization of queries with aggregates. *IEEE Data Engineering Bulletin*, 18(3), 1995.

5. Mostafa Elhemali, César Galindo-Legaria, Torsten Grabs, and Milind Joshi. Execution strategies for SQL sub-queries. In *Proceedings of the ACM International Conference on Management of Data (SIGMOD)*, 2007.

6. César A. Galindo-Legaria and Arnon Rosenthal. Outerjoin simplification and reordering for query optimization. *ACM Transactions on Database Systems*, 22(1), 1997.

7. Jonathan Goldstein and Per-Ake Larson. Optimizing queries using materialized views: A practical, scalable solution. In *Proceedings of the*

ACM International Conference on Management of Data (SIGMOD), 2001.

8. Goetz Graefe. The Cascades framework for query optimization. *Data Engineering Bulletin*, 18(3), 1995.

9. Goetz Graefe and William McKenna. The Volcano optimizer generator: Extensibility and efficient search. In *Proceedings of the International Conference on Data Engineering (ICDE)*, 1993.

10. Laura M. Haas et al. Extensible query processing in Starburst. In *Proceedings of the ACM International Conference on Management of Data (SIGMOD)*, 1989.

11. Yannis E. Ioannidis. The history of histograms (abridged). In *Proceedings of the International Conference on Very Large Databases (VLDB)*, 2003.

12. C. Mohan, Donald J. Haderle, Yun Wang, and Josephine M. Cheng. Single table access using multiple indexes: Optimization, execution, and concurrency control techniques. In *Proceedings of the International Conference on Extending Database Technology (EDBT)*, 1990.

13. M. Muralikrishna. Improved unnesting algorithms for join aggregate SQL queries. In *Proceedings of the International Conference on Very Large Databases (VLDB)*, 1992.

14. Patricia G. Selinger et al. Access path selection in a relational database management system. In *Proceedings of the ACM International Conference on Management of Data (SIGMOD)*, 1979.

15. Weipeng P. Yan and Paul Larson. Performing Group-By before Join. In *Proceedings of the International Coference on Data Engineering (ICDE)*, 1994.

Chapter 3

Physical Database Design

Relational database systems provide physical data independence. That is, no matter which index configuration constitutes the physical design of the database, queries always return the same results. Of course, the performance of evaluating queries over different physical designs (i.e., different index configurations) can vary significantly. For that reason, together with the capabilities of the execution engine and query optimizer (discussed in Chapter 2), the physical design of a database determines how efficiently a query is executed.

There is no such a thing as the *optimal* physical design for a database, unless we state the problem in the context of a given workload. The reason is that indexes are useful only if they speed up queries without significantly slowing down updates. Good candidate indexes for some workloads might be completely irrelevant—or even harmful—for others. Additionally, indexes are redundant structures that consume disk storage. Since available storage is always limited, deciding which indexes to include in the physical design of a database becomes a difficult problem. The physical design problem can be stated as follows:

> **Physical design problem:** Given a workload W consisting of queries and updates, and a storage bound B, obtain the index configuration C that fits in B and results in queries in W executing as efficiently as possible.

To further clarify this statement, we next discuss alternative interpretations to the components of the problem statement. We also explain which interpretations we follow in the rest of the book and point to specific chapters that explore other alternatives.

First there is the question of what constitutes a workload W and how it is obtained. The most prevalent choice is to consider the workload W as a set of SQL queries and updates, possibly assigning a weight (or importance) to each query in W. Workloads can be generated after monitoring a production database system for some amount of time, by performing static analysis of database applications, or even after a careful manual design. We are agnostic to the specific approach to obtain a workload W and require only that W is a representative sample of the real-world workload that the database management system (DBMS) would process. Other alternative representations for W (and their implications) are explored in Chapter 10.

The second question is what exactly constitutes the optimizing function. The problem statement asks for "executing queries in W as efficiently as possible." While this is what ultimately matters in a production system, it introduces some technical difficulties. First, it requires us to measure actual execution times of queries (which could take a long time) and updates (which would change the database system) just to evaluate the quality of a given configuration or compare two alternative configurations. Additionally, it requires that the system executing queries is free from interference from other concurrent database queries or even from operating system processes. Since this is almost impossible to achieve in practice, execution times are usually nondeterministic, and it becomes difficult to reason with such an optimizing function. An alternative approach, which does not require executing queries, is to *model* the cost it would take a query to execute under a given configuration. If the model accurately predicts the execution time of a query *without actually executing it*, it can serve as a proxy for the actual metric, and all the previous problems no longer apply. As discussed in Chapter 2, the query optimizer models execution costs of queries as part of its own processing. This means that, associated with each execution plan, there is a notion of how costly is the plan in optimizer units. It could be argued that, in order to correctly distinguish among various execution plans, the cost model of the optimizer needs to be strongly correlated with actual execution costs (of course, the optimizer cost units need not be seconds but abstract units of work). We therefore define the efficiency of a query in terms of its estimated cost as given by the query optimizer.

The final question is how to aggregate individual query costs. The simplest and most widely used metric adds together the estimated cost of all queries and thus minimizes the total workload cost. Other alternatives include minimizing the cost of the slowest query, or the average improvement ratio (i.e., the average of the cost of each query under the final configuration divided by the cost of the query under the current configuration).

We are now ready to present a refined version of the physical design problem, which includes all aspects of the previous discussion:

> **(Refined) Physical design problem:** Given a workload $W = \{Q_1, \ldots, Q_n\}$, where each Q_i is a SQL query or update, and a storage bound B, obtain the index configuration $C = \{I_1, \ldots, I_k\}$ such that (1) $\sum_j size(I_j) \leq B$, and (2) $\sum_j cost(Q_j, C)$ is minimized, where $cost(Q,C)$ is the cost of the optimal plan for Q found by the optimizer when all and only indexes in C are available.

3.1   The Complexity of the Physical Design Problem

In this section we analyze the complexity of the physical design problem as defined previously. We first review some of the many rules of thumb that are widely applied in database installations and discuss why a more systematic approach is needed. We then show that such a systematic but still manual approach quickly becomes infeasible. Finally, we formalize this claim by showing that the physical design problem is in fact NP-complete.

3.1.1   Rules of Thumb in Physical Database Design

The problem of tuning the physical design of a database is very important in production systems and heavily depends on the specific workload and data distributions. Over time, a number of *rules of thumb* emerged providing some form of general guidance and best practices to follow during effective physical design sessions. Virtually every course in database systems or book that specializes in query performance discusses such rules. For illustration purposes, we next describe a few of these rules of thumb:

- *Index primary keys and most foreign keys.* Since most joins are performed between columns in primary and foreign keys, including such columns in indexes can improve performance of complex queries.

- *Columns frequently referenced in* WHERE *clauses are good candidates for indexes.* Columns that are referenced in equality or inequality predicates in WHERE clauses (especially those that are frequently referenced) can be efficiently fetched by appropriate indexes.

- *Avoid redundant indexes.* Indexes defined over the same (or almost the same) columns are rarely beneficial, as they do not provide additional utility over a single index but at the same time use additional space and need to be updated.

- *Use index columns with caution when they are frequently updated.* When database columns are updated, all indexes defined over such columns need to be maintained. A column that is frequently updated might transform an otherwise useful index into a performance bottleneck.

- *Consider covering indexes for critical queries.* Covering indexes (i.e., those indexes that contain all columns required in a query) are very good at improving performance, but at the same time they can be large and useful only for a few queries. Queries that are critical or very frequent, however, might benefit from covering indexes.

- *Avoid indexes on small tables.* Indexes on tables that fit in one or two pages often do not provide additional performance benefits but increase the number of structures to maintain and administer.

We can argue about specific rules or their conditions of applicability, but in general these best practices make sense and can be justified while taken in isolation. At the same time, they are mostly qualitative assertions and principles that do not easily lead to detailed and well-defined "recipes." It is therefore difficult to know exactly *when* and *how* to combine these rules, especially in the presence of multiple complex queries or storage constraints. In such scenarios, the good properties of various indexes need to be quantitatively balanced, as it becomes challenging to understand how indexes interact to answer a given query. In general, some form of quantitative and systematic analysis becomes crucial for an effective physical design, as illustrated next by using examples.

3.1.2   Systematic Physical Database Design

Consider a query that returns tuples satisfying a range predicate from a single table R:

```
Q1 =   SELECT A, B, C
       FROM R
       WHERE 10 < A < 20
```

Suppose that we want to obtain the best configuration of indexes for such a query. In this case, we can show that an index $I_1 = R(A|B, C)$ is optimal. In fact, we can seek I_1 to obtain all tuples that satisfy the range predicate on column A. Additionally, index I_1 includes columns B and C, which together cover the query and avoid additional RID lookups. With the exception of the initial traversal of index I_1 to obtain the first tuple that satisfies the predicate, the plan that uses I_1 accesses exactly the tuples that constitute the answer for the query and therefore cannot be improved.

Now consider a slight variation of Q1, with an additional range predicate on column B:

```
Q2 =   SELECT A, B, C
       FROM R
       WHERE 10 < A < 20
         AND 20 < B < 100
```

A plan using the previous index I_1 would seek the index and obtain all tuples that satisfy predicate 10 < A < 20. From this intermediate result, all tuples that do not satisfy predicate 20 < B < 100 would be eliminated. Note that in this case we do not scan just the query result. If most of the tuples satisfy the predicate on A but just a handful do so for the predicate on B, we would read many unnecessary tuples from disk, thus wasting several inputs/outputs (I/Os). Analogously, a strategy using index $I_2 = R(B|A, C)$ would first obtain all tuples satisfying predicate 20 < B < 100 and then filter those not satisfying the predicate on A. It can be shown that for any data distribution, either I_1 or I_2 results in the better plan, but it is not immediate which one is better for any specific instance. If we have access to statistics on base tables (e.g., histograms as discussed in Chapter 2) and a rough understanding of the cost model of the optimizer, we can calculate, for any data instance, which alternative between I_1 and I_2 is better. Specifically, we should choose the index whose key column corresponds to the more selective predicate.

Now consider the following query, which is very similar to Q2 but has a slightly more complex predicate in the WHERE clause:

```
Q3 =   SELECT B, C, D
       FROM R
       WHERE 50 < B < 100
             AND 61 < 2 * D + 1 < 81
```

On the surface, Q2 and Q3 are not very different. We can rewrite the predicate on D to 30 < D < 40 and then, applying the same argument as in the previous example, choose between $I_3 = R(B|C, D)$ and $I_4 = R(D|C, B)$ based on statistical information on columns B and D. However, we are making the additional assumption that the optimizer would recognize the algebraic manipulation that equates 61 < 2 * D + 1 < 81 and 30 < D < 40. If the optimizer is unable to derive and leverage this identity, it would not be able to use index I_4 to seek appropriate tuples (even when *we know* it is the best alternative). In this scenario, if only I_4 is present, the optimizer would perform a clustered index scan to answer the query, which in general would be worse than the index-based alternative leveraging index I_3.

To make the running example a bit more complex, suppose that our workload consists of both Q2 and Q3. Then, the best configuration would be the union of the best index for each query (since the workload does not have updates, there is no performance penalty in adding indexes). Suppose that, based on statistical information and knowledge about the optimizer's simplification logic, we determine that the best configuration is $I_1 = R(A|B, C)$ and $I_4 = R(D|B, C)$. Assume now that the storage required by both I_1 and I_4 is unacceptably high (e.g., it might not fit in the available storage). In this case, the situation is considerably more difficult. We can always decide to drop either I_1 or I_4 (specifically, the one that results in the smaller improvement) and obtain a configuration that, at least, benefits one of the two queries. However, consider an index like $I_5 = R(A|B, C, D)$, which is smaller in size than I_1 and I_4 combined and thus might fit in the available storage. This index is slightly worse than $I_1 = R(A|B, C)$ for Q2 because of the additional included column D, which makes it wider and therefore more expensive to scan. While we cannot seek I_5 for Q3 because its key column A does not occur in the WHERE clause of Q3, I_3 can still be scanned much more efficiently than the clustered index (it contains fewer columns). The net effect is that, although I_5 is suboptimal for *both* Q2 and Q3, it might still be better than having a configuration with a single index that is optimal for either Q2 or Q3. Of course, $I_6 = R(D|A, B, C)$ should also be considered, since it helps Q3 almost as much as the optimal I_4 and is better for Q2 than the plan using a clustered index. To make matters worse, other interesting alternatives are possible as well. Consider the scenario where the available storage is even more constrained and cannot accommodate index I_5. In this situation, indexes $R(A)$ and $R(D)$, which combined are smaller than I_5, can be useful if I_5 itself is too big. Depending on the number of tuples in the result of Q2 and Q3, using

```
SELECT n_name, SUM(l_extendedprice*(1-l_discount)) AS revenue
FROM customers, orders, lineitem, supplier, nation, region
WHERE c_custkey = o_custkey
   AND o_orderkey = l_orderkey
   AND l_suppkey = s_suppkey
   AND c_nationkey = s_nationkey
   AND s_nationkey = n_nationkey
   AND n_regionkey = r_regionkey
   AND r_name = 'AMERICA'
   AND o_orderdate BETWEEN '1997-01-01' AND dateadd(YY, 1, '1997-01-01')
GROUP BY n_name
ORDER BY revenue DESC
```

FIGURE 3.1   A synthetic query of moderate complexity.

such narrow indexes to seek the relevant tuples, followed by RID lookups to the primary index and a final filter for the remaining predicates, can still be better than having no indexes. Of course, combinations of all these indexes result in complex trade-offs between required storage and the resulting query performance.

To finish our example, suppose that we add an update query to our workload:

$$Q4 = \quad \begin{aligned} &\text{UPDATE R} \\ &\text{SET B = B + 1} \\ &\text{WHERE } 10 < C < 20 \end{aligned}$$

In this case, every index that contains column B needs to be updated by Q4. Obtaining the best set of indexes for a workload consisting of {Q2, Q3, Q4} requires a nontrivial analysis and understanding of the cost model, search space, and other optimizer internals.

To top it all, so far we have considered very simple single-table queries. Real queries are rarely so well behaved. For instance, Figure 3.1 shows query 5 from the synthetic TPC-H benchmark, which models queries of medium complexity in a decision support scenario. This query contains joins among six tables, predicates that involve built-in functions like dateadd, group-by clauses, and arithmetic operations in the SELECT clause. Obtaining index recommendations for workloads consisting of several such queries is very complex. We calculated the number of possible indexes that, if present, would be considered in a candidate plan by the query optimizer. Figure 3.2 shows these counts for each table in the database and different workloads. For instance, if we consider only query 5, there are around 80 possible indexes that are relevant overall. While this number might seem small, our task is to pick a good *subset* of these 80 indexes, which already introduces a combinatorial explosion in the number of possible index configurations. In any case, repeating the same experiment for the first five queries in the benchmark results in over 50,000 candidate indexes. Finally, the full 22-query workload results in over a billion candidate

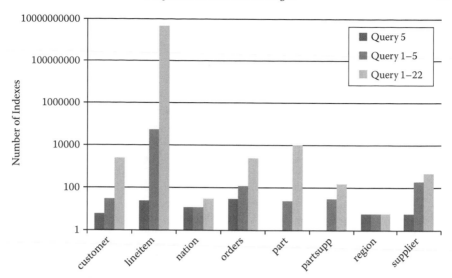

FIGURE 3.2 Number of possible relevant indexes for different query workloads.

indexes that, if present, would be considered by the query optimizer. Clearly, reasoning with such a large number of indexes is a very difficult task!

3.1.3 Formal Complexity Argument

We now show that in general the physical design problem is NP-complete. We provide a reduction from the 0-1 knapsack problem. The 0-1 knapsack problem takes as inputs an integer capacity C and a set of objects $O = \{o_1, \ldots, o_n\}$, where each o_i has volume c_i and is associated with a benefit b_i. The output is a subset of O whose combined volume fits in C (i.e., $\sum c_i \leq C$) and sum of benefit values is maximized (i.e. $maximize \sum b_i$).

Consider an arbitrary knapsack problem with capacity B and objects $O = \{o_1, \ldots, o_n\}$. We construct a physical design problem instance as follows. First, we associate each o_i with a table T_i. Table T_i contains n_i tuples and m_i columns (the first of such columns is called `col`). Values m_i and n_i are chosen such that the following properties are satisfied. First, a nonclustered index on column `col` fits in exactly c_i pages (since the number of pages is determined by the number of tuples n_i, this property essentially fixes the number of tuples of T_i). Second, table T_i fits in $b_i + 1$ pages. Note that the number of tuples in T_i is fixed, so this property determines how many additional columns m_i to create. Of course, the number of pages in the nonclustered index cannot be larger than the number of pages in the full table T_i, so a third constraint is that $b_i + 1 \geq c_i$. Note that b_i and c_i are given in the knapsack problem and might not satisfy the inequality. However, in such a case, we can always scale up all b_i values (and B) in the original problem by the same constant without changing the problem solution (and thus we assume that $b_i + 1 \geq c_i$ holds).

We populate table T_i with one tuple with value 0 for `col` and the remaining tuples with value 1 for `col`. Finally, we create a workload $W = \{Q_1, \ldots, Q_n\}$ where:

$$
\begin{aligned}
Q_i \; = \quad &\texttt{SELECT } \texttt{c}_i \\
&\texttt{FROM } \texttt{T}_i \\
&\texttt{WHERE } \texttt{c}_i \texttt{ = 0}
\end{aligned}
$$

and set a storag constraint of B disk pages. Now suppose that we can select only nonclustered indexes.* In such a case, the only candidate indexes that we consider are $I_i = T_i(c_i)$ since all queries refer to just one column. All such indexes are defined over different tables and therefore do not interact with each other with respect to the queries in W. Consider Q_i. If index I_i is present, the optimizer would pick an index-based strategy that seeks tuples where `col=0` using a single I/O (since there is a single tuple that satisfies the predicate). Alternatively, if index I_i is not present, the optimizer would scan table T_i to find the tuple satisfying $c_i = 0$ using $b_i + 1$ page I/Os. Therefore, the presence of index I_i results in an improvement of execution time given by $b_i + 1 - 1 = b_i$ I/Os. The physical design problem then reduces to finding the best subset of the original indexes I_i, each using c_i storage pages and improving the overall workload cost by a factor of b_i. Clearly, the optimal solution for this instance of the physical design problem directly translates into the optimal solution for the original 0-1 knapsack problem by selecting the objects o_i associated with tables T_i for which an index was chosen.

3.2   Toward Automated Physical Design

In the previous section we showed that even for moderate problem sizes it is very difficult to manually find the optimal physical database design for a given workload, and thus automated tools are a necessity. The fact that the physical design problem is NP-complete tells us that there is little hope for automated tools finding optimal physical designs except for small problem instances. A variant of this complexity result was originally proved in the early eighties and skewed much of the subsequent research in the area toward heuristic search and approximation algorithms.

Similar to the traditional optimization problem described in Chapter 2, the physical design problem can be seen as a very complex search problem.

---

*The more general case that additionally considers clustered indexes is slightly more involved, requiring an additional column `col2` and twice as many queries, but we omit such details for simplicity.

The analogy does not stop here, as we can describe and analyze the physical design problem in terms of the same three components that we used for the query optimization problem: the search space of index configurations, the cost model to evaluate configurations, and the enumeration strategy to traverse the search space. In the next section we briefly discuss these components in the context of the physical design problem and devote the next three chapters to an in-depth discussion and analysis of these concepts. At the end of this chapter we provide pointers to some earlier pieces of work in the context of the physical design problem that might be interesting to readers studying the evolution of ideas in the field.

3.2.1   Search Space

In the context of the physical design problem, the search space is the set of indexes that could be considered candidates for a given database and workload. We now discuss some choices that addressed this issue over the years. Some decisions are purely pragmatic, while others depend on specific infrastructure provided by the DBMS or its optimizer.

The first characterization of the search space that we discuss is very general and independent of the actual workload. Initial work in the physical design problem considered only single-column indexes. This choice was driven not only by simplicity but also by the fact that most workloads were generated by simple online transaction processing (OLTP) applications. In these scenarios, queries are rather simple (mostly navigational queries, where a single tuple is selected and possibly joined with other tables to obtain additional information), and therefore single-column indexes are a good alternative. Advances in query processing, coupled with ever-increasing application complexity, made the single-column index approach inadequate. Current decision support applications often generate complex queries that require elaborate access path selection and for which single-column indexes often fail to improve performance. To handle these new scenarios, newer solutions expand the search space to include indexes that have at most a certain number of columns, while others are unrestricted in that respect. Recent work in the physical design problem considers multicolumn indexes in the search space.

Another characterization of the search space that is independent of the workload concerns the search space of indexes for a single query. Driven by simpler applications and query engines, early designs assumed that any query would benefit from at most one index per table (and therefore excluded more complex strategies such as index intersections). As with the previous characterization, this restriction was lifted in more recent work.

After deciding on a generic characterization of the search space of indexes, we still need to decide what the *specific* search space would be for a given workload. After all, we would not want to include in the search space indexes that are guaranteed to be useless (i.e., indexes over tables that are never mentioned in the workload). The traditional way to define a search space for a given workload consists of two steps. First, there is a procedure to define the set of candidate indexes for each query in the workload. Different techniques are possible, ranging from purely syntactic ones that examine the query string to more sophisticated ones that leverage the query optimizer itself. Once we characterize the set of candidates for each query, the second step is to define the search space for the workload. Some earlier techniques restrict such space to simply the union of candidate indexes for each query, where more recent approaches also consider additional indexes that result from *combining* candidate indexes from different queries. In Chapter 4 we present a detailed discussion of all these alternatives.

3.2.2   Cost Model

To perform any sort of meaningful traversal over the search space of index configurations, we need the ability to calculate both the size of any given configuration C as well as the cost of evaluating the workload under C. Estimating the size of a configuration is not difficult, since it is essentially the sum of sizes of each index in the configuration. This can be calculated based on statistics of the corresponding base table (i.e., number of tuples and tuple length).

Calculating the cost of evaluating the workload under an arbitrary configuration is more challenging. The most accurate procedure involves creating the indexes in the configuration, optimizing all queries in the workload, and adding the estimated cost for all queries. While optimizing queries is relatively cheap, creating the indexes in the configuration is prohibitively expensive, as it requires repeatedly scanning and sorting tables in the database.

An early alternative to the accurate but expensive approach described already involved creating a cost model outside of the optimizer and predicting how query costs would vary with changes to the physical design. These models ranged from crude to sophisticated, in which histograms were built and used to compute selectivity of predicates and ultimately costs of queries. These approaches worked reasonably well when query engines were rather simple and workloads consisted of short OLTP queries. With modern query engines and complex decision support queries, however, these approaches quickly became impractical. The main problem is that indexes are useful only if the optimizer chooses a plan that leverages them. Even if an index might seem a great candidate, it would be irrelevant if the optimizer does not choose (or even considers) the corresponding execution plan. Therefore, it is not a good idea to second-guess the optimizer.

These issues result in an interesting conflict. On one hand, we need to be in sync with the optimizer to decide the cost of a workload under a given configuration. On the other hand, it seems that we cannot use the optimizer short of actually performing very expensive index materializations. A subsequent line of work solved this problem by implementing what is called a *what-if optimization layer*, which obtains estimated execution costs of plans under arbitrary configurations without actually materializing indexes. A detailed discussion on this component is the subject of Chapter 5.

3.2.3 Enumeration Strategy

Early enumeration strategies for the physical design problem relied on either simplified search spaces (e.g., only single-column indexes) or restricted execution environments (e.g., OLTP queries with external cost models). For that reason, several pieces of work considered the problem of obtaining the *optimal* physical design for a given workload. Motivated in part by complexity results in the area (see Section 3.1.3) but also by increasingly sophisticated query engines and workloads, recent techniques use heuristics to effectively traverse smaller but relevant portions of the search space. Some proposed alternatives leverage the fact that the physical design problem is in a way similar to the knapsack problem (however more general). Thus, they use modified heuristics for the knapsack problem to traverse the search space. Other techniques use greedy hill-climbing approaches, where configurations are built bottom-up by progressively adding high-impact indexes. A different approach starts with large configurations and progressively removes low-impact indexes, in what can be seen as a relaxation-based approach. In Chapter 6 we discuss these alternatives in detail.

3.3 Summary

- The physical design problem is computationally expensive and in general very complex even for moderate-sized inputs.
- The physical design problem can be seen as a complex search procedure that is specified by answering three questions:
  - Search space: What is the space of indexes that we consider for a given workload (Chapter 4)?
  - Cost model: How do we estimate the cost of a workload under a given configuration (Chapter 5)?
  - Enumeration strategy: How do we effectively traverse the space of configurations (Chapter 6)?

3.4 Additional Reading

The NP-completeness proof of Section 3.1.3 is one of several variants that appear in the literature.[1,2,10] Several books analyze the physical design problem and further discuss rules of thumb for physical database design.[9,13] Lahdenmaki and Leach give a very good and systematic approach for manually tuning SQL statements.[8] Chaudhuri and Narasayya give a historical perspective of the automated physical design problem.[3] Early work in the physical design problem[7,14] uses parametric models of the workload rather than an explicit workload as virtually all subsequent pieces of work. This early work focuses on optimal solutions due to the simplistic search space and query engine capabilities.[12,14] More recent work uses a cost model outside of that of the optimizer.[4,11] Another line of work uses the query optimizer itself to evaluate the goodness of configurations.[5,6] Early work suggested an enumeration strategy that heuristically identifies the best candidates for each query and subsequently searches through the union of alternatives.[11] More recent references are discussed in subsequent chapters.

References

1. Nicolas Bruno and Surajit Chaudhuri. Physical design refinement: The "Merge-Reduce" approach. In *Proceedings of the International Conference on Extending Database Technology (EDBT)*, 2006.

2. Surajit Chaudhuri, Mayur Datar, and Vivek R. Narasayya. Index selection for databases: A hardness study and a principled heuristic solution. *IEEE Transactions on Knowledge and Data Engineering*, 16(11), 2004.

3. Surajit Chaudhuri and Vivek R. Narasayya. Self-tuning database systems: A decade of progress. In *VLDB*, 2007.

4. Sunil Choenni, Henk M. Blanken, and Thiel Chang. Index selection in relational databases. In *Computer and Information*, 1993.

5. Sheldon J. Finkelstein, Mario Schkolnick, and Paolo Tiberio. Physical database design for relational databases. *ACM Transactions on Database Systems*, 13(1), 1988.

6. Martin R. Frank, Edward Omiecinski, and Shamkant B. Navathe. Adaptive and automated index selection in RDBMS. In *Proceedings of the International Conference on Extending Database Technology (EDBT)*, 1992.

7. M. Hammer and A. Chan. Index selection in a self-adaptive database management system. In *Proceedings of the ACM International Conference on Management of Data (SIGMOD)*, 1976.

8. Tapio Lahdenmaki and Michael Leach. *Relational Database Index Design and the Optimizers*. John Wiley & Sons, 2005.

9. Sam Lightstone, Toby Teorey, and Tom Nadeau. *Physical Database Design*. Morgan Kaufmann, 2007.

10. Gregory Piatetsky-Shapiro. The optimal selection of secondary indices is NP-complete. *SIGMOD Record*, 13(2), 1983.

11. Steve Rozen and Dennis Shasha. A framework for automating physical database design. In *VLDB*, 1991.

12. Mario Schkolnik. The optimal selection of secondary indices for files. In *Information Systems*, 1975.

13. Dennis Shasha and Phillippe Bonnet. *Database Tuning. Principles, Experiments, and Troubleshooting Techniques*. Morgan Kaufmann, 2003.

14. Michael Stonebraker. The choice of partial inversions and combined indices. In *Computer and Information Sciences*, 1974.

Part II

Automated Physical Database Design

Chapter 4

Characterizing the Search Space

The physical design problem introduced in Chapter 3 can be seen as a constrained optimization problem, in which the optimizing function is the overall cost of the workload (counting both queries and updates) and the constraint is the storage bound on the configuration size. In this chapter, we characterize the search space for the physical design problem. Specifically, we explain how to identify a set of indexes for a given workload and storage bound that includes the desired optimal index configuration. We do this in two steps. First, in Section 4.1 we present approaches that address a simpler problem. Specifically, we explain how to obtain a small set of indexes that include the optimal configuration for the case of a single SELECT query and no storage constraint. Then, in Section 4.2 we extend this basic approach to general workloads. We finish this chapter with a formal characterization of the search space for the physical design problem.

4.1 Candidate Indexes for a Single SELECT Query

When the workload consists of a single SELECT query and there is no storage bound, the physical design problem becomes much simpler. Adding indexes to a configuration does not hurt performance (because indexes are not updated) and does not invalidate the configuration (because there is no storage bound). We now discuss approaches to find a small set of candidate indexes that include the optimal configuration for a single SELECT query.

4.1.1 Parsing-Based Approach

The simplest way to obtain the candidate set of indexes for a given query is by performing a syntactic analysis of the query string. We first parse the input query and identify the set of *indexable* columns in the parse tree. A column c is indexable if there is a predicate of the form "c op *expression*" in the WHERE clause of the query, if c belongs to the set of columns in a group-by or order-by clause, or if c is updated in an **UPDATE** statement. For instance, consider the query following:

```
SELECT R.a, R.b
FROM R, S
WHERE R.x = S.y
ORDER BY R.a
```

The indexable columns in this case are **R.a** (because it belongs to the order-by columns) and both **R.x** and **S.y** (because they are part of a valid predicate in the **WHERE** clause).

Additionally, we need to identify the columns that are not indexable but still mentioned in the query string and therefore required during query processing. In the previous query, column **R.b** is not indexable but is required for the proper evaluation of the query.

Once all relevant columns have been identified, we can obtain the set of candidates for the query. There are different ways to define this initial candidate set, depending on the capabilities of the query engine. For instance, suppose that the query engine can leverage only single-column indexes. In that case, the candidate set for the query consists of one clustered index and one nonclustered index for each indexable column. The query would result in one clustered and one nonclustered index for columns **R.a**, **R.x**, and **S.y**, for a total of six candidate indexes.

Modern query engines, however, can handle multicolumn indexes. Suppose that I_T is the set of indexable columns of table T, and R_T is the set of non-indexable columns of table T for the input query. The candidate indexes for table T are all of the form $T(K|R_1 \cup R_2)$, where K is a permutation of $I \subseteq I_T$, $R_1 \subseteq (I_T - I)$, and $R_2 \in \{\emptyset, R_T\}$. That is, for each subset of the indexable columns I_T, we consider all its permutations as key columns, add subsets of the remaining indexable columns as included columns, and optionally add the nonindexable columns as additional included columns. For the previous query, the candidate set is {R(x), R(x|b), R(x|a), R(x|a,b), R(a), R(a|b), R(a|x), R(a|b,x), R(a,x), R(a,x|b), R(x,a), R(x,a|b), S(y)}. Additionally, the candidate set contains one clustered index for each nonclustered index in the previous set, with the same key columns.

Clearly the number of such indexes can be very large even for queries of moderate complexity. We can obtain a smaller candidate set that is very likely to contain the optimal configuration for the input query if we (1) consider covering only indexes (i.e., indexes that contain all columns required in the query), (2) restrict permutations of key columns to those that begin with all equality predicates in the **WHERE** clause or with all columns in the group-by or order-by columns, and (3) allow permutations only in which the remaining key columns are in decreasing order of selectivity. Using these heuristics, the candidate set for the previous query is {R(a,x|b), R(x,a|b), S(y)} plus the corresponding clustered indexes.

4.1.2   Execution Plan–Based Approach

We now discuss a variant of the parsing-based approach that works off the execution plan produced by the optimizer rather than off the query parse tree. To motivate this approach, consider again the example in the previous section:

```
SELECT R.a, R.b
FROM R, S
WHERE R.x = S.y
ORDER BY R.a
```

but suppose that there is a primary-key constraint on column S.y (all tuples in S have distinct S.y values), and a foreign-key constraint on R.x referencing the primary key of S (which guarantees that every tuple in R joins with exactly one tuple in S). In this case, since no column from S is present in the SELECT clause, an optimizer might choose to simplify the previous query by removing the *superfluous* join with S, obtaining the equivalent query:

```
SELECT R.a, R.b
FROM R
ORDER BY R.a
```

Performing such sophisticated analysis over the parse tree not only is very complex but also duplicates much of the work of the optimizer. An alternative approach to obtain candidate indexes for a query is to leverage the optimizer itself and process the resulting execution plan rather than the input query string. For the previous query, the execution plan would scan table R and then sort the result by R.a. We can then obtain indexable columns (e.g., those that are associated with Join, Aggregate, and Sort operators) and proceed as before. We would then obtain the candidate set {R(a|b)} for the original query and avoid considering indexes on columns R.x and S.y, which would not be exploited anyway by the database management system (DBMS).

In addition to the foreign-key constraint example above, optimizers rely on several rules to transform query fragments, such as detecting contradictions or tautologies in predicates, eliminating empty subexpressions, or inferring implied predicates through joins. The approach that leverages execution plans produced by the optimizer is therefore a more robust alternative to obtain candidate indexes for a query. Another benefit of this approach is that it is kept in sync with the optimizer. If a new simplification strategy is incorporated into the optimizer, it can be directly leveraged by the candidate selection module. Finally, this approach can be extended to mimic some of the features of the more accurate instrumentation-based approach discussed in the next section without requiring modifying the query optimizer.

4.1.3   Instrumentation-Based Approach

While the execution-plan-based approach discussed in the previous section is more robust than the parsing-based approach, it still suffers from certain shortcomings. In a way, it leverages only the final execution plan of the query, discarding important information that is obtained during optimization. In this section we present an instrumentation-based approach that piggybacks on top of regular query optimization and returns a very concise description of all access path requests of the input query. These access path (or index) requests can then be used to identify a small superset of the optimal set of indexes for the input query.

We assume that the optimizer has a unique entry point for single-table access path selection (see Chapter 2 for details on these procedures). In other words, there is one component responsible for finding physical index strategies for single-table logical subplans. For concreteness, in this section we assume a transformation-based optimizer, but the same ideas can be applied to other enumeration strategies as well.

4.1.3.1   Review of Access Path Selection

During the optimization of a single query, the optimizer issues several index requests via specific transformation rules. For an index request over a single-table subplan (see Figure 4.2), an access path generation module first identifies the columns in equality and range predicates, required sort columns, and the columns that are either part of complex predicates or additionally referenced upwards in the query tree. Then, it analyzes the available indexes and returns one or more alternative physical plans that might be optimal for the input logical subquery. In general, each generated plan is an instance of a template tree that (1) has one or more index seeks or scans at the leaf nodes, (2) combines the leaf nodes by binary intersections or unions, (3) applies an optional RID lookup to retrieve missing columns, (4) applies an optional filter operator for any remaining predicate, and (5) applies an optional sort operator to enforce order. Consider a single-table index request for the Standard Query Language (SQL) fragment below (note that this query fragment can be part of a larger query that joins multiple tables, but the optimizer calls only the access path selection module for single-table query fragments):

$$\Pi_{d,e}\left(\sigma_{a<10 \wedge b<10 \wedge a+c=8}(R)\right) \quad \text{(with a sort requirement over column } d)$$

In this case, the optimizer identifies columns a and b in sargable predicates (i.e., predicates that can leverage index seeks), column d as a required order, and columns e and c as additional columns that are referenced either by nonsargable predicates or upward in the tree. Suppose that indexes R(a) and R(b) are available. The optimizer can then generate the plan in Figure 4.1a. However, depending on selectivity values, the alternative plan in Figure 4.1b (that avoids intersecting indexes but performs more record id (RID) lookups) can be more attractive. Also, if a covering index R(d|a,b,c,e) is available, the alternative plan in Figure 4.1c might be preferable because it avoids sorting an intermediate result. A cost-based optimizer considers this space of alternative plans for the available indexes and returns the most efficient physical strategy.

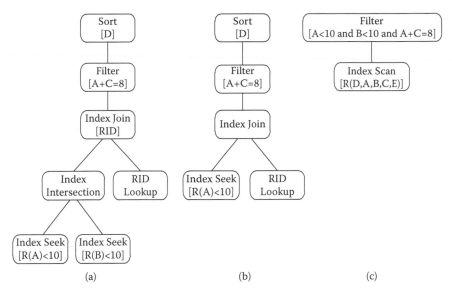

FIGURE 4.1 Alternative index strategies for the same single-table access path request. (Used with permission from Bruno, N. & Chaudhuri, S. In *Proceedings of the ACM International Conference on Management of Data [SIGMOD]*, 2005.)

This approach is also used to generate index-based join plans (which implement joins between an arbitrary outer relation and a single-table inner relation that is repeatedly accessed using an index to obtain join matches). In this case, the access path generation module works with the inner table only, and the joined column in the table is considered part of a sargable (equality) predicate. For instance, consider the query fragment $(Q \bowtie_{Q.x=T.y} T)$, where Q represents an arbitrary complex expression that returns the outer relation in the index-based join. Conceptually, the optimizer passes to the access path selection module the single-table expression $\sigma_{T.y=?}(T)$ and proceeds as before, considering $T.y$ a column in a sargable predicate with an (unspecified) constant value, which would be evaluated multiple times (once per each tuple returned by Q).

4.1.3.2 Instrumenting the Optimizer

Figure 4.2 shows how a query optimizer can be instrumented to enable reasoning with access path requests. Every time the optimizer issues an access path request through an implementation rule, we obtain the information that is relevant to such requests and store it at the root of the originating logical plan. At the end of optimization, we return, along with the execution plan, the set of all index requests generated during optimization. Intuitively, each index request encodes the properties of any index strategy that might implement the subtree

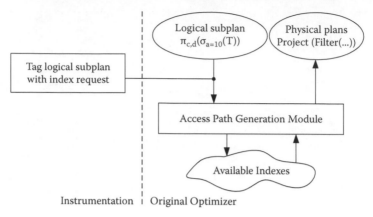

FIGURE 4.2   Instrumenting the query optimizer. (Used with permission from Bruno, N. & Chaudhuri, M. In *Proceedings of the ACM of Data [SIG-MOD]*, 1993.)

rooted at the operator over which the index request was issued. Specifically, an index request is an expression of the form $N \times (T, E, R, P, O, A)$, where:

- N is the number of times the subplan would be executed. It is greater than one when the subplan corresponds to the inner relation of an index-based join or is part of a correlated subquery (to simplify the notation, we omit this prefix when $N = 1$).

- T is the table over which the index request is issued.

- E is a set of tuples, $E = \{(c_i, card_i)\}$, where c_i is a column from T in a equality-based sargable predicate (e.g., a = 10), and $card_i$ is the estimated cardinality of the predicate.

- R is a set of tuples, $R = \{(c_i, card_i)\}$, where c_i is a column from T in a range-based sargable predicate (e.g., 5 < a < 10), and $card_i$ is the estimated cardinality of the predicate.

- P is a set of tuples $P = \{(C_i, card_i)\}$, where C_i is a subset of columns from T corresponding to a nonsargable predicate (e.g., a * b < 10), and $card_i$ is the estimated cardinality of the predicate.

- O is a sequence of columns for which an order has been requested.

- A is the set of additional columns from T required upward in the execution plan.

Figure 4.3 illustrates this procedure for some fragments of the following query:

```
SELECT R.a
FROM R, S, T
WHERE R.x = S.y AND R.w = T.z
    AND R.a = 5 AND R.b < 8
    AND T.c = 8 AND T.d + T.e = 100
```

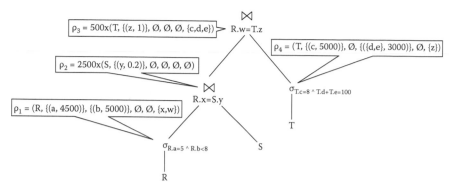

FIGURE 4.3   Sample requests for different nodes in a subquery.

As an example, request ρ_1 is associated with the selection condition on table R and specifies that there are (1) a sargable column a associated with an equality predicate expecting to return 4,500 tuples, (2) a sargable column b associated with a range predicate expecting to return 5,000 tuples, (3) no columns in nonsargable predicates, (4) no order requested, and (5) additional required columns w and x. Similarly, request ρ_2 was generated when the optimizer considered an index-based join alternative with R and S as the outer and inner relations, respectively. Request ρ_2 specifies that $T_2.y$ is part of an equality-based predicate that would be executed 2,500 times (once for each outer row). The average number of tuples matched and returned from S is 0.2, and therefore the corresponding index join would produce $2,500 \cdot 0.2 = 500$ rows overall.

From an engineering point of view, the instrumentation approach is appealing because it is not very intrusive. In fact, the modifications required to enable this instrumentation are restricted to a single component in the optimizer. From an algorithmic point of view, the instrumentation technique does not rely on guesswork to reason with access path requests. Since requests are intercepted *during* optimization, we do not miss candidates that might not be apparent by looking at the final execution plan, nor do we propose many candidates that are syntactically valid but might not be exploitable during optimization.* From a practical point of view, the number of requests that are generated for input queries is not very large. As an illustration, Figure 4.4 shows the total number of requests for a typical TPC-H workload. We can see that even for relatively complex queries, the number of requests is moderate (compare these numbers with the total number of candidate indexes in Figure 3.2).

---

*Note that we can approximate access path requests from inspecting resulting execution plans as described in Section 4.1.2. This procedure is not as accurate as the instrumentation-based approach but requires no changes to the query optimizer.

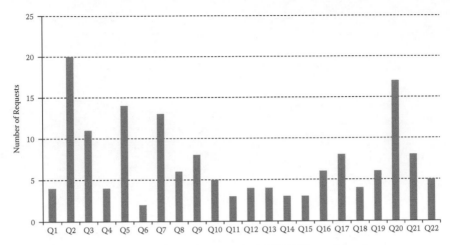

FIGURE 4.4   Index requests for a typical TPC-H workload.

4.1.3.3   Finding the Best Indexes for a Request

The instrumentation approach described in the previous section returns a concise encoding of all access path requests performed by the optimizer for an input query. If we obtain the indexes that best implement each of these requests and unite them, the result would be a superset of the optimal configuration for the input query.

In general, if we can choose the physical design, the optimal execution plan for a given request cannot use index intersections. Consider an execution plan that intersects a number R_A and R_B of rows from table R that are produced, respectively, by indexes I_A (stored in P_A pages) and I_B (stored in P_B pages). The number of inputs/outputs (I/Os) required by this plan is $C_{AB} = P_A \frac{R_A}{|R|} + P_B \frac{R_B}{|R|} + \Delta$, where Δ is the number of I/Os used to intersect RIDs (we assume fixed-size records, but this does not change the main result). Now, assume without loss of generality that $R_A < R_B$, and consider index I_D, which consists of all columns of I_A followed by the columns in I_B that are not in I_A. Index I_D can be stored in $P_D \leq P_A + P_B$ pages because some columns (at least RIDs) are duplicated in I_A and I_B. Seeking I_D with the predicates used in I_A results in $R_D = R_A$ rows. Therefore, the total number of I/Os by using I_D is $C_D = P_D \frac{R_D}{|R|} \leq (P_A + P_B) \frac{R_A}{|R|} = P_A \frac{R_A}{|R|} + P_B \frac{R_A}{|R|} \leq C_{AB}$, since $R_A < R_B$ and $\Delta \geq 0$. The optimal execution plan therefore uses at most one index (and optional RID lookups).

We next show how to obtain the indexes that would lead to the best execution plan implementing a given access path request, for progressively more complex scenarios. Specifically, we assume that $N = 1$ since the best index for a request is independent of the number of times the corresponding subplan would be executed.

Scenario 1: $|R| \leq 1$, $P = \emptyset$, $O = \emptyset$. Suppose first that the index request contains no sort columns (i.e., $O = \emptyset$), no columns in nonsargable predicates (i.e., $P = \emptyset$), and at most one column associated with a sargable range predicate (i.e., $|R| = 1$). In this case, we can show that no strategy using RID lookups is optimal. To see this, consider an execution plan that looks up R_A rows from index I_A (stored in P_A pages) and subsequently performs that many RID lookups to obtain the remaining columns. The number of I/Os required by this plan is $C_A = P_A \frac{R_A}{|R|} + \min(R_A, P_R)$, where P_R is the number of pages used to store R in a clustered index or heap. Consider now index I_B, which contains all columns in I_A followed by all other required columns in the query execution plan, and denote $P_B (\geq P_A)$ as the number of pages used to store I_B. Since I_B is a covering index, we can retrieve the same result as before by seeking I_B with the same predicates we used on I_A but without doing RID lookups. The number of I/Os of such a plan is $C_B = P_B \frac{R_A}{|R|}$. We consider two cases. If $R_A \geq P_R$, then $C_A = \frac{R_A}{|R|} + P_R \geq P_R \geq P_B \geq C_B$. Otherwise, if $R_A < P_R$, $C_A = P_A \frac{R_A}{|R|} + R_A = \frac{R_A}{|R|}(P_A + |R|)$. Then, $C_A < C_B$ if $P_A + |R| < P_B$. This is not possible, however, because each row fits in one page, and therefore $|R| \geq P_B$.

Therefore, we can guarantee that the optimal plan does not use index intersections or RID lookups, so it must seek a covering index. To obtain this index we proceed as follows. First, we define the key columns of the index as the set of columns in equality-based sargable predicates (in any order), followed by the column in the range-based sargable predicate with the smallest selectivity.* Modern query engines can seek multiple equality predicates (and one final range predicate) using a multicolumn index simultaneously by concatenating the predicate values in the search key. Therefore, the key columns of the index previously described are the ones resulting in the seek with the smallest number of false positives. The included columns in the index are all those in R, P, O, and A that are not already in the index key. As an example, consider an index request over table T with $E = \{(a, 100)\}$, $R = \{(b, 200)\}$, $P = O = \emptyset$, and $A = \{c, d\}$. In this case, the optimal index would be $T(a, b|c, d)$.

Scenario 2: $P = \emptyset$, $O = \emptyset$. Suppose first that there are multiple range-based sargable predicates in R but that P and O are still empty. In this case, the key columns for the optimal index are obtained in the same way as in scenario 1. However, obtaining the included columns of the index is more complex. A covering index guarantees that no RID lookups would be necessary. At the same time, it can be more expensive than a strategy that relies on a narrow index that includes a few columns

---

*If there are no columns in sargable predicates (i.e., $E = R = \emptyset$), the key of the index is the column, among those in P, O, and A, with the smallest size.

from R, filters many tuples after the index seek (using the corresponding predicates in R) and then performs a very small number of lookups. As an example, consider an index request over table T with $E = \{(a, 100)\}$, $R = \{(b, 10), (c, 20)\}$, $P = O = \emptyset$, and $A = \{d\}$. A covering index $I_c = T(a, b|c, d)$ scans all tuples satisfying the predicates on a, b, and c without requiring RID lookups. Consider the alternative index $I_n = T(a, b|c)$. In this case, after obtaining tuples from the index we need to fetch column d from the primary index. The scan over the narrower (and therefore smaller) index I_n, however, might compensate the additional RID lookups, especially if column d is wide.

In this case, assuming independence among predicates, it can be shown that the optimal index is either that of scenario 1 or has the same key columns as in scenario 1 followed by a prefix of the columns in R sorted by increasing cardinality (requiring an optional fetch to obtain the remaining columns). The best index can therefore be efficiently identified by progressively including new columns from R to the included columns of the index until no further benefit is obtained.

Scenario 3: $O = \emptyset$. If the index request contains nonsargable predicates (i.e., $P \neq \emptyset$), the situation is more complex since there can be interaction between columns. For instance, a predicate a + b > 10 can be evaluated when we consider an index for other sargable predicates over columns a and b. While the main ideas remain the same as for scenario 2 (i.e., we obtain the index that results in the best plan using seeks followed by optional RID lookups), the details are more complex. If the number of columns in R and P is not very large (as is commonly the case), an exhaustive approach for subsets of such columns is feasible. If this is not possible, we can use a greedy heuristic leveraging the fact that cardinality estimation routines would typically use magic numbers to estimate cardinality values of complex predicates (e.g., the selectivity of predicate d*d = 100 might be guessed as 0.1). Although subsets of columns in P are different, they might all have roughly the same selectivity and can be greedily picked maximizing the number of predicates in P covered by the index. Finally, note that in a very large number of cases, choosing the covering index results in either the optimal strategy or very close to it, and some techniques heuristically choose such covering index.

Scenario 4: General case. Consider now the general case of an index request $N \times (T, E, R, P, O, A)$. If the index obtained using scenario 3 produces rows in the desired order O, this is the best plan overall. Otherwise, we need to introduce a sort operator at the root of the plan obtained with such an index. However, there might be an alternative plan that does not require sorting and is more efficient. To obtain this alternative plan, we create an index as follows. The key columns are all those in E followed by those in $O - E$ (note that since columns in E are associated with equality predicates, scanning such index still satisfies the order in O). The included columns in this case are obtained as in the previous scenarios. We finally compare the cost of the two alternatives (i.e., the one derived from scenario 3 with an additional sort operator and the one that natively returns tuples in the right order) and return the one with the minimal expected cost.

Consider an index request over table T with $E = \{(a, 100)\}$, $R = \{(b, 10)\}$, $P = \emptyset$, $O = \{c\}$, and $A = \{d\}$. The best index ignoring the sort column is $I_1 = T(a, b|c, d)$. This index does not return tuples in the right order, so the resulting plan would have a sort operator on top. The alternative index that returns tuples in the right order is $I_2 = T(a, c|b, d)$. The best index is the one that results in the cheaper execution plan for the request.

4.1.4 Reducing the Candidate Set

The approaches discussed earlier obtain a candidate set of indexes that likely contains the optimal configuration. Although the resulting candidate set is usually small, there might be opportunities to further reduce its size. Specifically, indexes in the candidate set can be helpful for the query but nevertheless conflicting among each other. For instance, an index on table S that is part of an index-based join between an outer table R and S conflicts with another index that seeks a single-table predicate in S and performs a hash join with R (because both indexes cannot be used in the same execution plan).

A common mechanism to reduce the set of indexes is to rely on the query optimizer itself. Suppose that we create all candidate indexes and optimize the query. The optimizer can now leverage the good properties of each such index and obtain the overall optimal plan. In such a case, we can inspect this plan and identify which of the candidate indexes are used and can refine our candidate set so that it contains only these. A well-behaved optimizer, faced with this subset of indexes, would result in the same optimal plan.

Some clarifications are needed to further understand this idea. First, it seems that we need to create a large set of indexes just to optimize a query and obtain a reduced set of candidate indexes. Creating indexes is very expensive and thus can be seen as a crucial drawback of this approach. However, as we explain in Chapter 5, we can simulate the optimization of the input query without actually creating the indexes. Second, there is a problem if the initial candidate set contains multiple clustered indexes for the same table, because the resulting configuration is invalid and cannot be materialized. In general, to guarantee optimality, we need to perform the optimization step for each combination of clustered indexes. Some approaches avoid this time-consuming step by heuristically choosing a small set of alternatives (e.g., coordinate clustered indexes in different tables so that join predicates can be answered directly) and performing a few optimization calls, retaining the indexes of the best plan overall. If the query engine supports covering indexes, the problem is simplified. In fact, in such situations a single optimization call is enough because the set of candidate indexes need not include clustered indexes (a covering index has the same capabilities but is no larger than the corresponding clustered index).

In the instrumentation approach described earlier, we can combine the instrumented optimization and the postoptimization step and obtain the reduced set of candidate indexes in a single optimization call as follows. Each time the optimizer issues an access path request, we suspend optimization and analyze the request. We then obtain the index that results in the most efficient plan for such request as explained earlier, create the index (again, see Chapter 5), and resume optimization. The optimizer would now consider the newly created indexes and obtain the "optimal" execution subplan for each request. Since we repeat this procedure for each access path request, the optimizer is always given the optimal set of indexes to implement execution plans. Therefore, the execution plan returned by the optimizer would be the most efficient one over the space of all possible configurations.

4.2   Candidate Set for a Workload

In the previous section we discussed different ways to obtain a small superset of the optimal configuration for a single SELECT query. When the workload consists of multiple queries and updates, the situation is more complex. A simple approach to obtain a candidate set for a workload W is to obtain candidate sets for each individual query in W and join the results. As we show next, this simple approach misses opportunities in the presence of updates or storage constraints.

4.2.1   Suboptimal Indexes in Optimal Configurations

We now introduce two scenarios that can result in indexes, which are not optimal for any query in the workload, to be part of the optimal configuration.

4.2.1.1   Storage Constraints

Storage constraints are very common in practice. No matter how good is a configuration, it has to fit in the available disk space. Consider the following queries:

```
Q1 =   SELECT A, B, C
       FROM R
       WHERE 10 < A < 20
```

```
Q2 =    SELECT A, B, D
        FROM R
        WHERE 50 < A < 100
```

In this case, the best index for Q1 is I_1=R(A|B,C) and the best index for Q2 is I_2=R(A|B,D). In the absence of storage constraints, obviously the best configuration is $\{I_1, I_2\}$. Now, suppose that the space taken by I_1 and I_2 together exceeds the storage budget. If the candidate set is $\{I_1, I_2\}$, the only alternative is to pick either I_1 or I_2 as the final configuration. In such scenario, either Q1 or Q2 would result in optimal performance, but the performance of the other query would not improve much. For instance, suppose that we pick I_1. The best plan for Q2 would be either the original one (which scans R and filters tuples based on the predicate on A) or an alternative one that uses I_1 to obtain columns A and B and then performs RID lookups to the primary index *for each* tuple in the result to obtain column D. Clearly, if many tuples satisfy 50 < A < 100, the index-based alternative would be more expensive than the original scan, and Q2 would not benefit at all from I_1.

Consider now index I_3=R(A|B,C,D). This index is almost as good as I_1 and I_2 for queries Q1 and Q2. Both queries can seek I_3 to obtain tuples that satisfy predicates on A, and the index covers all columns required by both Q1 and Q2. Since I_3 includes one more column than either I_1 or I_2, seeking I_3 would be slightly more expensive than doing so for the narrower indexes. However, I_3 is smaller than I_1 and I_2 combined and therefore could fit in the storage budget, and the overall performance for both Q1 and Q2, while not optimal, could be better than the alternatives discussed before (which would pick either I_1 or I_2). In this case, an index that was not optimal for either Q1 or Q2 is part of the optimal configuration for the workload $\{Q1,Q2\}$.

4.2.1.2   Updates

Updates make the physical design problem harder. The reason is that indexes that are very useful in the absence of updates can lose all their benefits when we additionally consider maintenance costs. Consider the following UPDATE query:

```
Q3 =    UPDATE R
        SET D = D + 1
        WHERE B < 5
```

Updates are composed of an inner SELECT query, which determines which tuples to update, and an UPDATE shell, which performs the actual update. For that reason, the techniques in the previous section can be used on the inner SELECT query to obtain indexes that can improve the performance of the update. For Q3, index I_4 = R(B) would be optimal to obtain the RIDs of all tuples in R that satisfy B<5 and thus need to be updated.

Update statements also require that all relevant indexes be maintained. Specifically for Q3, any index on R that contains column D needs to be updated. Consider now a workload {Q2, Q3}. The optimal index for Q2, I_2, contains column D and thus needs to be maintained. Consider now index I_5=R(A). Query Q2 can use index I_5 in conjunction with RID lookups to obtain the result (assuming that few tuples satisfy the predicate on A). Using I_5 to evaluate Q2 is certainly worse than using I_2. However, I_5 does not contain column D and therefore does not need to be maintained for Q3. It certainly can be the case that a configuration {I_5, I_4} is better than {I_2, I_4} due to the update statement. In this case, I_5, which was not optimal for any query in the workload, would be part of the optimal configuration.

4.2.2   Index Transformations

As described already, some situations require considering candidate indexes that are not part of the optimal candidate set of any query in the workload. In this section we formally describe a set of transformations that can generate these derived indexes from an initial candidate set. The transformations exploit knowledge about how indexes are used in the DBMS. To simplify the notation, we assume that if S_1 and S_2 are sequences, the expression $S_1 \cap S_2$ (similarly, $S_1 - S_2$) returns the sequence that has elements in the intersection (similarly, difference) of S_1 and S_2 *in the same order* as they appear in S_1.

4.2.2.1   Merging

Index merging is an operation that takes two input indexes and produces a new index that eliminates redundancy resulting from shared columns. The resulting index is smaller than the two input indexes combined while preserving, as much as possible, their querying capabilities. We define the (ordered) merging of two indexes I_1 and I_2 as the best index that can answer all requests that either I_1 and I_2 do and can be efficiently used to seek tuples in all cases that I_1 can (some requests that can be answered by seeking I_2 might need to scan the merged index, though). Specifically, we define the merging of I_1 and I_2 (denoted $I_1 \oplus I_2$) as an index that has all key columns in I_1 as key columns and the remaining columns in I_2 as well as the included columns in I_1 as included columns. That is, given $I_1 = R(K_1|S_1)$ and $I_2 = R(K_2|S_2)$, we define $I_1 \oplus I_2 = R(K_1|(S_1 \cup K_2 \cup S_2) - K_1)$. As an optimization, if K_1 is a prefix of K_2, we define $I_1 \oplus I_2 = R(K_2|(S_1 \cup S_2) - K_2)$. For instance, consider indexes $I_1 = R(a, b|c, d)$ and $I_2 = R(b, d, e|f)$. Then, $I_1 \oplus I_2 = R(a, b|c, d, e, f)$ and $I_2 \oplus I_1 = R(b, d, e|a, c, f)$.

4.2.2.2 Splitting

Index splitting aims to introduce suboptimal index intersection plans by rearranging overlapping columns of existing (wider) indexes. Consider $I_1 = R(K_1|S_1)$ and $I_2 = R(K_2|S_2)$. Splitting I_1 and I_2 (denoted $I_1 \otimes I_2$) produces a common index I_C and at most two additional residual indexes I_{R1} and I_{R2}. The idea is that we could replace usages of index I_1 (respectively, I_2) by a less efficient index intersection between I_C and I_{R1} (respectively, I_{R2}), or RID lookups over I_C's result if I_{R1} (respectively, I_{R2}) does not exist. Specifically, we define $I_C = R(K_C, S_C)$, where $K_C = K_1 \cap K_2$ and $S_C = S_1 \cap S_2$, provided that K_C is nonempty (index splits are undefined if K_1 and K_2 have no common columns). If K_1 and K_C are different, $I_{R1} = R(K_1 - K_C|I_1 - I_C)$ and if K_2 and K_C are different, $I_{R2} = R(K_2 - K_C|I_2 - I_C)$. Consider, as an example, $I_1 = R(a, b, c|d, e, f)$, $I_2 = R(c, a|e)$, and $I_3 = R(a, b|d, g)$. In this case, $I_1 \otimes I_2 = \{I_C = R(a, c|e), I_{R1} = R(b|d, f), I_{R2} = R(d)\}$. In turn, we have that $I_1 \otimes I_3 = \{I_C = R(a, b|d), I_{R1} = R(c|e, f)\}$.

4.2.2.3 Reduction

Index reductions transform an index into another one with fewer columns. Specifically, consider $I = R(K|S)$. We can reduce I with respect to any subset $K' \subseteq K$ (denoted $\rho(I, K')$), to obtain a new index with K' as key columns and no included columns. That is, $\rho(I, K') = R(K')$. The reduced index can be used to answer requests for which I was useful (generally requiring RID lookups to get the remaining columns in $K \cup S - K'$) Alternatively, rather than allowing all possible subsets $K' \subseteq K$, a simpler family of reductions considers only prefixes of K. Then, a reduction is specified by an integer k, and $\rho(I, k) = R(K')$, where K' is a prefix of K of length k.

4.2.2.4 Promotion

Any index $I = R(K|S)$ can be promoted to a clustered index with key columns K, denoted $\Gamma(I)$. The clustered index $\Gamma(I)$ provides the same query capabilities as the original index I. However, since we can get one clustered index "for free" for each table, promoting one index to a clustered index results in new opportunities for other indexes to be part of the final configuration.

4.3 Defining the Search Space Using Closures

The transformations in the previous section provide a framework to characterize the search space for the physical design problem with input workload W and use it to further refine our problem statement. Let $cand(Q)$ be the set of candidate indexes for query Q, obtained by any of the techniques of Section 4.1. Let C_i ($i \geq 0$) be a family of candidate indexes defined as follows:

$$C_0 = \bigcup_{Q \in W} cand(Q)$$

$$C_{i+1} = C_i \ \cup$$

$$\{I_1 \oplus I_2 \text{ for each } I_1, I_2 \in C_i\} \ \cup$$

$$\{I_1 \otimes I_2 \text{ for each } I_1, I_2 \in C_i\} \ \cup$$

$$\{\rho(I, K') \text{ for each } I = R(K, S) \in C_i, K' \subseteq K\} \ \cup$$

$$\{\Gamma(I) \text{ for each } I \in C_i\}$$

That is, C_{i+1} is obtained by considering all possible merges, splits, reductions, and promotions of indexes in C_i. We define $closure(W){=}C_k$, where k is the smallest integer that satisfies $C_k{=}C_{k+1}$. In words, the closure of a workload W is the set of all indexes that either are in the candidate set of a query in W or can be derived from these candidates through a series of merging, splitting, reduction, and promotion operations. Our goal is then to obtain a subset of this closure that fits in the available storage and is as efficient as possible for a given representative workload. Thus, the physical design problem can be stated as follows:

Physical design problem: Given a workload $W = \{Q_1, \ldots, Q_n\}$, where each Q_i is a SQL query or update, and a storage bound B, obtain the index configuration $C = \{I_1, \ldots, I_k\}$ such that:

1. $C \subseteq closure(W)$
2. $\sum_{I \in C} size(I) \leq B$
3. $\sum_{q_i \in W} cost(q_i, C)$ is minimized, where $cost(q, C)$ is the optimizer estimated cost of query q under configuration C

Note that the definition of $closure(W)$ just specifies all possible indexes that can be considered as part of the final configuration, but in general it is not feasible to evaluate each subset of $closure(W)$ except for *extremely* simple cases. In Chapter 6 we introduce different approaches to effectively traverse the search space of a physical design problem instance and to obtain good configurations in reasonable amounts of time.

4.4   Summary

- The search space for the physical design problem can be defined as the closure of an initial set of query-specific candidates under suitable transformations.

- The initial set of candidates is the union of the candidates for each query, which can be obtained by either syntactically analyzing the query string, processing the final execution plan or instrumenting the query optimizer.

- The transformations to generate indexes that, while not optimal for any query, can be part of the optimal configuration are *merging* and *splitting* two indexes and *reducing* and *promoting* an index.

4.5   Additional Reading

Earlier work on physical database design assumed single-column indexes, and thus the resulting search space was invariably of moderate size.[5-7] The main technical problem in this setting is how to pick feasible indexes for each individual query. Then, the combined search space is just the union of candidates for each query in the workload (since early work considers only single-column indexes, there is not much else that can be done). More recent work infers a candidate set of indexes for each query in the workload by relying on internal query representations,[8] execution plans,[3] and instrumented optimizers.[1] In addition to the candidate set of indexes, some work considers additional indexes obtained through transformation, such as index merging,[4] splitting, and reduction transformations.[1,2]

References

1. Nicolas Bruno and Surajit Chaudhuri. Automatic physical database tuning: A relaxation-based approach. In *Proceedings of the ACM International Conference on Management of Data (SIGMOD)*, 2005.

2. Nicolas Bruno and Surajit Chaudhuri. Physical design refinement: The "Merge-Reduce" approach. In *Proceedings of the International Conference on Extending Database Technology (EDBT)*, 2006.

3. Surajit Chaudhuri and Vivek Narasayya. An efficient cost-driven index selection tool for Microsoft SQL Server. In *Proceedings of the International Conference on Very Large Databases (VLDB)*, 1997.

4. Surajit Chaudhuri and Vivek Narasayya. Index merging. In *Proceedings of the International Conference on Data Engineering (ICDE)*, 1999.

5. Sheldon J. Finkelstein, Mario Schkolnick, and Paolo Tiberio. Physical database design for relational databases. *ACM Transactions on Database Systems*, 13(1), 1988.

6. Martin R. Frank, Edward Omiecinski, and Shamkant B. Navathe. Adaptive and automated index selection in RDBMS. In *Proceedings of the International Conference on Extending Database Technology (EDBT)*, 1992.

7. Steve Rozen and Dennis Shasha. A framework for automating physical database design. In *Proceedings of the International Conference on Very Large Databases (VLDB)*, 1991.

8. Gary Valentin, Michael Zuliani, Daniel Zilio, Guy Lohman, and Alan Skelley. DB2 advisor: An optimizer smart enough to recommend its own indexes. In *Proceedings of the International Conference on Data Engineering (ICDE)*, 2000.

Chapter 5

Designing a Cost Model

As we discussed in previous chapters, physical database design can be seen as a complex search problem over a potentially very large space of feasible configurations. Although there are different approaches to conducting this search (we discuss different alternatives in Chapter 6), a common requirement of any solution is the ability to evaluate the expected cost of a query under a given candidate configuration in the search space. In Section 3.2.2 we discussed why early designs, which were based on a cost model outside of the query optimizer, cannot be trusted and in general produce undesirable results. At the same time, it is fairly obvious that materializing each candidate configuration in the database management system (DBMS), optimizing the workload queries, and obtaining their costs are not feasible in practice.

Therefore, an important challenge for designing scalable physical design algorithms is to efficiently and accurately estimate query costs under arbitrary configurations. To address this problem, we need a new component that is able to *simulate* a hypothetical configuration in the DBMS and to optimize queries without actually materializing new indexes (we call this process *what-if optimization*). In this chapter we explain different challenges that appear in a robust implementation of this component. We then introduce additional improvements that further increase the performance of this what-if optimization component without significantly compromising the quality of results.

5.1 What-If Optimization

The key observation that enables what-if optimization is that the query optimizer does not actually leverage the *content* of the indexes (i.e., internal and leaf nodes in the B^+-*trees*) during query optimization but instead exploits only *metadata information*. Specifically, to determine whether an index is useful in an execution plan, the optimizer leverages information about the table over which the index is defined, the collections of key and included columns, the size of the index, and existing integrity constraints (e.g., uniqueness).

Suppose then that we can create a version of an index that contains only metadata information but not actual data (we call it a *hypothetical* index). From the point of view of the optimizer, such a hypothetical index is exactly like any ordinary materialized index. Optimization can proceed in the usual manner considering both regular and hypothetical indexes simultaneously. The final execution plan can even include operators that reference hypothetical indexes. Of course, such execution plans are not actually *executable* because hypothetical indexes do not really exist. However, the final execution plan and cost of a query that uses hypothetical indexes are indistinguishable from the alternative obtained by materializing all hypothetical indexes. We can therefore effectively simulate the presence of an index by creating the corresponding metadata in the system catalogs. Since such metadata are very small and independent of the index size, this process is very efficient and allows performing what-if optimizations with almost no overhead compared with regular optimizations.

5.1.1   What-If Optimization Interface

Figure 5.1 shows a schematic interface that extends a DBMS to enable what-if optimization. The key aspects of this what-if interface are:

1. A command to create a hypothetical index in the DBMS, which populates the system catalogs with the index metadata. This command could be as simple as a regular index creation statement with a specific flag that marks the index as hypothetical, such as:

   ```
   CREATE HYPOTHETICAL INDEX empNameIndex ON Emp(name)
   ```

2. A mechanism to create any supporting information about the hypothetical index. This step depends on the specific DBMS implementation. Recall that a hypothetical index must be indistinguishable from a regular index during optimization. Therefore, any information that is obtained while creating a regular index and later exploited during optimization must be recreated in this step. A common example is statistical information on index columns. We discuss this topic in more detail in the next section.

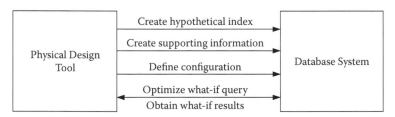

FIGURE 5.1 What-if interface for optimizing under hypothetical configurations.

3. A mechanism to define a configuration for what-if optimization. This interface allows defining a set of existing and hypothetical indexes as the configuration for doing subsequent what-if optimization calls. Without this component, it would not be possible to generate configurations that do not contain some of the indexes that currently exist in the DBMS. Additionally, by decoupling the creation of a hypothetical index and the inclusion of such index in a candidate configuration, we can create a large number of hypothetical indexes up front and then repeatedly optimize queries under different index subsets.

4. Finally, a small extension to the regular optimization call to inform the optimizer that it should consider a given hypothetical configuration as the true underlying physical design and thus optimize the query assuming that all and only the indexes in such configuration are available. Other than a reference to the desired configuration, no additional changes are required in the optimizer itself.

5.1.2   Statistics Management

As explained already, any information obtained by creating an index that can be exploited by the optimizer must be simulated during a what-if optimization call. The most common piece of information is statistics on the index columns. In Chapter 2 we described how optimizers maintain histograms on the distribution of column values and how these histograms are used during cardinality estimation. On some systems, the creation of an index with key column c also returns a histogram for column c. The reason is that the index contains all values in the column in sorted order, and thus the histogram construction procedure can be piggybacked on top of the index creation task proper. The net effect is that, by creating an index in the database system, the optimizer is additionally given better estimates for certain predicates, which could in turn make a difference in the choice of the optimal plan.

Therefore, creating a hypothetical index must be accompanied by the creation of the relevant histogram as supporting information (see Figure 5.1). However, creating a histogram requires at least reading the values for the column over all tuples in the table. This is clearly expensive and would quickly become the bottleneck for what-if optimization calls. To alleviate this problem, a number of techniques can be used:

Sampling-based construction of statistics. Histograms are already approximations of data distributions of table columns. Therefore, we can create a histogram over a uniform random sample of the underlying data, and the resulting histogram would be very close to the one built over the full data distribution. The advantage of creating histograms using samples is that only a fraction of the table needs to be processed, which improves performance. However, the basic unit of retrieval from disk is a page, which in general contains many tuples not needed for the sample. In general, a uniform random sample of 1 to 10% can effectively require reading all pages of a given table. For that reason, rather than performing a uniform random sample of tuples in a table, we can randomly sample pages in disk and use all tuples in the page as part of the sample. Of course, this mechanism works whenever there is no correlation between the values of the column and the page the tuple belongs to, which is not always the case. A common approach to remedy this problem is to use an adaptive page-level sampling algorithm. The idea is to start with a "seed" sample of $\sqrt{P}$ pages, where P is the number of pages in the table. We then retrieve a new sample of $\sqrt{P}$ pages for cross-validation purposes. If it is determined that both samples are not statistically similar, we combine both samples into one and repeat the procedure of obtaining a new sample. When the cross-validation step is successful, the accumulated sample is used to obtain the final histogram. Each hypothetical index creation thus requires that we sample the corresponding table and build a histogram on the index key column.

Decoupling of statistics and indexes. While using sampling to create histograms significantly improves performance, we still need to obtain a random sample for each index that is created. Alternatively, we can decouple statistics and the corresponding indexes and build statistics only once for each column. In this case, histograms would be shared among any index that shares the same leading key column. Additionally, if some histogram already exists in the DBMS (due to an existing index, or because the histogram itself was manually generated) we do not need to duplicate it and can reuse the existing histogram instead.

Sharing multicolumn statistics. If the DBMS supports multicolumn statistics, the techniques discussed previously need to be extended. The reason is that different indexes with the same leading column would be associated with different statistics that cannot be shared. Depending on the properties of such multicolumn statistics, however, we might be able to improve the basic scheme. For instance, some multicolumn statistics (e.g., multidimensional histograms) satisfy some notion of "commutativity" (i.e., statistics on (a, b) and (b, a) are essentially the same). Other commonly used statistics (e.g., a single-column histogram plus the number of distinct values for each prefix of columns in a given set) satisfy a "containment" property (i.e., (a, b, c) contains all the information of (a) and (a, b)). These properties allow us to reduce the set of statistics to materialize without significantly compromising quality. As an example, suppose that we want to consider indexes on (a), (b), (a, b), (b, a), and (a, b, c). In principle, we would need to create all five multicolumn statistics. However, if statistics satisfy the containment property, we can obtain the same result by materializing only (a, b, c) and (b, a). Obtaining the minimal set of statistics to create is a challenging problem, and there exist greedy algorithms that approximate the exact solution in a short amount of time.

5.2 Reducing the Overhead of What-If Optimization Calls

The what-if abstraction described in the previous section makes it possible to design complex search algorithms that rely on such a fast mode of evaluating workloads under arbitrary configurations. However, the overhead of a what-if optimization call is essentially that of a regular optimization call. For relatively complex queries, this overhead can still be significant. In fact, in some cases over 90% of the search time is spent issuing what-if optimization calls. In the rest of this chapter we introduce techniques to reduce the overhead of what-if optimization calls without significantly compromising the quality of results.

5.2.1 Atomic Configurations

An interesting approach to reduce the number of optimization calls is based on the notion of *atomic configurations*. A configuration C is atomic for a query q if there is a possible execution plan from q that uses all indexes in C (in turn, a configuration is atomic for a workload W if it is atomic for at least one query in W). An interesting consequence of this definition is that if a configuration is not atomic for a query q, we can derive the cost of q for this configuration accurately from costs of atomic configurations only, thus saving what-if optimization calls.

Assume that C is a nonatomic configuration and q is a SELECT query. Since C is not atomic, there is no plan that uses all indexes in C. Therefore, optimizing q under C would result in a plan that uses all and only indexes in some $C' \subset C$ (i.e., some atomic configuration C'). A well-behaved optimizer will choose the plan using indexes in the atomic configuration C' that has the minimal cost. Therefore, we can derive the cost of q under C as follows:

$$cost(q, C) = min_{C' \subseteq C \wedge atomic(C')} cost(q, C')$$

For an UPDATE query, the analysis is more complex. The cost of an UPDATE query for a nonatomic configuration C can be divided in three components: (1) the cost of the inner SELECT query, (2) the cost of updating the indexes that are used in the inner SELECT query, and (3) the cost for updating the remaining indexes. Similar to the case of a SELECT query, we can derive the minimum costs over all atomic configurations of q that are subsets of C to account for components (1) and (2). Note that the costs for updating indexes in component (3) are independent of each other and also of the chosen plan.

To obtain this cost, we calculate $cost(q, \{I\}) - cost(q, \emptyset)$ (either by using optimization calls or by leveraging the cost model of the optimizer). Therefore, we derive the cost of a nonatomic configuration C for an UPDATE query q as

$$cost(q, C) = min_{C' \subset C \wedge atomic(C')} cost(q, C') + \sum_{I \notin inner\ \text{SELECT}} cost(q, \{I\})$$
$$- cost(q, \emptyset)$$

So far we have discussed the definition of atomic configurations and how they can be used to avoid some optimization calls but have given no procedure to identify such configurations for a given query. We next introduce two approaches to address this issue.

5.2.1.1 Static Strategy Based on Query Processor Restrictions

The characteristics of the query processor can determine what constitutes an atomic configuration. Suppose, for instance, that for any execution plan for q, the DBMS will not use more than j indexes per table. This restriction reflects the design point in the DBMS that no more than a small number of indexes may be intersected to identify tuples of one table (query engines that do not support index intersection strategies result in $j = 1$). In these scenarios, we can easily determine whether a given configuration C is atomic and, if not, generate all atomic configurations that consist of subsets of indexes from C. Once we characterize the space of atomic configurations, these can be evaluated on demand during the search strategy. Specifically, when we need to evaluate $cost(q, C)$, we first optimize q under all atomic configurations that are subsets of C and have not yet been evaluated and then derive the cost of q under C. While initially there would be more optimization calls for atomic configurations than the originally requested ones, the trend eventually reverses as atomic configurations represent a small fraction of the search space.

5.2.1.2 Adaptive Strategy Based on Index Benefit Graphs

The previous technique makes assumptions on the characteristics of the query processor. We now describe an alternative approach that detects atomic configurations for a query based on interaction among indexes. Specifically, we leverage the concept of an *index benefit graph* (or *IBG* for short), which efficiently encodes the properties of optimal plans under reasonably "well-behaved" query optimizers.

The *IBG* for a query q is a directed graph, where each node is defined by (1) a subset C of indexes, (2) the indexes $U \subseteq C$ that were part of the plan for q under configuration C, and (3) the estimated cost of such a plan. Additionally, there is a directed edge between nodes $N_1 = (C_1, U_1, cost_1)$ and $N_2 = (C_2, U_2, cost_2)$ if $C_1 = C_2 \cup \{I\}$ for some $I \in U_1$. Figure 5.2 shows an *IBG* for indexes $\{I_1, I_2, I_3, I_4\}$, where the used indexes U are underlined, and plan costs are shown in parentheses within each node. Based on the definition

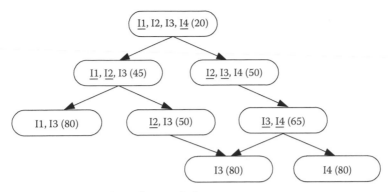

FIGURE 5.2 Index benefit graph for a query.

of the *IBG* we can obtain a recursive top-down algorithm to compute graph instances (see Figure 5.3). Specifically, we start with all candidate indexes in C and perform a what-if optimization call. Suppose that the resulting plan uses indexes U ⊆ C. We then create node N=(C, U, cost(q,C)). Then, for each I ∈ U we recursively obtain the root N' of the *IBG* graph calculated from q and C - { I } and connect N and N'. The size of the resulting *IBG* might be, in the worst case, exponential in the number of indexes. In general, however, *IBG* sizes are much smaller (the example in Figure 5.2 has 8 of 16 possible index subsets).

An interesting property of an *IBG* graph is that we can infer the cost of the input query under arbitrary configurations without making additional optimization calls. In fact, the used indexes U in each node N=(C,U,cost) correspond to atomic configurations for the input query, since a well-behaved optimizer would return the same plan under C or U. For instance, the atomic configurations in Figure 5.2 are $\{I_1, I_4\}$, $\{I_1, I_2\}$, $\{I_2\}$, and $\{I_3\}$. Additionally, it can be shown that all atomic configurations are represented in *IBG* nodes. Therefore, after an *IBG* has been computed, it can be used to infer all atomic configurations and thus query costs under arbitrary configurations.

```
buildIBG (q:Query, C:Configuration)
return root note of the IBG for q and C
01  P = plan for q under C (using indexes U ⊆ C)
02  N = new node (C, U, cost(q,C))
03  foreach I ∈ U
04      N' = buildIBG(q, C-I)
05      add edge between N and N'
06  return N
```

FIGURE 5.3 Obtaining the *IBG* for a given query and initial set of indexes.

5.2.2   Upper Bounds

Some search strategies (discussed in Chapter 6) require approximating a large number of query costs under different—but similar—configurations. In such situations, performing a large number of what-if calls quickly becomes prohibitively expensive. These strategies, however, can be adapted to work off approximations of query costs, as long as such approximations are (tight) upper bounds of the true cost of the queries. We now describe how to obtain an upper bound on the cost of a query under a given configuration without making an explicit optimization call. The techniques discussed in this section are also useful in the more advanced strategies that we discuss later in this chapter.

To begin with a simple example, suppose that we optimized a SELECT query q under configuration C, and we want to obtain an upper bound on the cost for q under $C' = C - \{I\}$. If the execution plan for q under C does not use index I, the execution plan for q under C' would be unchanged. The reason is that the optimal plan for q under C' is no better than that under C because $C' \subset C$ and is no worse either, because the one under C uses only indexes that are available in C'. Then, a tight upper bound for $cost(q, C')$ is $cost(q, C)$ itself.

5.2.2.1   Local Plan Transformations

In general, however, the optimal execution plan for q under C would use an index I that is not in C'. Consider the execution plan P at the left of Figure 5.4. Index $I = R(a|b, c)$ is used to seek tuples that satisfy $a < 10$

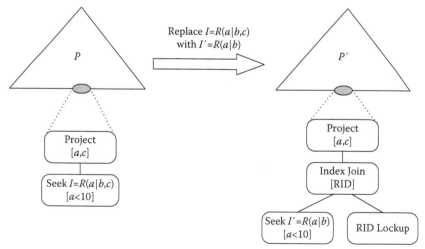

FIGURE 5.4   Estimating execution cost upper bounds. (Used with permission from Bruno, N. & Chaudhuri, S. In *Proceedings of the ACM International Conference on Management of Data [SIGMOD]*, 2005.)

and also to retrieve an additional column c, which is eventually needed at higher levels in the execution plan. In general, the optimal execution plan under $C' = C - \{I\}$ might be arbitrarily different from that under C. However, we can always *locally transform* P into P' by adjusting the execution subplan that uses I so that it depends only on indexes in C'. To simplify the presentation, we define the *internal subplan* of an execution plan p as the portion of p that remains after removing all index-based execution subplans (i.e., scans, seeks, index intersections, and RID lookups). An important property of the local transformations previously described is that the cost of the internal subplan does not vary across transformations, because the transformed subplan returns the same sequence of tuples as the original subplan. Therefore, estimating the cost of the transformed plan can be done by just comparing the original and transformed index-based subplans. Since P was optimal, the local transformation would result in a less efficient plan P'. However, we know that the locally transformed plan P' is valid under C', and therefore its cost is an upper bound on the cost of the optimal plan for C', as desired. As an example, the alternative plan at the right of Figure 5.4 locally transforms the original plan so that it uses $I' = R(a|b)$ instead of $I = R(a|b, c)$. To do that, it additionally looks up the primary index to obtain the required c column and returns the same sequence of tuples as the original subplan in P.

So far we discussed examples for which C' has strictly fewer indexes than C. In general, the configuration C' that we try to approximate might have additional indexes not found in a previously evaluated configuration C. Of course, we can ignore indexes in $C' - C$, proceed as before, and still obtain an upper bound on the cost of q under C'. The upper bound would be looser in this case, because we are not leveraging indexes in $C' - C$. In general, we have to consider each subplan that is defined over a table associated with at least one index in $C' - C$ and locally transform such execution subplans by leveraging all indexes in C'.

To summarize this discussion, the algorithm in Figure 5.5 obtains an upper bound on the cost of a query q under a configuration newC, leveraging information on past optimizations over configurations CS but without issuing a new optimization call. We first obtain the optimal execution plan P for q under each configuration C $\in$ CS. We then transform some index-based subplans of P depending on the indexes in both C and newC. Specifically, for each subplan p of P that uses an index present in C but not available in newC, we construct an alternative, equivalent plan that uses only available indexes in newC. Similarly, for each subplan p of P over a table that has indexes in newC but not in C, we try to improve the current plan by additionally using indexes in newC-C. We keep the best transformed execution plan for every previous configuration and return its expected cost. This returned plan is valid and should be considered by the optimizer. However, the optimizer might return some even better execution plan for newC, and that is the reason that the execution cost of the returned plan is an upper bound of $cost$(q, newC).

```
upperBound (q:Query, newC:Configuration, CS:set of)
            Configurations
return upper bound on cost(q, newC)
01   result = null
02   foreach C in CS
03       P = plan for q under C
04       foreach index-based subplan p of P such that
                (i) uses indexes in (C-newC), or
                (ii) is defined over a table compatible with an
                    index in (newC-C)
05           replace p in P with the best alternative using
                indexes in newC
06       if expected cost of P is better than expected cost of
                result, result = P
07   return expected cost of result
```

FIGURE 5.5   Obtaining upper bounds on query costs.

Note that the best we can do by following this approach is to obtain a *locally optimal* execution plan. That is, we replace only some physical subplans associated with index strategies with alternatives that are as efficient as possible under the new configuration. We would not be able, however, to obtain a plan with different join orders or in general with a different internal subplan. In that sense, we are giving up some opportunities to obtain the globally optimal execution plan but avoid an expensive what-if optimization call.

5.2.2.2   Gathering Information to Transform Subplans

The first step to transform an index-based subplan is to understand which task the subplan is performing so that the transformed subplan returns the same result. To that end, an available source of information is the query execution plan itself. In general, DBMSs return rich supporting information along with query execution plans. Specifically, it is common to be able to extract or infer information about each index-based subplan by inspecting the corresponding execution plan. Such information includes the estimated input/output (I/O) and central processing unit (CPU) cost of the subplan, the estimated number of rows returned, the type of index usage (i.e., whether the indexes are used to seek a fraction of the rows or to scan all rows), the resulting order of the returned rows, and the set of additional columns that are required upward in the tree. An alternative and more accurate way to obtain this information is by means of the access path requests intercepted during query optimization (see Section 4.1.3). Access path requests encode the requirements of any possible index strategy that might implement the corresponding subtree. Also, since access path requests are intercepted during optimization, we can avoid the extraction and inference of the logical requirements of an index-based subtree based solely on execution plans.

Assuming that the optimizer returns the access path requests associated with each index-based subtree in the query execution plan, we can transform the relevant subplans by simply reimplementing each request based on the set of available indexes. Consider a physical request $\rho = N \times (T, E, R, P, O, A)$ (see Section 4.1.3), and suppose that we want to calculate the cost of an alternative subplan that uses index $I = T(c_1, \ldots, c_n)$ to implement ρ. In order to do so, we can conceptually simulate the implementation rules in the optimizer that produced ρ in the first place and can approximate what the optimizer would have obtained under the hypothetical configuration that contains index I. As an example, let I_ρ be the longest prefix $(c_1, \ldots, c_k)$ that appears in E (equality predicates), optionally followed by c_{k+1} if c_{k+1} appears in R (range predicate). We can then implement ρ by (1) seeking I with the predicates associated with columns in I_ρ, (2) filtering the remaining predicates in $E \cup R \cup P$ that can be answered with all columns in I, (3) looking up a primary index to retrieve columns that are required by ρ but not available in I, (4) filtering the remaining predicates in $E \cup R \cup P$, and (5) optionally sorting the result if O is not already satisfied. Figure 5.6a shows the pattern for single-index execution plans that implement this logical tree.

As a simple example, consider the single-table logical expression $\Pi_d(\sigma_{a+b=2 \wedge c=4}(T))$ and the associated request $\rho = (T, E=\{c\}, R=\emptyset, P= \{(a, b)\}, O=\{d\}, A=\{a, b, d\})$ (note that there is a sort requirement of column d). Figure 5.6b shows the resulting execution subplan for an index

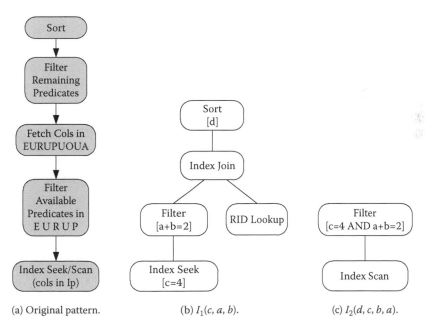

(a) Original pattern.   (b) $I_1(c, a, b)$.   (c) $I_2(d, c, b, a)$.

FIGURE 5.6 Generic plan pattern to implement local transformations.

$I_1=(c, a, b)$. This execution plan seeks I_1 for tuples satisfying $c=4$, filters tuples satisfying $a + b = 2$, looks up the remaining columns from the primary index, and performs a final sort to satisfy the required order. Analogously, Figure 5.6c shows the execution subplan for index $I_2=(d, c, b, a)$. This subplan scans index I_2 and filters all predicates simultaneously but does not explicitly sort the output since it is already ordered in the right way.

Configurations generally contain multiple indexes over the table of a given request. In principle, we could use more than one index to obtain a physical subplan that implements a request (e.g., by using index intersections) or even could consider hash-based alternatives to replace index joins for which no suitable index exists anymore. These alternatives effectively trade the accuracy of the estimation and the efficiency/complexity to obtain the subplan.

5.3   Index Usage Model (INUM)

The approach described in the previous section returns upper bounds on the cost of a query under a given configuration. It does so by means of local transformations to subplans that correspond to index strategies. It is important to note that the upper bounds are obtained without considering changes to the internal subplan, which is configuration independent. Sometimes, the resulting upper bounds are very accurate, as we discuss next.

Consider a restricted query optimizer that handles only hash-based join alternatives. We will show that in this scenario, the optimal plan under any configuration must follow the same join order. Suppose we optimize a query q under a configuration C_1 and obtain plan P_1. Figure 5.7 shows an example of a three-way join query q, where each single-table index strategy is depicted with a triangle. Let us denote IP_1 as the internal subplan of P_1. Now suppose that

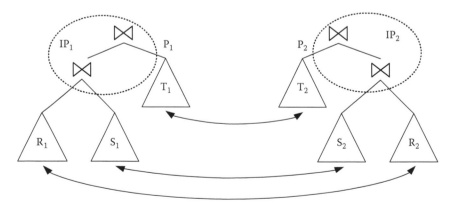

FIGURE 5.7   Replacing index strategies in different inner subplans.

we optimize q under C_2 and obtain plan P_2 and moreover that the internal subplan IP_2 for P_2 is different from IP_1 (see again Figure 5.7). Note that both IP_1 and IP_2 are just different join reorderings of the same query. As such, we can instantiate all index-based subplans from P_1 (i.e., R_1, S_1, and T_1 in the figure) in the internal subplan IP_2 and obtain a valid plan for q under configuration C_1. Since the optimizer did not return such a plan for q under C_1, and the cost of R_1, S_1, and T_1 is independent of the internal subplan they belong to, we can conclude that the cost of IP_1 is smaller than that of IP_2. But then we can construct a plan that uses IP_1 and index subplans R_2, S_2, and T_2 from P_2. This plan, called P_2', is valid for q under configuration C_2. Additionally, it is more efficient than P_2 because, as we have shown before, IP_1 is more efficient than IP_2, and R_2, S_2, and T_2 have the same cost in both P_2 and P_2'. We conclude then that P_2 is not optimal for C_2, which is a contradiction. Therefore, every optimal plan in this restricted scenario must contain the same internal subplan, and the upper-bound technique of the previous section would return accurate values of $cost(q, C)$ for arbitrary configurations.

Of course, the previous example relies on a drastically simplified query processor. In reality, indexes on join columns can result in plans that use merge- or index-based joins. Therefore, a better execution plan that is based on a different join order would be missed by the algorithm in Figure 5.5. INUM is a technique that extends the upper-bound approach of the previous section in the following way. During a preprocessing step, several optimization calls are issued for a given query until the resulting inner subplans are sufficient to infer execution plans for as many configurations as possible. The resulting inner subplans constitute INUM's space. Then, INUM considers the inner subplans in its space as the input CS in Figure 5.5 (with some additional improvements to avoid considering each inner subplan for every call).

The set of optimization calls required in the preprocessing step of a given query depends on the capabilities of the query engine. In the trivial (and unrealistic) case described in Figure 5.7, a single optimization call would be enough to obtain the internal subplan needed to infer optimal plans for arbitrary configurations (using hash-based joins only). When we additionally consider merge joins, INUM needs to optimize query q for configurations that include indexes for each combination of interesting orders of q. Interesting orders are derived from columns that are mentioned in a join predicate or a group-by clause. Consider a query q referencing tables $T_1, \ldots, T_n$ and let O_i be the set of interesting orders for table T_i. The set $O = O_1 \times \ldots \times O_n$ contains all possible combinations of interesting orders that a configuration can cover. Making some general assumption on the optimizer cost model, it can be shown that for every member of O there exists a single optimal inner subplan using hash- or merge-based joins. Thus, to compute the INUM space in this case, it is enough to optimize the query once for each member of O using some representative configuration. Although in the worst case this technique requires an exponential number of optimization calls in the number of query tables, there exist heuristics to reduce the number of optimization calls.

When additionally considering index-based joins, the analysis of INUM becomes more complex. The problem is that some properties in the cost model of hash- and merge-based join operators are not applicable when considering index-based joins. For that reason, INUM uses a simplified cost model and additional optimization calls to be able to handle index-based joins. Although the number of optimization calls in the preprocessing step might be high, INUM is able to perform very quick reoptimizations afterward and results in performance improvements during tuning sessions that explore large numbers of configurations.

5.4   Configuration-Parametric Query Optimization (CPQO)

The INUM technique described earlier can be used to infer costs of queries under arbitrary configurations at a fraction of the cost of a what-if optimization call. However, INUM is not fully integrated with the query optimizer. For that reason, it is not clear how to extend the approach for more complex execution plans (such as correlated subqueries). INUM also relies on some assumptions to reduce the number of regular optimization calls per query in the precomputation phase (which could be exponential in the number of tables in the worst case). As an example, for TPC-H query 15, INUM requires over a thousand regular optimization calls for simpler variations of the input query before it can start optimizing arbitrary configurations. In this section we present a technique called *configuration-parametric query optimization*, or *CPQO* for short. The idea is to issue a single optimization call per query (possibly with a larger overhead than that of a regular optimization call) and obtain back a compact representation of all possible internal subplans that allows us to efficiently generate execution plans for arbitrary configurations. Then, the modest overhead during the first (and only) optimization call is amortized when the same query is reoptimized for different configurations. We next introduce *CPQO* in the context of a transformation-based optimizer such as Cascades (see Chapter 2 for details).

Figure 5.8 shows a high-level, conceptual illustration of *CPQO*. Consider the final MEMO structure after optimizing an input query q. If we consider only physical operators, this final MEMO is a directed acyclic graph, where each node is a physical operator and edges going out of a node G connect G with its best children. The rule set in a transformation-based optimizer contains a small subset that deals with access path selection (see Section 2.3.3.3). Intuitively, these are the few rules that might make a difference when optimizing the same query under different configurations. Now suppose that we identify the subgraphs in the MEMO that were produced by a rule that deals with access path selection (e.g., $P_1, \ldots, P_4$ in Figure 5.8a). Then, everything that is above

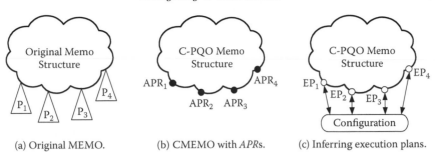

(a) Original MEMO.   (b) CMEMO with *APR*s.   (c) Inferring execution plans.

FIGURE 5.8 High-level overview of *CPQO*. (Used with permission from Bruno, N. & Nehme, R. In *Proceedings of the ACM International Conference on Management of Data [SIGMOD]*, 2008.)

P_i is independent of the configuration and corresponds to all combinations of internal subplans considered by the optimizer.

Leveraging the instrumentation approach described in Section 4.1.3, we create a new physical operator, which we call *APR*, that contains an access path request $N \times (T, E, R, P, O, A)$. Then, we modify the generation of substitutes for all the rules that are related to access path selection so that they return an *APR* operator rather than an actual physical execution subplan. In this way, we make access path selection rules configuration independent, and we do not miss any potential execution subplan (see the resulting MEMO, denoted CMEMO, in Figure 5.8b). Intuitively, the information in *APR* nodes encodes the properties satisfied by any physical execution subplan implementing the logical operator tree that triggered the implementation rule. Note that this mechanism results in the following two crucial properties. First, the leaf nodes in the resulting CMEMO are always *APR* physical operators. Second, there are no rules in the optimizer that depend on the specific configuration, so query optimization is truly configuration independent.

Whenever we want to reoptimize the query under a different configuration we can just focus on the *APR* nodes and infer small execution subplans that satisfy their requirements under the new configuration (obtained as described in Section 5.2.2 and denoted EP_1 in Figure 5.8c). We can then extract the best execution plan from the resulting CMEMO (whose bulk was precomputed) in a much more efficient manner.

5.4.1 Obtaining the CMEMO Structure

Transformation-based, top-down optimizers such as Cascades use a variant of branch-and-bound pruning to avoid exploring alternatives that are guaranteed to be suboptimal. Specifically, line 7 in Figure 2.9 (see Chapter 2) completely discards a *groupExpression*—without even optimizing all its children—if it costs more than the upper bound UB. While this pruning makes sense in a traditional optimizer, it would be wrong to apply it for *CPQO* since the ultimate cost of an expression in fact depends on the actual configuration, and thus any aggressive pruning might result in the loss of optimal plans for some valid configurations.

5.4.1.1   Pruning the Search Space

A simple solution for this problem would be to simply remove the pruning altogether. While this approach is correct, it might result in much longer optimization calls. We can, however, improve this approach by eliminating candidates that cannot be part of a solution *under any configuration*. One of the difficulties of handling *APR* operators is that they are really a specification of the required properties that any execution subplan must satisfy. Therefore, there is no precise notion of the *cost* of an *APR*, since it depends on the actual configuration. However, there are precise bounds on the cost of such *APR*. On one hand, there exists a configuration with the right indexes that makes a given *APR* execute as fast as possible. We can obtain such configuration by analyzing the access path request as explained in Section 4.1.3.3. Also, the configuration that contains no indexes results in the worst possible implementation of an *APR*. Therefore, instead of having a single cost for each physical operator in the tree, we maintain two costs, denoted *bestCost* (which is the smallest possible cost of any plan implementing the operator tree under any configuration) and *worstCost* (which is the largest possible cost of any execution plan over all configurations). Once we calculate *bestCost* and *worstCost* values for leaf *APR* nodes, we can propagate such values easily in the CMEMO. The *bestCost* of an operator is the local cost of the operator plus the sum of the minimum *bestCost* of each child (*worstCost* values are calculated analogously).

With the ability to calculate *bestCost* and *worstCost* values for arbitrary physical operators in the CMEMO structure, we can rely on a relaxed pruning rule. Specifically, every time that the partial *bestCost* of a *groupExpressions* g is larger than the *worstCost* of a previous solution for the group under the same optimization context, we can eliminate g from consideration.

5.4.1.2   Modifying the Enumeration Strategy

Figure 5.9 shows *OptimizeGroup$_{CPQO}$*, a modified version of the original *OptimizeGroup* procedure described in Figure 2.9, which produces the CMEMO structure. One difference in *OptimizeGroup$_{CPQO}$* is the input/output signature. The new version does not accept an upper bound UB as input, since this is used in the original branch-and-bound pruning strategy, which we do not rely on anymore. Also, the output of the new procedure consists not of a single *groupExpression* but of the full set of *groupExpressions* for group G and required properties RP. We also replace the original *winnerCircle* structure with the more general *alternativePool* associative array, which returns the set of all valid *groupExpressions* for a given group and required properties.

```
OptimizeGroup_CPQO (G: Group, RP: Properties)
return set of groupExpressions in G satisfying RP
01  allP = alternativePool[G,RP]
02  if (allP ≠ NULL) return allP
// No precomputed solution, enumerate plans
03  candPool = ∅
    UB = ∞
04  foreach enumerated physical groupExpression candP
05      candP.bestCost = localCostForBest(candP)
        candP.worstCost = localCostForWorst(candP)
06      foreach input p_i of candP
07          if (candP.bestCost ≥ UB)
                continue to 4    // out of bounds
08          G_i = group of p_i
            RP_i = required properties for p_i
09          allP_i = OptimizeGroup_CPQO(G_i, RP_i)
10          if (allP_i = ∅) continue to 4    // no solution
11          candP.allChildren[i] = allP_i
12          candP.bestCost += min_{c_i ∈ allP_i} c_i.bestCost
            candP.worstCost += min_{c_i ∈ allP_i} c_i.worstCost
            // Have valid solution, update state
13          candPool = candPool ∪ {candP}
14          if (candP.worstCost < UB)
                UB = candP.worstCost
15  alternativePool[G,RP] = candPool
16  return candPool
```

FIGURE 5.9 Modified *OptimizeGroup* task for *CPQO*. (Used with permission from Bruno, N. & Nehme, R. In *the ACM International Conference on Management of Data [SIGMOD]*, 2008.)

For a given input group G and required properties RP, algorithm *OptimizeGroup_CPQO* first checks the alternativePool data structure for a previous call compatible with RP. If it finds one, it returns the *groupExpressions* previously found, effectively implementing memoization. Otherwise, line 4 iterates over all enumerated physical *groupExpressions* in G (note that this line encapsulates the changes to the rules that select access paths and now return *APR* operators). For each such root *groupExpression* candP, line 5 estimates the local values of *bestCost* and *worstCost* for candP (in case of *APR* operators, we use the procedure of Section 5.4.1.1, while in the remaining cases both *bestCost* and *worstCost* values are equal to the original local cost of the operator). Then, line 8 calculates the input *group* and required properties for each input of candP, and line 9 recursively calls *OptimizeGroup_CPQO* to optimize them. After each input is successfully optimized, lines 11 and 12 store the candidates for each of candP's children in the array allChildren and update its partial values of *bestCost* and *worstCost*.

Note that if at any moment the current *bestCost* of `candP` becomes larger than the *worstCost* of a previously calculated solution, the candidate is discarded and the next one is considered (line 7). Otherwise, after `candP` is completely optimized, line 13 adds it to the candidate pool for the `G` and `RP`, and line 14 updates the upper bound with the *worstCost* value of `candP` if applicable. After all candidates are explored, line 15 updates the `alternativePool` array, and line 16 returns the candidate *groupExpressions*.

5.4.1.3   Generating the `CMEMO` Structure

After executing *OptimizeGroup$_{CPQO}$* on the root node of the initial `MEMO` with the global set of required properties, we need to prepare the output of a *CPQO* optimization. We do so by extracting an `AND/OR` subgraph of physical operators from the final `MEMO`. Each node in the output graph can be of one of two classes. On one hand, `AND` nodes contain the actual physical *groupExpressions* along with their *bestCost* and *localCost* values (the *local-Cost* value is the one defined in line 5 of Figure 5.9 and can be obtained back by subtracting the *bestCost* values of the best children of a *groupExpression* from its own *bestCost* value). Each outgoing edge of an `AND` node represents a child of the corresponding *groupExpression* and goes into an `OR` node. `OR` nodes, in turn, correspond to candidate choices, represented by outgoing edges into other `AND` nodes. Additionally, each `OR` node distinguishes, among its choices, the one that resulted in the minimum *bestCost* value (i.e., the child that contributed to `candP.bestCost` in line 12 of Figure 5.9). Finally, we add a *root* `OR` node that has outgoing edges toward every `AND` node that corresponds to a *groupExpression* in the root node of the final `MEMO` satisfying the original required properties (since there might be many alternatives to implement the query, this root `OR` node represents the highest-level choice). Figure 5.10 shows a sample `AND/OR` graph induced by a partial `MEMO`

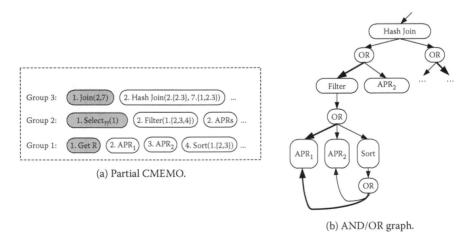

(a) Partial CMEMO.

(b) AND/OR graph.

FIGURE 5.10   AND/OR graph induced from a MEMO.

```
bestCostForConfiguration (n:Node in AND/OR graph for query q,
                     C:Configuration)
return cost(q, C)
01  if n is APRᵢ
02      return leafNodeCalculation(APRᵢ, C)    // (Section 5.2.2)
03  else if n is AND( op, {g₁, g₂, ..., gₙ})
04      return localCost(op) + ∑ᵢ bestCostForConfiguration(gᵢ,C)
05  else   // n is OR( {g₁,g₂, ..., gₙ} )
06      return minᵢ bestCostForConfiguration(gᵢ,C)
```

FIGURE 5.11   Reoptimizing queries in *CPQO*. (Used with permission from Bruno N. & Nehme, R. In *Proceedings of the ACM International Conference on Management of Data [SIGMOD]*, 2008.)

structure (the notation 7.{1, 2, 3} in physical operators refers to the set of *groupExpressions* {7.1, 7.2, 7.3}, and the best alternative for an OR node is shown with a bold arrow). In summary, the CMEMO structure is effectively the AND/OR graph induced from the final MEMO produced by a *CPQO* optimizer.

5.4.2   Fast Reoptimization in CPQO

The CMEMO encapsulates all the optimization state that is possible to obtain without knowing a specific configuration instance. Additionally, it contains enough information to derive configuration-specific execution subplans. For a given configuration C and CMEMO M, algorithm bestCostForConfiguration(*root(M)*, C) in Figure 5.11 returns the cost of the best execution plan for the query represented by M under configuration C. The algorithm operates depending on the type of input node n. If n is a leaf node (i.e., an *APR* node), we estimate the cost of the best configuration as explained in Section 5.2.2. Otherwise, if it is an internal AND node, we calculate the best cost by adding to the *localCost* of the *groupExpression* in n the sum of the best costs of each of n's children (calculated recursively). Finally, if n is an OR node, we return the minimum cost among the choices.

5.4.3   Handling Updates

So far we implicitly discussed SELECT-only workloads. In reality, *CPQO* must take into consideration UPDATE queries as well. The main impact of an update query is that some (or all) indexes defined over the updated table must also be updated as a side effect. To address updates, *CPQO* similarly modifies the configuration-dependent implementation rules that deal with updates and replaces them with internal *UAPR* nodes that encode the relevant update information. At reoptimization time, we calculate the cost of updating all relevant indexes in the configuration for each *UAPR* node in a similar way to what was described for regular *APR* nodes earlier in this section.

5.5   Summary

- Materializing a configuration to obtain the estimated cost of a query is not scalable.

- What-if calls allow optimizing queries under arbitrary configurations by simulating the metadata of hypothetical indexes along with supporting statistical information.

- What-if optimization calls can be avoided in some scenarios by inferring costs from previous optimizations of atomic configurations.

- INUM and CPQO are techniques that can reoptimize queries under different configurations much more efficiently than by doing separate what-if optimization calls.

5.6   Additional Reading

After initial work on parametric cost models, a new line of work used the optimizer cost model itself to evaluate the goodness of a configuration.[6] The *what-if* optimization concept was later extended for the case of complex engines and multicolumn indexes, acknowledging the difficulties involved in materializing statistics,[5] whose creation cost can be reduced by using sampling.[3] Other performance improvements include the notion of atomic configurations,[6] which can be computed based on assumptions of the query engine[4] or by leveraging index benefit graphs.[7,9] More advanced strategies like INUM[8] and CPQO[2] further reduce the cost to perform what-if optimization calls.

References

1. Nicolas Bruno and Surajit Chaudhuri. Automatic physical database tuning: A relaxation-based approach. In *Proceedings of the ACM International Conference on Management of Data (SIGMOD)*, 2005.

2. Nicolas Bruno and Rimma Nehme. Configuration-parametric query optimization for physical design tuning. In *Proceedings of the ACM International Conference on Management of Data (SIGMOD)*, 2008.

3. Surajit Chaudhuri, Rajeev Motwani, and Vivek Narasayya. Random sampling for histogram construction: How much is enough? In

Proceedings of the ACM International Conference on Management of Data (SIGMOD), 1998.

4. Surajit Chaudhuri and Vivek Narasayya. An efficient cost-driven index selection tool for Microsoft SQL Server. In *Proceedings of the International Conference on Very Large Databases (VLDB)*, 1997.

5. Surajit Chaudhuri and Vivek Narasayya. Autoadmin "What-if" index analysis utility. In *Proceedings of the ACM International Conference on Management of Data (SIGMOD)*, 1998.

6. Sheldon J. Finkelstein, Mario Schkolnick, and Paolo Tiberio. Physical database design for relational databases. *ACM Transactions on Database Systems*, 13(1), 1988.

7. Martin R. Frank, Edward Omiecinski, and Shamkant B. Navathe. Adaptive and automated index selection in RDBMS. In *Proceedings of the International Conference on Extending Database Technology (EDBT)*, 1992.

8. Stratos Papadomanolakis, Debabrata Dash, and Anastasia Ailamaki. Efficient use of the query optimizer for automated physical design. In *Proceedings of the International Conference on Very Large Databases (VLDB)*, 2007.

9. Karl Schnaitter, Neoklis Polyzotis, and Lise Getoor. Index interactions in physical design tuning: Modeling, analysis, and applications. *Proceedings of the VLDB Endowment*, 2(1), 2009.

Chapter 6

Enumerating the Search Space

In Chapter 4 we characterized the search space for the physical design problem, and in Chapter 5 we discussed how to approximate the cost of a workload and required storage for arbitrary configurations. As we showed in Chapter 3, however, the number of configurations in the search space is very large, which rules out any exact solution. In this chapter we introduce different heuristic approaches to enumerate the search space and thus solve the physical design problem.

Enumeration strategies can be categorized as bottom-up or top-down, with each one associated with different challenges and advantages. Bottom-up strategies begin with an empty (or preexisting) configuration and progressively add indexes. This approach can be efficient when available storage is low, since the best configuration is likely to consist of only a few indexes. In contrast, a top-down approach begins with a globally optimal configuration, which generally exceeds the storage bound, and thus it is not valid. It then progressively refines the configuration until it meets the storage constraints. Top-down strategies have several key desirable properties, especially when the storage constraint is not very tight. It remains an interesting open problem whether hybrid schemes based on specific input characteristics can improve upon the aforementioned approaches.

6.1 Bottom-Up Enumeration

The bottom-up techniques discussed in this section begin by identifying a subset of the full set of indexes that can be part of the final configuration, called the *enumeration space*. Since the full set of indexes for a given workload is generally too large to manipulate, the enumeration space implements the first heuristic to reduce the complexity of the optimization problem. The enumeration strategy proper is therefore conducted over the enumeration space. Figure 6.1 illustrates a high-level overview of a generic bottom-up approach.

The simplest way to define the enumeration space for a given workload is as the union of candidate indexes for each query in the workload, as described

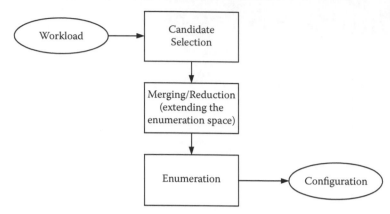

FIGURE 6.1   Generic bottom-up search framework.

in Section 4.1. Since the number of candidate indexes for a given query is typically small, an enumeration space defined in this way has a reasonable size that can be handled by the enumeration strategies. At the same time, however, it will miss some interesting candidates that result from operations such as merge and reduction (see Section 4.2), especially in the presence of storage constraints. For that reason, some approaches consider additional indexes in the enumeration space.

A common addition to the enumeration space is all the single-column indexes that result from taking the original set of candidate indexes and removing all but the leading key column. This extended set is designed to heuristically cover the reduction and splitting operations discussed in Section 4.2. Similarly, the clustered index associated to each index in the original enumeration space is also included, which covers the promotion operation. It is generally a good idea to additionally consider some merged indexes. There are different approaches to add merged indexes to the enumeration space. A simple *syntactic* strategy consists of including all indexes obtained by merging a pair of indexes from the original candidate set. This approach can be refined to consider only indexes that are candidates for many queries or those that are candidates for the most expensive queries under the current configuration. A more adaptive approach is shown in Figure 6.2 and works as follows. We start with the initial enumeration space **ES** and consider merging every pair of indexes I_1 and I_2 in **ES** into I_{12}. We then obtain the cost of the workload under **ES** and also under **ES**—$\{I_1, I_2\} \cup \{I_{12}\}$ (that is, the configuration that contains the merged index but none of its "parents"). If the new configuration is no worse than the original by a factor δ (e.g., $\delta = 1.1$), we keep the merged index. We repeat this procedure until no new merged index is added in an iteration.

Once the enumeration space is defined by any of the approaches previously described, we can conduct the enumeration phase proper. In the rest of this section we discuss some common alternatives.

```
adaptiveMerge (ES: enumeration space)
1    NS = ES
2    while (NS ≠ ∅)
3        ES = ES ∪ NS; NS = ∅
4        foreach (I1, I2 in ES)
5            I12 = merge(I1, I2)
6            if (I12 is not valid or I12 ∈ ES) continue
7            if (cost(W, ES-{I1,I2}∪{I12}) < δ· cost(W, ES))
8                NS = NS ∪ {I12}
9    return ES
```

FIGURE 6.2 Adaptive merging of indexes to obtain the enumeration space.

6.1.1 Hill-Climbing Approach

We now describe a hill-climbing approach, which we call *greedy(m,B)*. The *greedy(m,B)* approach results in a spectrum of alternatives that includes the exhaustive enumeration strategy at one extreme and a pure greedy strategy at the other. Rather than exhaustively traversing all subsets of the enumeration space, *greedy(m,B)* starts by evaluating all configurations with at most m indexes and then continues considering the remaining indexes greedily. Figure 6.3 illustrates this approach. Lines 1–4 consider all subsets of the enumeration space ES and obtain the configuration C that fits B and results in the smallest execution cost for the workload W. Then, lines 5–11 greedily attempt to add a single index to C that improves the cost the most (if possible). Lines 7–9 consider each index in the enumeration space that is not already part of C and keep track, in newC, of the configuration that fits in B and improves over

```
greedy-mB (ES: set of indexes, m:integer, B:size constraint)
01   C = null
02   foreach (valid CS ⊆ ES such that |CS| ≤ m and size(CS) ≤ B)
03       if (cost(W, CS) < cost(W, C))    // cost(W,null)=∞
04           C = CS
     // C contains the best configuration with at most m indexes.
05   while (true)
06       newC = C
07       foreach (I in ES-C such that size(C ∪ {I}) ≤ B)
08           if (cost(W, C ∪ {I}) < min(cost(W, newC)))
09               newC = C ∪ {I}
10       if (newC = C) break
11       C = newC
12   return C
```

FIGURE 6.3 Greedy(m,B) approach to traverse the enumeration space.

C the most. If no such configuration is found in line 10, the best configuration found so far is returned in line 12. Otherwise, the improved configuration newC takes the place of C, and the greedy strategy repeats.

Note that if m=0, *greedy(m,B)* results in a pure greedy approach. On the other hand, when m = |ES|, *greedy(m,B)* degenerates into the exhaustive approach. Therefore, the algorithm is computationally efficient only if m is small relative to |ES|. In such a case, the enumeration strategy exhibits "near greedy behavior." The reason that *greedy(m,B)* generally performs well is that in many cases the largest cost reductions often result from indexes that are good candidate indexes by themselves. At the same time, however, it is important to capture significant *index interactions*. These correspond to situations in which a single index is not useful unless another index is also present in the configuration (e.g., consider the case of a merge-based join simultaneously using two covering indexes). Such index interactions justify the exhaustive phase of *greedy(m,B)*, which helps capture interactions that have the most significant effect on cost.

6.1.1.1   Variants

A variant of the previously given enumeration algorithm additionally relies on branch-and-bound. The idea is to use *greedy(m,B)* with a low value of m to quickly generate a first-cut solution. Subsequently, configurations are enumerated with *greedy(m', k)* for some $m' > m$. While we are calculating the cost of the workload under a specific configuration, we can stop (and discard the configuration) as soon as the cost of any prefix of the workload exceeds the total cost of the first-cut solution. This approach executes *greedy(m,B)* twice, but it might save significant what-if calls for undesirable configurations during the second execution.

Alternatively, we can obtain several *seed* configurations (either by keeping the top configurations found in lines 1–5 of Figure 6.3 or as result of using other heuristics) and apply the greedy phase in lines 6–11 over each seed. Such alternatives help prevent local minima and in general traverse a larger search space with only a modest overhead.

We finally note that the initial formulation of *greedy(m,B)* was used to enumerate multicolumn indexes after obtaining an enumeration space with only single-column indexes. The idea is to call *greedy(m,B)* with just single-column indexes in the enumeration space and to obtain back a configuration C_1. Then, we add to the enumeration space all two-column indexes that can be extended from an index in C_1 and call *greedy(m,B)* again with this new set, obtaining back C_2. We repeat this procedure until indexes of a certain length have been considered and return the best configuration overall. Since new candidate selection mechanisms do consider multicolumn indexes, however, this procedure is not widely used in practice anymore.

6.1.2 Knapsack-Based Approach

The enumeration strategy for the physical design problem can also be seen as an application of the classical *knapsack* combinatorial optimization problem. Suppose we are given a set of items, each with a *weight* and a *benefit* value. The knapsack problem consists of determining how many instances of each item to put in a knapsack of capacity B so that the combined weight of all instances is below B and the overall benefit is maximized. There are several variations of the knapsack problem, and in this section we consider the 0-1 knapsack problem, in which we can pick each item at most once.

To model the enumeration strategy as a knapsack problem, we consider each index in the enumeration space as an item. We then need to determine appropriate values for the weight and benefit of each index. The weight of an index is its estimated size, so the combined weight of a configuration is the overall storage required to materialize it. Determining the benefit of an index is more complex. A simple strategy to determine the benefit of an index is as follows. Consider the configuration that has all indexes in the enumeration space, and call it C_{ES} (we pick only one clustering index per table from the enumeration space so that the resulting configuration is valid). Also consider the configuration with no indexes (or alternatively, the current configuration) and call it C_0. The benefit of an index I can then be obtained by finding all queries that use I under C_{ES} and adding their benefits in terms of execution cost with respect to configuration C_0. That is, the benefit for an index I, denoted as $b(I)$, is defined as follows:

$$b(I) = \sum_{q \in W \text{ that uses } I \text{ under } C_{ES}} \big(cost(q_S, C_0) - cost(q_S, C_{ES}) - updateCost(q, I)\big)$$

where q_S is the inner select query of an UPDATE query q (or q itself if q is a SELECT query), and $updateCost(q, I)$ is the estimated cost of updating index I in the update shell of an UPDATE q (or zero if q is a SELECT query). That is, the benefit of an index I is roughly measured by how much I can decrease the cost of the workload in the best case.

Once we define weight and benefit values in this way, we can use well-known approaches to solve the resulting knapsack instance. The knapsack problem, however, is NP-hard, and therefore finding the optimal solution is unfeasible in practice. A heuristic to solve the 0-1 knapsack problem is to sort indexes in order of decreasing ratio of benefit to weight and to pick indexes in this order until the available space is exhausted. This assignment performs very well in practice, and a very simple refinement guarantees a factor 2 approximation to the optimal solution.

There are, however, a few complications in this straightforward application of the knapsack problem. First, the technique to assign benefits to index would not produce accurate results for merged indexes, which would not be picked by the optimizer to evaluate any query in the workload whenever the original candidate indexes are also present. Additionally, indexes usually interact with each other, and therefore assigning a fixed *benefit* value to each index will miss opportunities (see our discussion in the previous section in the context of *greedy(m,B)*). Finally, the simple heuristic to solve the knapsack problem is efficient but can be twice as bad as the optimal solution, and we might want to trade additional optimization time with the quality of the resulting configuration. We next comment on some approaches to address these limitations.

6.1.2.1 Improving Benefit Values

Rather than assigning the full benefit of a query q to all indexes used to evaluate it under C_{ES}, we can instead scale down this benefit value by the number of indexes used in q's plan. Additionally, we can assign a fraction of the benefit of an index to all the derived candidates via merging, reduction, or other operations. In this way, the benefit of an index more accurately describes the reality during query optimization.

Even with these adjustments, we have the problem that index benefits are not independent of one another. Therefore, any strategy that assigns benefits to individual indexes and ignores interaction among them will incur approximation errors. That is, when the individual benefits of indexes are added up, they will either underestimate or overestimate the actual benefit of such set of indexes for the query. To alleviate this problem, we could try to assign benefits to indexes in a more principled manner such that the previous approximation error is the least. That is, suppose that $\beta(C)$ is the true benefit of configuration C for workload W, that is, $\beta(C) = \sum_{q \in W}(cost(W, C_0) - cost(W, C))$. We would like to obtain benefit values $b(I)$ for indexes I in the enumeration space such that for each configuration C we have that $\beta(C) = \sum_{I \in C} b(I)$. Since the overall benefit function $\beta(C)$ can be arbitrary, it may not be possible to get such an assignment for $b(I)$ values. The aim is to obtain an assignment that minimizes the error between $\beta(C)$ and $\sum_{I \in C} b(I)$. Specifically, we would like to obtain an assignment of $b(I)$ values that results in

$$\forall C \subseteq C_{ES} : \frac{\beta(C)}{k} \leq \sum_{I \in C} b(I) \leq k \cdot \beta(C)$$

for the smallest possible value k. This problem can be decomposed into finding $b(I)$ values for each query q in the workload and then adding up all the partial benefits. For a given query and fixed value of k it is possible to obtain such assignment (if it exists) by solving a linear program with the inequalities above (a pair of equations for each $C \subseteq C_{ES}$). Note that since we solve a linear program for each query, and indexes that are not relevant for the query have zero benefit, the number of valid subsets $C \subseteq C_{ES}$ is not that big (we need to consider subsets that contain candidate indexes only for the query in consideration). Having a subroutine that solves the linear program for a fixed value of k allows us to obtain the smallest k by performing a binary search on k (solving a linear program at each iteration) and thus to calculate our desired benefit assignment. Consider two indexes I_1 and I_2, and suppose that for a given query, $\beta(\{I_1\})=20$, $\beta(\{I_2\})=10$, and $\beta(\{I_1, I_2\})=25$. The original formulation for benefit values would result in $b(I_1) = b(I_2) = 25$ (or 12.5 if we divide the whole benefit equally per index in the query). Using the approach described already, we would obtain $b(I_1) = 16.67$ and $b(I_2) = 8.33$, which minimizes the deviation from the true benefit as little as possible.

6.1.2.2   Extending the Enumeration Strategy

Even when using more accurate benefit values, these are still an approximation. If we base our search purely on such benefit values, we might miss configurations that have a combined benefit value that is underestimated when we add individual index benefits. It makes sense then to explore some additional points in the search space beyond what is traversed by the heuristic solution to the 0-1 knapsack problem. For that purpose, a common approach is to randomize the initial solution produced by the knapsack heuristic and thus to explore nearby points in the search space. Specifically, we swap a small number δ of indexes in the current configuration with indexes not in the configuration and thus obtain a configuration that is in the "neighborhood" of the original one. We repeat this procedure and improve the current solution until a prespecified time bound is reached returning the best configuration overall.

Figure 6.4 illustrates the knapsack-based approach discussed in this section. Lines 1–3 calculate the weight and benefit values for each index in the enumeration space using any of the techniques discussed already. Lines 4 and 5 implement the heuristic approach to knapsack, and lines 6–8 implement the randomized postprocessing of the initial solution.

```
knapsack (ES: set of indexes, B:size constraint)
1    foreach I ∈ ES
2        w_I = size of I
3        b_I = benefit of I for workload W    // See Section 6.1.2.1
4    sort ES by decreasing b_I/w_I
5    C = longest prefix in ES that fits B
6    while (time does not expire)
7        C' = C - C⁻ ∪ C⁺ // C⁻ ⊆ C, C⁺ ⊆ ES-C, | C⁻ | ≤ δ, |C⁺| ≤ δ
8        if (cost(W,C') < cost(W,C)) C = C'
9    return C
```

FIGURE 6.4   Knapsack-based approach to traverse the enumeration space.

6.1.3　Integer Programming Approach

The technique presented in Section 6.1.2.1 calculates more accurate benefit values by solving several linear programs. These benefit values are subsequently fed to the knapsack heuristic. We can alternatively cast the full physical design problem as an integer programming instance and use existing solvers to obtain the desired configuration. Note that this approach is not strictly bottom-up, but we include it in this section since it generalizes some ideas and techniques discussed earlier.

For that purpose, suppose that the indexes in the enumeration space are $ES = \{I_1, \dots, I_n\}$, and the queries in the workload are $W = \{q_1, \dots, q_m\}$. Now assume that the set of atomic configurations for W and ES are $\{C_1, \dots C_p\}$. Recall that a configuration C is atomic for a query q if q uses all indexes in C (see Section 5.2.1 for more details). We then calculate the benefit of each query q_i ($1 \leq i \leq m$) under atomic configurations C_k, denoted as $b_{ik} = cost(q_i, C_0) - cost(q_i, C_k)$, where C_0 is the base configuration (using the notation in the previous section, we have that $\beta(C_k) = \sum_{q_i} b_{ik}$).

Let y_j be a decision variable that is 1 if index I_j is part of the final configuration, and 0 otherwise. Additionally, let x_{ik} be a decision variable that is 1 if query q_i uses all indexes in C_k when optimized under the final configuration, and 0 otherwise. Then, the corresponding integer program is defined as follows:

$$maximize \sum_{i=1}^{m} \sum_{k=1}^{p} b_{ik} \cdot x_{ik}$$

subject to

$$\sum_{i=1}^{p} x_{ik} \leq 1 \qquad \forall i \tag{6.1}$$

$$x_{ik} \leq y_j \qquad \forall i, \forall j, k : I_j \in C_k \tag{6.2}$$

$$\sum_{j=1}^{n} size(I_j) \cdot y_j \leq B \tag{6.3}$$

Constraints 6.1 guarantee that a query uses a single atomic configuration, and Constraints 6.2 guarantee that all the indexes in such atomic configuration are defined in the final configuration. Constraint 6.3 expresses the storage limit. Finally, the optimizing function sums the benefits of all queries over all possible atomic configurations. A single atomic configuration is used for each query (Constraints 6.1), all indexes in such atomic configuration are present in the final configuration (Constraints 6.2), and the final configuration fits in the available storage (Constraint 6.3). Note that we require an additional constraint to prevent more than a single clustered index per table, but we omit it for simplicity.

This integer program can be adapted to handle updates by slightly modifying the optimizing function so that it takes into account the negative benefit of indexes that are updated (i.e., using the traditional separation of an UPDATE query into an inner SELECT and an UPDATE shell). Once the integer program is defined, it can be solved exactly or approximately by one of many existing general purpose solvers.

In order to define an integer problem for a given physical design problem instance, we need to calculate $size(I_j)$ and b_{ik} values. While sizes are easy to approximate, obtaining b_{ik} benefit values is more challenging. Specifically, we need to obtain the cost of each query under every atomic configuration defined from the enumeration space. If the enumeration space is moderately large or contains merged, split, or reduced indexes, there can be a combinatorial explosion in the number of such benefit values (note that integer programming itself is NP-hard). For small problem instances, however, the integer programming approach can quickly return the optimal configuration.

6.2 Top-Down Enumeration

The techniques for enumerating the physical design search space discussed in the previous section rely on the following generic pattern:

1. Identify a set of candidate indexes that speed up each query in isolation.

2. Extend this set by means of index transformations into an enumeration space.

3. Search the enumeration space for a subset of indexes that satisfies the space constraint and results in the largest improvement in execution cost for the workload.

In all previous approaches, steps 2 and 3 are performed separately, and step 3 generally follows a bottom-up strategy that starts with an empty configuration and progressively adds indexes until the space constraint is no longer satisfied. In Section 4.3 we showed how to (conceptually) characterize the full enumeration space as the closure of an initial set of candidates under certain index transformations. This approach suggests a completely different approach to enumerate the space of configurations. Specifically, in this section we describe an alternative enumeration scheme that begins with an "optimal" configuration that is generally too large to fit in the available space and progressively transforms it into configurations that consume less space and at the same time are less efficient (we first assume that there are no updates in the workload and lift this restriction in Section 6.2.2). Conceptually, this approach results in the following additional benefits (note that some of the following features are also applicable in a bottom-up strategy, but they are more difficult to design and implement in such a context):

- The *merging/reduction* and *enumeration* steps in Figure 6.1 are interleaved. It is not required to obtain all merged indexes before starting enumeration, but instead these can be generated lazily, on demand, while traversing the enumeration space.

- Configurations are always transformed by replacing some indexes by others that are smaller but less efficient, so estimating the cost of the workload under a transformed configuration can be done more efficiently (we need only to reoptimize queries that originally used some of the transformed indexes). In a bottom-up strategy, adding a new index to an existing configuration requires reoptimizing all queries that reference the index table (or resort to heuristics, which introduces additional inaccuracies).

- A top-down approach provides additional information to the database administrator. Since we progressively transform efficient configurations so that they use less space while performing slightly worse, at the end of the tuning process we have many alternative configurations that are more efficient than the final recommendation but that use more resources. This might provide hints about the distribution of more efficient configurations to the database administrator and help in making decisions (e.g., increasing the disk storage in the current database installation). Figure 6.5 shows a sample output of a top-down strategy described in this section for a TPC-H workload. Using the initial configuration (requiring 1.25 GB), the workload is estimated to execute in 2,469 time-units. The optimal configuration can bring the execution cost down to 540 time-units but requires over 6 GB of space. The best configuration under 1.75 GB (the input constraint) is estimated to result in 1,388 time-units (56% of the original estimated cost). The figure shows that adding up to 250 MB of additional disk space can result in an additional 10% improvement (a reasonable trade-off). It also shows that having more than 4 GB improves the situation only by a marginal 3% and therefore is not advisable (see the steep slope in Figure 6.5 for configurations larger than 4 GB).

6.2.1 General Architecture

Figure 6.6 shows a high-level overview of a top-down enumeration architecture. We begin the search from an initial configuration (step 1 in the figure). This initial configuration does not need to fit in the available space but is the most efficient one that the search strategy would explore during enumeration (in terms of SELECT queries). We then progressively traverse the search space

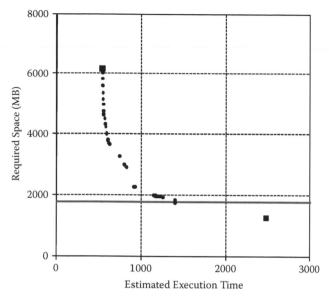

FIGURE 6.5 Top-down search output for a TPC-H database.

until a stopping condition is satisfied (typically a time bound). Each iteration during enumeration consists of the following steps. First, we evaluate the current configuration and store it in the global cache of configurations (step 2 in the figure). Then, we consider transformations that generate new candidate configurations from the current one (step 3 in the figure). We transform a

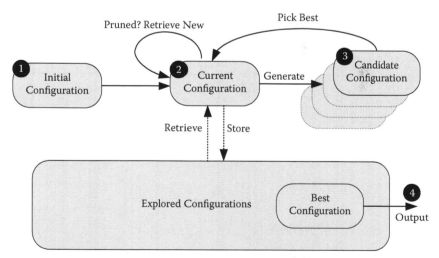

FIGURE 6.6 Architecture of a top-down search framework. (Used with permission from Bruno, N. & Chaudhuri, S. In *Proceedings of the International Conference on Very Large Databases [VLDB]*, 2008.)

configuration by replacing a subset of its indexes by another one so that the resulting configuration is smaller at the cost of being generally less efficient. We then rank the resulting candidate configurations based on their expected promise and pick the best candidate that is not already in the global cache, which becomes the current configuration. This cycle repeats until the stopping condition is met, and we output the best configuration found so far (step 4 in the figure). Note that each time a configuration is evaluated, we check whether we should prune the current configuration. If so, we retrieve from the global cache a previously explored configuration that is not pruned and continue (this step effectively implements a backtracking mechanism). In the rest of this section we give additional details on each step in Figure 6.6.

6.2.1.1　Choosing the Initial Configuration

Although any configuration can be chosen to be the starting point in the search, the initial configuration effectively restricts the search space. Specifically, the enumeration architecture eventually considers any configuration that is a subset of the closure of the initial configuration under the set of transformations. Therefore, if we consider as the initial configuration the union of all candidate indexes for each query in the workload, the resulting enumeration space is the same as the full search space as defined in Section 4.3. If the workload consists of SELECT queries only, this configuration is the optimal one in absence of storage constraints or results in a lower bound for estimated cost if there is a storage constraint.

6.2.1.2　Evaluating the Current Configuration

Each search iteration requires evaluating a previously unexplored configuration, which consists of two tasks. First, we need to determine whether the storage constraint is satisfied and, if not, how close is the current configuration to a viable state. With a storage constraint of B, we simply estimate the size of the current configuration, size(C). If size$(C) \leq B$, the storage constraint is satisfied. Otherwise, the value size$(C) - B$ quantifies how close we are to a valid configuration. Second, we need to evaluate the optimizing function, that is, the expected cost of the workload under the current configuration. In order to do so, we need to optimize the queries in the workload in *what-if* mode, which returns the expected cost of each query without materializing the configuration. This step is usually the bottleneck of the whole process, since optimizer calls are typically expensive. Chapter 5 explores different ways to reduce this overhead.

6.2.1.3　Generating Candidate Configurations

After evaluating the current configuration, we apply transformations to generate a set of new, unexplored configurations in the search space. For that purpose, we use the family of transformations introduced in Section 4.2.2.

Specifically, given the current configuration C, we generate the following configurations:

- **Merging:** $C - \{I_1, I_2\} \cup \{I_1 \oplus I_2\}$ for each pair of compatible indexes (I_1, I_2) in C.
- **Splitting:** $C - \{I_1, I_2\} \cup \{I_1 \otimes I_2\}$ for each pair of compatible indexes (I_1, I_2) in C.
- **Reduction:** $C - \{I\} \cup \{\rho(I, K)\}$ for each index I in C and prefix K of I.
- **Promotion:** $C - \{I\} - \{I_{cl}\} \cup \{\Gamma(I)\}$ for each index I in C, where I_{cl} is the clustered index of I's table (if defined).
- **Deletion:** $C - \{I\}$ for each index I in C. If the removed index is a clustered index, it is replaced by the corresponding table heap.

The number of transformations for a given configuration C is $\mathcal{O}(n \cdot (n+m))$, where n is the number of indexes in C, and m is the maximum number of columns in an index in C. In real situations this number is likely to be much smaller, because indexes are spread throughout several tables (and therefore merging and splitting are valid for only a subset of cases) and also because not all reductions need to be considered. To clarify the latter point, consider index $I = R(a, b, c, d, e)$ and the single-query workload:

```
SELECT a, b, c, d, e
FROM R
WHERE a = 10
```

In this situation, the only useful reduction for the index is $I' = R(a)$, since any other prefix of I is going to be both larger than I' and less efficient for processing the query.

6.2.1.4 Ranking Candidate Configurations

After generating all candidate configurations from the current one via transformations, we need to rank them in decreasing order of "promise," so that better configurations are chosen and explored first. For that purpose, we estimate both the expected cost of the workload and the expected size (i.e., the storage constraint) of each resulting configuration. While estimating sizes can be done efficiently, estimating costs is more challenging. The reason is that often there are several candidate configurations to rank, and the cost of performing what-if optimization calls (even when using the optimizations described in Sections 5.3 and 5.4) is too costly. To reduce overheads, we can use the upper-bound approach of Section 5.2.2 and obtain upper bounds on the cost of queries for each candidate transformation.

Once we obtain estimates for both the optimizing function and the deviation from the storage constraint for each of the alternative configurations, we need to put together these values to rank the different candidate transformations. Consider some transformation that goes from the current configuration

C to a new candidate C_{tr}. We can efficiently estimate the expected decrease in storage space $\Delta S_{tr} = size(C) - size(C_{tr})$ and the maximum increase in cost $\Delta T_{tr} = CostBound(C_{tr}) - Cost(C)$. The value $penalty(C_{tr}) = \Delta T_{tr}/\Delta S_{tr}$ estimates the increase in execution cost per unit of storage expected for C_{tr}. Penalty values are opposed to promise values, and thus we can rank configurations by increasing values of $penalty(C_{tr})$. The reason is that we are interested in configurations that are significantly smaller in space without increasing the expected cost too much (note that a slight variation of this heuristic is used in the greedy approximation to the knapsack problem in Section 6.1.2). Suppose that the space constraint is B (i.e., we are interested in the best configuration that fits in B). Any decrease in space beyond B is not strictly useful, but we might artificially decrease the value of $penalty(C_{tr})$ whenever $size(C_{tr})$ is significantly below B. For that reason, we refine the penalty function for C_{tr} obtained by transforming C as follows:

$$penalty(C_{tr}) = \frac{\Delta T_{tr}}{\min(size(C) - B, \Delta S_{tr})}$$

6.2.1.5   Pruning and Backtracking

As explained in Figure 6.6, we keep transforming the current configuration until it is pruned, at which point we backtrack to a previous configuration and start another iteration. Consider a storage constraint B, and assume a SELECT-only workload. Suppose that the current configuration C exceeds B, but after transforming C into C' we observe that C' is within the storage bound B. In this case, no matter how we further transform C', we would never obtain a valid configuration that is more efficient than C'. The reason is that all the transformations (e.g., merges and reductions) result in configurations that are less efficient for the input workload. Therefore, C' would be more efficient than any remaining configuration obtained by transforming C' and also fits in the storage constraint. We can therefore stop the current iteration and prune C'. After we prune a configuration (or whenever the current configuration cannot be further transformed), we need to pick a suitable configuration to backtrack to and continue the search space enumeration. One approach to choose a new configuration is as follows. We first obtain the chain of transformed configurations from the initial to the current one. We then pick the configuration that resulted in the *actual* largest penalty when transformed (with the aim of "correcting" what went wrong in the estimation of penalty values). Other alternative ways to pick a new configuration include choosing the unpruned configuration with the smallest cost, the smallest storage surplus, or the best ratio of such quantities.

6.2.2   Handling Updates

So far we focused on SELECT-only workloads. The main impact of an update query is that some (or all) of the indexes defined over the table updated by the query must also be updated as a side effect. Therefore, it is not true anymore that adding more indexes would always reduce the expected cost of a workload. We next briefly explain how the different components in the top-down approach change when updates are present in the workload.

Choosing the initial configuration: When updates are present, the initial configuration is not optimal anymore because indexes also need to be updated, raising the overall workload cost. However, the resulting configuration is still optimal for the SELECT component of each update query, and we can use this fact to obtain a lower bound. Specifically, the expected cost for the SELECT portion of the queries in the workload is added to the cost of all the UPDATE shells under the base configuration (which contains only indexes that must be present in any configuration). We then obtain a cost that cannot be improved by any configuration. This bound is not tight (i.e., there might be no configuration that meets the lower bound) but offers valuable additional information to a database administrator.

Evaluating the current configuration: Updates can be handled by the traditional approach of separating an update query into an inner SELECT and an UPDATE shell. Specifically, we calculate, for each index I and update query q in the workload, the cost of updating I for each update shell in the workload. Later, when evaluating a configuration, we first consider the inner SELECT portion of an update query q and then add, to the resulting partial cost, the update cost of all indexes in the configuration over the table referenced by q.

Ranking candidate configurations: For workloads with updates, the upper-bound on the cost of a transformed configuration can be negative (sometimes the cost of removing an index can be outweighed by the benefit of not having to update it). In those cases the penalty function correctly chooses transformations with negative over positive cost upper bounds but sometimes makes poor decisions comparing two transformations with negative costs. If $\Delta T_{t1} = -10$, $\Delta S_{t1} = 10$, $\Delta T_{t2} = -20$, and $\Delta S_{t2} = 30$, then $penalty(C_{t1}) = -1$ is smaller than $penalty(C_{t_2}) = -2/3$. However, configuration C_{t_2} is clearly better than C_{t_1} in terms of both space and cost (we say that t_2 dominates t_1). To remedy those situations, we first obtain the skyline of candidate configurations (i.e., we consider only candidate configurations that are not dominated by any other transformation) and then use the original *penalty* definition over this restricted subset. Also, note that the denominator in the definition of *penalty* is given by $\min(size(C) - B, \Delta S)$. Since now we can relax a configuration that requires less than B storage (see above), the denominator might become negative, which is undesirable. However, in those situations space is not relevant since the configuration already fits in B. Therefore, when the current configuration requires less than

B storage, we simply use ΔT_{tr} as the penalty associated with each transformation tr.

6.2.3   Variations and Optimizations

We next briefly describe some minor optimizations and variations to the top-down approach introduced in this section.

Shortcut evaluation: When evaluating the cost of a configuration C, we might reach a point in which the SELECT cost of a subset of queries in C is larger than the total cost of the current best configuration C_{best}. In this case, we know that neither C nor any configuration that is further relaxed from C would be more efficient than C_{best}. Therefore, we can stop evaluating C (thus saving optimization calls) and can backtrack to a different configuration (thus pruning the search space). For this heuristic to be effective, it is useful to evaluate the workload so that more expensive queries are first (this ranking of queries can be static depending on the cost of the query under the initial configuration or adaptive based on the configuration that was transformed to obtain the current one).

Multiple transformations per iteration: The current strategy applies a single transformation to relax the current configuration. In general, we might apply more than one transformation. We need to be careful that we do not select conflicting transformations (such as merging I_1 and I_2 after removing I_1). This alternative might reduce the overall time to arrive to a valid transformation but introduces additional inaccuracies because often transformations strongly interact with each other.

Shrinking configurations: Another variation consists of removing, at each iteration, all indexes from the current configuration that are not used to evaluate any query in the workload. While this approach would reduce the search space because fewer transformations are available, it might also decrease the quality of the final recommendation, since some structures that are not used in the current configuration might become useful after applying some transformation.

6.3   Summary

- The search space for the physical design problem is too large to expect exact solutions in reasonable amounts of time, even for moderately sized input instances.

- Heuristic enumeration strategies typically follow bottom-up approaches (which start with an empty configuration and add indexes incrementally) or top-down approaches (which start with an optimal configuration that is too large and keep relaxing it into smaller and less efficient ones).

    - Bottom-up approaches include the *greedy(m,B)* approach (which performs an exhaustive search of a subspace followed by a hill-climbing greedy heuristic), the *knapsack-based* approach (which models the physical design problem as an instance of the 0-1 knapsack problem), and the *integer-programming* approach (which uses known techniques in combinatorial optimization to find solutions for small problem instances).
    - Top-down approaches interleave enumeration and generation of derived indexes (via merging, reduction, and other operators), can exploit certain properties of derived indexes to speed up reoptimization, and can result in better quality configurations than bottom-up approaches when the storage constraint is not too tight.

6.4   Additional Reading

The *greedy(m,B)* technique[5] was first introduced in a slightly different context (specifically, the algorithm is called *greedy(m,k)* and performs an exhaustive enumeration of up to m indexes followed by a greedy choice of $k - m$ additional indexes). Subsequent work describes a knapsack-based approach to the physical design problem,[8] improvements to calculate index benefits by using linear programming,[4] and an integer programming approach.[6] All these techniques are concerned about the effect of index interactions, a topic that is discussed in recent work[7] based on the concept of *index benefit graphs*. A different approach to enumerate the search space uses relaxation of indexes[1] via transformations to the current configuration.[2,3]

References

1. Nicolas Bruno and Surajit Chaudhuri. Automatic physical database tuning: A relaxation-based approach. In *Proceedings of the ACM International Conference on Management of Data (SIGMOD)*, 2005.

2. Nicolas Bruno and Surajit Chaudhuri. Physical design refinement: The "Merge-Reduce" approach. In *Proceedings of the International Conference on Extending Database Technology (EDBT)*, 2006.

3. Nicolas Bruno and Surajit Chaudhuri. Constrained physical design tuning. In *Proceedings of the International Conference on Very Large Databases (VLDB)*, 2008.

4. Surajit Chaudhuri, Mayur Datar, and Vivek R. Narasayya. Index selection for databases: A hardness study and a principled heuristic solution. *IEEE Transactions on Knowledge and Data Engineering*, 16(11), 2004.

5. Surajit Chaudhuri and Vivek Narasayya. An efficient cost-driven index selection tool for Microsoft SQL Server. In *Proceedings of the International Conference on Very Large Databases (VLDB)*, 1997.

6. Stratos Papadomanolakis and Anastassia Ailamaki. An integer linear programming approach to database design. In *Workshop on Self-Managing Database Systems*, 2007.

7. Karl Schnaitter, Neoklis Polyzotis, and Lise Getoor. Index interactions in physical design tuning: Modeling, analysis, and applications. *Proceedings of the VLDB Endowment*, 2(1), 2009.

8. Gary Valentin, Michael Zuliani, Daniel Zilio, Guy Lohman, and Alan Skelley. DB2 advisor: An optimizer smart enough to recommend its own indexes. In *Proceedings of the International Conference on Data Engineering (ICDE)*, 2000.

Chapter 7

Practical Aspects in Physical Database Design

This chapter complements the various approaches for the physical design problem that we introduced earlier by discussing practical aspects that need to be addressed in a real-world tuning tool. Figure 7.1 gives an overview of the various issues that we discuss in this chapter. Specifically, we cover (1) how to gather representative workloads, (2) how to clean and compress workloads for scalable tuning, (3) variations on tuning models, (4) variations to limit tuning time, (5) practical aspects of tuning production servers, (6) generation of reports, and (7) scheduling scripts for deploying the recommended configurations.

7.1   Workload Gathering

The physical design problem consumes a query workload W and a storage constraint B and produces the configuration C that minimizes the cost of W while fitting in B. It is therefore very important that the input workload W be representative of the real-world scenario on which configuration C would be deployed. Otherwise, the resulting configuration, while very appropriate for the input workload, might not be effective in the production system. We now discuss different approaches to gather a representative input workload for the physical design problem [see Figure 7.1(1)].

Manually designed queries: This approach is commonly used when we have a good understanding of the database application and want to do some amount of localized performance tuning. Suppose that a commonly executed query suddenly becomes much more expensive. In that case, we can tune such query and obtain a configuration that solves the performance problem (without considering other updates or storage constraints). We can then use this configuration as a starting point in a more comprehensive performance tuning investigation. If we need

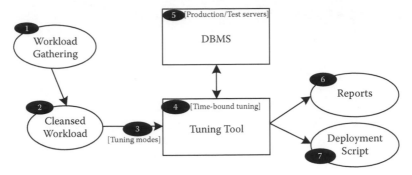

FIGURE 7.1   Overview of practical aspects in physical database design.

to additionally consider updates, we can include queries that modify the corresponding tables and therefore can analyze a specific problem instance in detail.

Synthetically generated queries: Before deploying a new application, developers are usually aware of the set of queries that would be executed in the production environment via stored procedures. However, database administrators (DBAs) might not know in advance additional details about the query mix, or the specific values for which stored procedures would be instantiated and executed. In that case, a common approach is to synthetically generate query workloads that follow expected distributions and common parameter values. These workloads can be useful to tune a system before it goes into production.

Automatically profiled queries: The best approach to obtain representative workloads is to actually monitor and capture queries as they are processed by the database system. This approach results in the most representative workloads but is usually associated with larger overheads. The reason is that each query that is executed needs to be additionally logged by a query profiler. There are, however, some mechanisms to mitigate this overhead. First, we can profile queries for short periods of time, effectively sampling the workload. Alternatively, some sophisticated profiling tools can selectively capture queries that satisfy certain predicates, such as those issued by a given user or defined over a specific set of tables. Finally, we can piggyback on top of existing database functionality and obtain relatively good approximations of recent queries being executed. An example of this approach leverages the plan cache (which stores frequently used plans and therefore avoids reoptimizing queries). Since the plan cache contains queries that are either expensive or frequently executed, periodically flushing the content of the plan cache into a local repository can result in representative workloads that are obtained without incurring significant overhead.

Some workloads consist of a mixture of high-priority queries (which should be evaluated as efficiently as possible) and low-priority queries (which are not critical to the business and can tolerate some amount of delay). After gathering a representative workload, we can handle such scenarios by assigning weights to input queries. A common approach is to replace each query q by a pair (q, w), where w is a number that represents the *weight* or *importance* of q. Then, the cost of the workload W under a given configuration C is extended to be $\sum_i w_i \cdot cost(q_i, C)$, and the search strategy stays unchanged.

7.2 Workload Compression

After a representative workload has been gathered (especially under the profiling approach described previously), it is usually a good idea to postprocess it before passing it to a tuning tool [see Figure 7.1(2)]. On one hand, the workload might have many queries (or in general, profiled *events*) that are not relevant to a specific physical design problem. Examples are queries that are defined over tables that do not require tuning or those that do not access database tables directly but instead set database parameters or are invoked from utilities such as backup/restore. If the query profiler did not filter out such events (as described in the previous section), a postprocessing filtering step is required.

Even after discarding such nonrelevant queries, the resulting workload can sometimes be very large. This issue affects the scalability of physical design tools, since we would need to evaluate the cost of a large number of queries for each candidate configuration. In such cases, a natural question is whether tuning a smaller subset of the workload would be sufficient to give a recommendation with approximately the same reduction in cost as the recommendation that would have been obtained by tuning the entire workload.

A simple strategy to handle very large workloads is to eliminate duplicate queries. Specifically, we keep a single instance of each distinct query in the workload and assign it a weight that is equal to the number of times that the query appears in the original workload. In general, however, queries in the workload are parameterized and invoked with specific values via stored procedures. In such cases, very few instances would be truly duplicates due to varying parameter values, and this technique would not be effective. In such cases, it is useful to use relax the duplicate elimination strategy. The idea is to leverage the inherent parametrization in query workloads by partitioning the queries in equivalence classes based on their "signatures." Concretely, two queries have the same signature and therefore belong to the same equivalence class, if they are identical in all respects except for their constant values. In many cases, it is not enough to pick a single representative query from each equivalence class. The reason is that constants themselves might impact the choice of physical designs. Consider, for instance, an equivalence class that contains all queries that share the following template and have specific values for parameters @v1 and @v2:

```
SELECT R.a
FROM R
WHERE R.b < @v1 AND R.c > @v2
ORDER BY R.d
```

Depending on specific values of @v1 and @v2, the best index for the resulting query could be $R(b, c, d, a)$ if R.b < @v1 is very selective, $R(c, b, d, a)$ if instead R.c < @v2 is very selective, or even $R(d, c, b, a)$ if both predicates are not selective. If we pick only a single query from this equivalence class, we might bias the resulting configuration toward a specific set of indexes. To address this problem, we can pick a random subset from each equivalence class. For instance, we can pick $\max(5, 0.1 \cdot |EC|)$ queries from equivalence class EC (i.e., a 10% random sample of the equivalence class or five queries, whichever is larger). In that way, each *interesting* combination of values in a partition would probably be represented in the compressed workload, and the resulting configuration would be close to the optimal one when considering the full workload.

Note that the previous approach can be seen as an instance of a clustering problem. The idea is to create clusters of queries in the workload, where each cluster contains queries that are *similar* to each other and different from queries in other clusters, based on a given distance function. We then select a representative subset of queries from each cluster and thus obtain the compressed workload. The technique discussed previously considers a distance function between queries defined as follows:

$$distance(q_1, q_2) = \begin{cases} 0 & \text{if } q_1 \text{ and } q_2 \text{ are identical except for constant values} \\ 1 & \text{otherwise} \end{cases}$$

More advanced distance functions take into account domain-specific knowledge but are more expensive to compute. For instance, we can define a distance function as follows:

$$distance(q_1, q_2) = \frac{|\mathcal{I}(q_1) \cap \mathcal{I}(q_2)|}{|\mathcal{I}(q_1) \cup \mathcal{I}(q_2)|}$$

where $\mathcal{I}(q)$ is the set of candidate indexes for query q as defined in Section 4.1. In this way, the more similar the candidate sets of two queries, the closer the queries in terms of distance. This technique is more sophisticated than the syntactic approach but requires optimizing each query in the workload at least once, which can be expensive.

7.3 Tuning Modes

The traditional physical design problem asks for the best configuration that fits in a storage constraint and is expected to improve the execution time of the input workload as much as possible. Certain scenarios, however, require slight variations of this problem statement [see Figure 7.1(3)]. In this section we discuss some common alternatives.

Keep existing structures. If the current physical design is reasonably tuned for performance and there are a few queries that require additional tuning, a common alternative is to require that the final configuration include the current one. That is, we can add new indexes to the current configuration but not remove existing indexes. Note that the current configuration can also include hypothetical indexes, with the implicit meaning that the final configuration should include them as well. The techniques discussed in previous chapters can be easily adapted to this scenario, by adding the desired set of indexes to each candidate configuration and disallowing invalid configurations (e.g., those for which two clustered indexes are defined over the same table).

Remove unused indexes. This approach is useful when we want to reduce the size of the current configuration without significantly compromising the quality of execution plans. In this scenario, the enumeration space is composed of all and only indexes in the current configuration, and we look for the subset of indexes that result in the smallest execution time. Usually, indexes are removed because of updates in the workload or simply because they are not useful for any query in the workload (note that, naturally, given two configurations with the same expected cost for the workload, we should pick the smallest one). A variation of this technique is to consider only indexes that are either in the original configuration or can be obtained by merging, splitting, or reduction operations from them. In a sense, the idea is to *refine* the original configuration so that it is not much worse than the original one but is significantly smaller in size.

Index restrictions. Sometimes it is useful to restrict the search space to a certain subset of candidate indexes. A common alternative, when the clustered indexes of a database are predefined by design choices, is to consider tuning only nonclustered indexes in the configuration. Other alternatives include recommending indexes for only a subset of the tables in the database or indexes that satisfy certain constraint (e.g., with at most a certain number of columns or a given size).

Database scaling. An interesting variant of the physical design problem results from using scaling factors for database tables. Suppose that we want to understand how the physical database design should change if the data volume grows by 500%. In this case, we can scale the actual table cardinalities appropriately by temporarily modifying the statistical information used by the optimizer. Specifically, if we change metadata information so that table sizes appear to the optimizer to be five times larger than the current values, for all practical purposes the tuning session would be indistinguishable from one that uses tables that are truly five times larger than the current ones.

Evaluate only. An *evaluate-only* mode is useful when trying to analyze the performance of a given workload under one (or several) manually designed configurations. Although not an automated tuning process per se, this scenario exposes the what-if optimization component of the tuning tool so that a DBA can evaluate different designs. This functionality is commonly used after a configuration is recommended. The DBA can take this configuration, make a small amount of changes (say, removing or adding an index), and evaluate these variations before deciding which alternative to deploy.

7.4   Time-Bound Tuning

As we discussed in previous chapters, the physical design problem is NP-hard, which motivates the use of heuristics during enumeration. Even when applying such heuristics, and especially for large workloads, a tuning tool might run for too long before returning a recommendation. This might be a problem if the DBA has a limited window of opportunity to tune a database. In this case, it is preferable to have algorithms that run to completion within a reliable period of time or that can be interrupted at any time obtaining the best solution found so far. In this section we describe some common alternatives for this *time-bound* tuning approach [see Figure 7.1(4)].

Anytime approach. An anytime algorithm does not need to run to completion to give an answer but instead is able to return partial answers, whose quality depends on the amount of computation that was performed until it was interrupted. Since the physical design problem is essentially a complex search over a large space of configurations, most algorithms can be adapted to provide partial answers early. In general, we need some fixed amount of computation to obtain the first solution, which is then refined over time. After this first solution is found, we can interrupt the various enumeration strategies and obtain the best configuration found so far. Details naturally depend on each specific technique. For instance, consider the knapsack-based technique discussed in Section 6.1. The idea is to first obtain weights and benefits for all indexes in the enumeration space and then greedily pick indexes to form the initial solution. After the first solution is found, the algorithm tries variations by slightly modifying the current configuration. This process can be stopped at any time, returning the best configuration found so far. The original *greedy(m, B)* starts from multiple seeds and performs a partial exhaustive search on each one followed by a hill-climbing step. This technique can be redesigned to return the best solution found after evaluating each seed. It is not clear, however, how to provide more fine-grained capabilities during the execution of *greedy(m,B)* for a single seed. The top-down approach of Section 6.2 begins with an optimal configuration that is too large and transforms it until the resulting configuration fits in the available space and cannot be further improved. At that point, the technique backtracks to a previous solution and starts a new iteration. Therefore, after the first solution is found, we can stop the search at any moment and return the best solution found so far.

Incremental approach. In the previous approach we cannot interrupt the enumeration strategy before the first solution has been calculated. When the workload is large, this step can take a long time in which no partial solutions are generated. To overcome this limitation, we can randomly partition the workload into pieces and incrementally tune larger query subsets over time. If we interrupt the algorithm before the whole workload has been processed, we would get a configuration that is good for a subset of the original workload. In that sense, the longer the algorithm runs, the more accurate is the solution.

Pause/resume approach. The previous approaches allow a DBA to continuously monitor the quality of the best configuration found over time and to interrupt the tuning session whenever the current solution looks good enough. In some scenarios, it might be useful to pause the tuning process for some time and to resume it later. For instance, suppose that a DBA has a fraction of time per day to tune workloads, but the window of opportunity is not large enough to allow a full tuning session to finish. It is important to have checkpoint mechanisms that allow us to pause a tuning session and restart it later from the point it was suspended. A common denominator approach to enable such functionality is to cache the result of optimizing every *(configuration, query)* pair. When we suspend a tuning session, we save this information to disk. At restart time, we read back the cache and *rerun* the tuning session without performing optimization calls up to the time it was suspended.

This process should take little time since no real *what-if* calls are made, after which the session continues normally. However, the enumeration strategy itself is repeated. More advanced alternatives need to cache the state of the tuning session itself, so that at restart time the tuning proceeds exactly where it was interrupted (the specific details depend on actual implementations). For such pause/restart functionality to be effective, no changes can occur while the tuning session is suspended. For instance, if a table is dropped and the tuning session is restarted, there would be metadata inconsistencies that prevent resuming the session correctly. For that reason, when the tuning session is suspended, all metadata information needs to be saved along with the state of the session, which is checked at resume time to validate that the session is able to continue.

7.5   Production/Test Tuning

Tuning tools perform complex search procedures invoking many what-if optimization calls to the database management system (DBMS). For that reason, tuning large workloads imposes a significant overhead on the server being tuned and can severely reduce the performance of applications on production servers [see Figure 7.1(5)]. In large installations, however, it is common to rely on *test servers* in addition to production servers. A test server can be used for a variety of purposes, including performance tuning and evaluation of application changes before they are deployed on the production server. A straightforward way to reduce the impact of tuning on a production server is to use a test server as follows:

1. Copy the relevant databases from the production server to the test server.
2. Tune the workload on the test server.
3. Deploy the recommendation obtained on the test server into the production server.

The advantage of such a simplistic approach is that once the databases are copied into the test server, there is no additional tuning overhead imposed on the production server. However, this approach suffers from many drawbacks that severely limit its applicability. First, databases can be very large (production databases can be hundreds of gigabytes in size or more) or changing frequently. In such situations, copying large amounts of data from production to test servers for the purposes of tuning can be time-consuming and resource intensive. Second, the hardware characteristics of test and production servers can be very different. Production servers tend to be much more powerful than

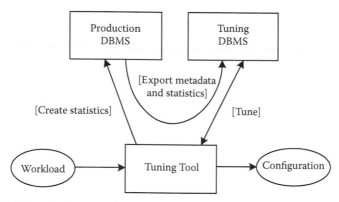

FIGURE 7.2 Tuning production servers with limited overhead.

test servers in terms of processors, memory, and disk capabilities. For that reason, it might not be even possible to copy the full databases from the production server into the test server. Additionally, since the tuning process relies on the optimizer to arrive at a recommendation and that in turn is tied to the underlying hardware, this can lead to vastly different results on the test server.

We next discuss an interesting approach to exploit a test server for physical design tuning that does not require copying database tables from the production server. The key observation that enables this functionality is that the query optimizer relies on metadata and statistics when generating execution plans for input queries. We leverage this observation to enable tuning on the test server as follows (see also Figure 7.2):

1. Copy the metadata of the relevant databases from the production server to the test server, *without* importing actual data from tables. Metadata can be imported using scripting capabilities that are available in current DBMS. This is generally a very fast operation as it processes only system catalog entries, which is independent of data size.

2. Tune the workload on the test server. For getting the same plan on the test server as we would have obtained on the production server, we require two important functionalities from the database server. First, the tuning tool might need certain statistics to be present during what-if optimization calls. However, statistic creation procedures (even those that use sampling) require access to the actual data, which is stored on the production server. Therefore, whenever the tuning tool determines that certain statistics are needed, it communicates with the production server and imports such statistical information (note that this step might require the production server to actually create such statistics on demand). Second, the hardware parameters of the production server that are modeled by the query optimizer when it generates a query plan (e.g., the amount of memory or number of central processing units [CPUs])

need to be appropriately *simulated* on the test server. This functionality might easily be incorporated into an existing query optimizer by parameterizing hardware-dependent values and having the possibility of importing/exporting hardware configuration across different servers.

3. Deploy the recommendation obtained on the test server into the production server.

Note that the only overhead introduced on the production server during tuning is the creation of additional statistics that are necessary as tuning progresses (if any). The rest of the tasks, such as performing what-if optimizations or the enumeration strategy proper, are done on the test server. In practice, this approach results in drastic reductions of overhead in production servers without compromising the quality of the resulting configurations.

7.6   Reports

After a physical design session finishes, it is useful to complement the resulting configuration with analytical reports [see Figure 7.1(6)]. This additional information gives insights to DBAs, who can then either accept the recommended configuration with no changes or slightly modify it until they are satisfied. These reports provide information such as the cost of queries occurring in the workload under the current and recommended configurations, the fraction of queries that increase their cost under the new configuration, or the relationships between queries and the indexes they reference. Figure 7.3 shows some examples of reports that are generated and returned along with physical design recommendations.

7.7   Deployment Scripts

At the end of a physical design session, we obtain a new configuration to deploy into the database server. This configuration might contain new indexes that are not present in the current configuration and might also require removing existing indexes. A common way to recommend a configuration is in the form of a deployment script [see Figure 7.1(7)]. This script can be immediately executed or postponed to a later time in which the system is not heavily loaded. A simple deployment script contains one *create-index* statement for each new index in the configuration and one *drop-index* statement for each

Sample Report	Description
Query frequency	Lists all queries in the workload sorted by frequency of occurrence
Current query cost	Lists all queries in the workload sorted by estimated cost under the current configuration
Recommended query cost	Lists all queries in the workload sorted by estimated cost under the recommended configuration
Current indexes	Lists information about each index in the current configuration, the fraction of queries in the workload that use the index, and the different ways the index is used in the workload
Recommended indexes	Same as *current indexes* but with respect to the recommended configuration
Query improvement	List of all queries along with the respective improvement in execution cost under the recommended workload
Statement/index usage	Lists each query along with the indexes that it would use in the recommended configuration
Workload information	Lists number of queries in the workload, and fraction of queries whose cost decreases/stayed the same/increased under the recommended configuration

FIGURE 7.3 Reports that can be returned along with the recommended configuration.

existing index that needs to be deleted (to avoid running out of space, *drop* statements precede *create* statements).

Interestingly enough, the creation of the deployment script itself can be challenging if we are concerned about performance. The reason is that the presence of an index can speed up the creation of a subsequent index. For example, to create index $R(c)$ we need to sort a vertical fragment of R on column c. If an index with leading column c already exists in the database, we can build $R(c)$ without sorting by just scanning such existing index. If an index with a leading column other than c (but also including c) exists, we can still scan the index faster than the clustered index, resulting in a better alternative. In this section we formally describe this task and show that it can be seen as a search problem.

Let C_0 be the current configuration, and C_f be the desired configuration to deploy. A physical schedule consists of a sequence of *create-index* and *drop-index* statements that starts in configuration C_0 and ends in configuration C_f. The *physical design scheduling problem* consists of finding the minimum cost schedule using no more than B storage, where $B \geq \max\left(size(C_f), size(C_0)\right)$. As an example, consider the following configurations over a database with a single table R:

$$C_0 = \{R(c, d), R(e)\}$$
$$C_f = \{R(a, b), R(a, c), R(c), R(e)\}$$

A simple schedule first removes all indexes in $(C_0 - C_f)$ and then creates the indexes in $(C_f - C_0)$, that is:

[drop $R(c, d)$, create $R(a, b)$, create $R(a, c)$, create $R(c)$]

The following schedule, however, can be more efficient than the previous one (assuming that the indexes at each intermediate step fit in the storage constraint):

[create $R(c)$, drop $R(c, d)$, create $R(a, b)$, create $R(a, c)$]

In this case, we use $R(c, d)$ to avoid sorting table R in c order to create $R(c)$, thus saving time. However, in this case we need to be able to store $R(c)$ and $R(c, d)$ simultaneously. There might be more efficient schedules that create *additional* intermediate indexes not in $(C_f - C_0)$. Consider the following schedule:

[create $R(c)$, drop $R(c, d)$, create $R(a, b, c)$,

create $R(a, b)$, create $R(a, c)$, drop $R(a, b, c)$]

In this schedule, we create a temporary index $R(a, b, c) = R(a, b) \oplus R(a, c)$ before creating $R(a, b)$ and $R(a, c)$. Therefore, we need to perform a full sort only once, and then $R(a, b)$ and $R(a, c)$ can be built by scanning $R(a, b, c)$ and doing a minor sort on column c for the case of $R(a, c)$ (if a is a key, no minor sorting is required for $R(a, c)$). The general physical design scheduling problem can be defined as follows. Given configurations C_0 and C_f and a space constraint B, obtain a schedule $(s_1, s_2, \ldots, s_n)$ that transforms C_0 into C_f such that:

1. Each s_i drops an existing index or creates a new index in $closure(C_f)$, as defined in Section 4.3.

2. The size of each intermediate configuration is bounded by B.

3. The cost of implementing $(s_1, s_2, \ldots, s_n)$ is minimized.

The two main challenges of the physical design scheduling problem are the explosion in the search space due to the ability to add elements in the closure of C_f and the presence of the space constraint B, which invalidates more obvious approaches based on topological orders. We now show an interesting property that connects the scheduling problem with a shortest-path algorithm in an induced graph.

Consider an instance of the physical design scheduling problem (C_0, C_f, B), and let $G = (V, E)$ be a graph defined as follows. Each vertex in the graph represents an index in the search space, $V = \{v | v \in (C_0 \cup closure(C_f)) \land size(v) \leq B\}$. Additionally, there is a directed edge $e = (v_1, v_2)$ in E if the symmetric difference between v_1 and v_2 has a single element (that is, if $|(v_1 - v_2) \cup (v_2 - v_1)| = 1$). The weight of e is equal to the cost of creating the index in $v_2 - v_1$ starting in configuration v_1 (if $v_1 \subset v_2$), or the cost of dropping the index in $v_1 - v_2$ (if $v_2 \subset v_1$). The label of edge e is the corresponding *create* or *drop* action.

In that case, the solution for (C_0, C_f, B) is the sequence of labels of the shortest path between C_0 and C_f in the graph defined previously. While this property does not directly lead to an efficient algorithm (i.e., the induced graph has an exponential number of nodes in the worst case), it can be used as a starting point to define search strategies.

7.8 A Case Study: Database Engine Tuning Advisor

We conclude this chapter with an example of a physical design tuning tool that is part of a commercial DBMS. Specifically, we focus on the *Database Engine Tuning Advisor*, or *DTA* for short, found in *Microsoft SQL Server 2005* and above (see Section 7.10 for information about physical design tools found in other database systems).

DTA uses *named sessions* to manipulate, store, and tune different scenarios over time. Each set of input parameters, output configuration, logs, and reports is gathered in a session, which is stored in the database server itself and can be retrieved later by its name. Figure 7.4 shows three sessions (named *GLS*, *NREF*, and *TPCH22*). While the first two are previous sessions that were already processed, the last one is being currently defined. In addition to the session name, the figure shows that the input workload comes from a file named `d:\dta\workloads\tpch-all.sql`, and the database to be tuned is called `tpch1g`. Alternatively, workloads can be obtained from profiled tables, and the database administrator can choose subsets of tables to perform tuning (implicitly discarding queries that refer to other tables).

Technically, this information is sufficient to start a tuning session. *DTA* exposes several additional tuning options, some of which are shown in Figure 7.5. For instance, the DBA can set a time limit that specifies when the tuning session has to finish (and return the best configuration found so far). To meet the time constraint, *DTA* uses several techniques, including clustering-based workload compression and a combination of caching optimization calls and an incremental approach that progressively tunes workload fragments (as described in Section 7.4). Additionally, different tuning modes can be set by the user, as shown in the figure. For instance, we can choose to recommend only non-clustered indexes and to additionally consider clustered indexes and also

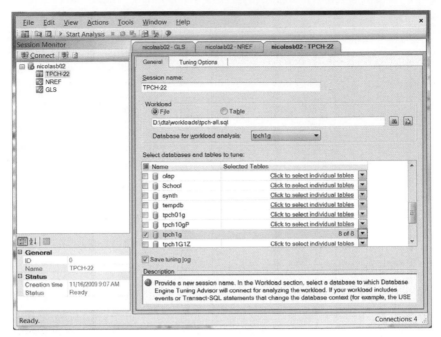

FIGURE 7.4   Session-based tuning in *DTA*. (Used with permission from Microsoft.)

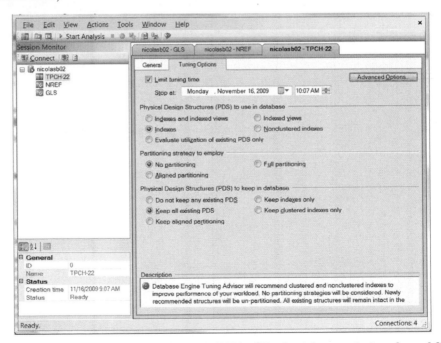

FIGURE 7.5   Tuning options in *DTA*. (Used with permission from Microsoft.)

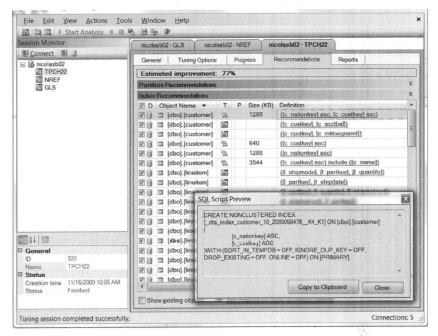

FIGURE 7.6 Recommendation produced by *DTA*. (Used with permission from Microsoft.)

other access paths (e.g., materialized views, which we cover in Chapter 8). The user can also choose to keep all existing indexes in the current configuration or just the clustered indexes or to start a new recommendation from scratch. There are additional options not shown in the figure, which let DBAs specify other aspects of tuning (e.g., storage bounds or the maximum number of columns in any recommended index).

After the input session is defined, we can launch the tuning task proper. *DTA* uses variations of the original *greedy(m,B)* technique discussed in Section 6.1 (adapted to work in incremental mode). After the tuning is finished (or the time bound is exceeded), *DTA* returns the best recommendation, as shown in Figure 7.6. The figure shows an estimated improvement of 77%. This is a quick report that quantifies how much the recommendation is expected to speed up the workload. The improvement of a recommended configuration C_R over the current configuration C_0 for workload W is defined as

$$improvement(C_R, C_0, W) = 100\% \cdot \left(1 - \frac{cost(W, C_R)}{cost(W, C_0)}\right)$$

Improvement values can be negative (when the recommended configuration is less efficient than the current one due to stricter space constraints) but is always smaller than 100%. Additionally, the figure shows the configuration that was recommended by *DTA*. The recommendation includes both indexes

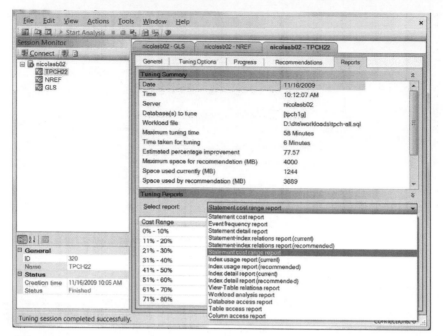

FIGURE 7.7   Additional reports produced by *DTA*. (Used with permission from Microsoft.)

and supporting statistics that should be created. For instance, the first item in the recommendation is an index on table `customer` over columns `c_nationkey` and `c_custkey`, and the second item is a multicolumn statistic on columns `c_custkey` and `c_acctbal`. Selecting any such item produces a preview script with the Standard Query Language (`SQL`) statement that can be used to create the index or statistic in the DBMS.

In addition to the recommended configuration, *DTA* produces reports that give information back to the user. Figure 7.7 shows reports for the last tuned session, including the time taken for tuning, the storage requirement and cost improvement of the recommended configuration, and over a dozen customized reports, similar to those discussed in Section 7.6. After analyzing the reports, the DBA can deploy the recommended configuration or schedule a task to do it at a later time.

DTA defines a public Extensible Markup Language (XML) schema for physical database design that forms the basis of input and output. The user interface shown in Figures 7.4 to 7.7 is a front end that translates user requests into input XML files and output XML files into recommendations and reports. Figure 7.8a shows a fragment of the input XML file that was generated for the tuning session described earlier, and Figure 7.8b shows a fragment of the corresponding output XML file. Through customized XML input files, *DTA* can use test servers for tuning and can evaluate arbitrary configurations for workloads without tuning and other advanced features.

```
<?xml version="1.0" encoding="utf-16" ?>
- <DTAXML xmlns:xsi="http://www.w3.org/2001/XMLSchema-instance"
  xmlns="http://schemas.microsoft.com/sqlserver/2004/07/dta">
  - <DTAInput>
    - <Server>
      <Name>nicolasb02</Name>
      - <Database>
        <Name>[tpch1g]</Name>
        + <Schema>
        </Database>
      </Server>
    - <Workload>
      <File>D:\dta\workloads\tpch-all.sql</File>
      </Workload>
    - <TuningOptions>
      <TuningLogTable />
      <TuningTimeInMin>58</TuningTimeInMin>
      <StorageBoundInMB>4000</StorageBoundInMB>
      <MaxColumnsInIndex>16</MaxColumnsInIndex>
      <FeatureSet>IDX</FeatureSet>
      <Partitioning>NONE</Partitioning>
      <KeepExisting>ALL</KeepExisting>
      <OnlineIndexOperation>OFF</OnlineIndexOperation>
      <DatabaseToConnect>[tpch1g]</DatabaseToConnect>
      </TuningOptions>
    </DTAInput>
  </DTAXML>
```

(a) Input

```
<?xml version="1.0" encoding="utf-16" ?>
- <DTAXML xmlns:xsi="http://www.w3.org/2001/XMLSchema-instance"
  xmlns="http://schemas.microsoft.com/sqlserver/2004/07/dta">
  - <DTAOutput>
    + <TuningSummary>
    - <Configuration>
      - <Server>
        <Name>nicolasb02</Name>
        - <Database>
          <Name>tpch1g</Name>
          - <Schema>
            <Name>dbo</Name>
            - <Table>
              <Name>lineitem</Name>
              - <Recommendation>
                - <Create>
                  - <Index IndexSizeInMB="309.632813">
                    <Name>_dta_index_lineitem_11</Name>
                    - <Column Type="KeyColumn" SortOrder="Ascending">
                      <Name>[l_partkey]</Name>
                      </Column>
                    - <Column Type="KeyColumn" SortOrder="Ascending">
                      <Name>[l_suppkey]</Name>
                      </Column>
                    - <Column Type="KeyColumn" SortOrder="Ascending">
                      <Name>[l_orderkey]</Name>
                      </Column>
                    - <Column Type="IncludedColumn">
                      ...
```

(b) Output

FIGURE 7.8 XML input/output descriptions for advanced tasks in *DTA*.

7.9   Summary

In addition to the basic functionality required to produce a configuration for
a given workload and storage constraint, physical design tools need to address
several practical aspects:

- Provide means to gather, clean, and compress input workloads.
- Present different tuning options for specific user needs, such as different tuning models, the ability to pause and restart sessions, or the possibility to offload most of the tuning overhead to a test server.
- Generate useful reports that explain and complement the recommended configurations as well as efficient scripts to deploy the resulting physical designs.

7.10 Additional Reading

Several ideas described in this chapter can be found in white papers, academic publications, and book chapters.[1,4,6,9] Some references discuss in more detail specific topics, such as workload compression[3] and the physical design scheduling problem.[2] The reader can consult, for more information, the documentation of commercial physical design tools, such as the Database Engine Tuning Advisor in Microsoft SQL Server,[7] the `db2advis` utility in IBM DB2,[5] and automatic SQL tuning capabilities in Oracle.[8]

References

1. Sanjay Agrawal, Surajit Chaudhuri, Lubor Kollar, Arun Marathe, Vivek Narasayya, and Manoj Syamala. Database Tuning Advisor for Microsoft SQL Server 2005. In *Proceedings of the International Conference on Very Large Databases (VLDB)*, 2004.

2. Nicolas Bruno and Surajit Chaudhuri. Physical design refinement: The "merge-reduce" approach. *ACM Transactions on Database Systems*, 32(4), 2007.

3. Surajit Chaudhuri, Ashish Gupta, and Vivek Narasayya. Compressing SQL workloads. In *Proceedings of the ACM International Conference on Management of Data (SIGMOD)*, 2002.

4. Benoit Dageville, Dinesh Das, Karl Dias, Khaled Yagoub, Mohamed Zait, and Mohamed Ziauddin. Automatic SQL tuning in Oracle 10g. In *Proceedings of the International Conference on Very Large Databases (VLDB)*, 2004.

5. IBM. *The Design Advisor*. Available at http://publib.boulder.ibm.com/ infocenter/db2luw/v9r5/topic/com.ibm.db2luw.admin.perf.doc/doc- /c0005144.html.

6. Sam Lightstone, Toby Teorey, and Tom Nadeau. *Physical Database Design*. Morgan Kaufmann, 2007.

7. Microsoft. *Tuning the Physical Database Design*. Available at http:// msdn.microsoft.com/en-us/library/ms191531.aspx.

8. Oracle. *Automatic SQL Tuning*. Available at http://download.oracle. com/docs/cd/B19306_01/server.102/b14211/sql_tune.htm#i22019.

9. Daniel Zilio, Jun Rao, Sam Lightstone, Guy Lohman, Adam Storm, Christian Garcia-Arellano, and Scott Fadden. DB2 design advisor: Integrated automatic physical database design. In *Proceedings of the International Conference on Very Large Databases (VLDB)*, 2004.

Part III

Advanced Topics

Chapter 8

Handling Materialized Views

Similar to indexes, materialized views are redundant data structures that can be used to speed up query processing. A view is a virtual table whose content is derived from base tables by using a subset of Standard Query Language (SQL) (we discuss the language used to define views in Section 8.1). A view is *materialized* by defining an appropriate clustered index. Then, the content of the view is persisted and maintained as if it were a regular table, which can be indexed and leveraged to answer queries efficiently. Consider again the query from Chapter 2 that returns the names of employees working in departments with budgets larger than $10 million:

```
Q1 =   SELECT Emp.name
       FROM Emp, Dept
       WHERE Emp.DId = Dept.DId
         AND Dept.Budget>10M
```

Suppose that we create a materialized view MV1 that precomputes the join between employees and departments. This view, which we denote MV1, is defined as follows:

```
MV1 =   SELECT Emp.EId, Dept.DId, Emp.name, Dept.Budget
        FROM Emp, Dept
        WHERE Emp.DId = Dept.DId
```

Using MV1, we can rewrite the original Q1 into an equivalent form as follows:

```
Q2 =   SELECT MV1.name
       FROM MV1
       WHERE MV1.Budget>10M
```

In general, a view must *subsume* a query subexpression to be useful in answering the full query (i.e., the view definition must contain at least all the tuples required in the query subexpression as well as means to filter out the tuples that are not relevant). MV1 subsumes the whole Q1, since the results of MV1 are a superset of those of Q1. For Q1 and Q2 to be equivalent, we add the filter condition MV1.Budget > 10M in Q2, generally referred to as a *compensating action*. Just by syntactically looking at Q1 and Q2, it cannot be determined which alternative would lead to the most efficient execution plan. If only a few departments satisfy the budget constraint, and there are appropriate indexes in the base tables but not in the materialized view, Q1 can be efficiently answered by seeking an index on Dept(Budget, DId) to obtain the departments with budgets over $10M$ and then performing an index-based join leveraging a clustered index on Emp(DId). If, instead, most departments satisfy the predicate on Budget, scanning MV1 and filtering tuples with low-budget departments might be much more efficient because the join is avoided. If an index on MV1(Budget, Name) is available, then the plan that seeks such index is always better than the alternative that does not rely on MV1.

Materialized views therefore *may* significantly speed up queries, especially if they define the right indexes. At the same time, materialized views can use significant storage (e.g., MV1 needs space that is proportional to the size of the join) and need to be maintained for UPDATE queries. It is therefore very natural to extend the traditional physical design problem so that it returns the best set of materialized views and indexes, which together fit a storage constraint and for which the given workload is expected to execute as fast as possible. In this chapter we revisit the traditional physical design problem discussed in previous chapters and explain how to extend the main ideas to additionally handle materialized views.

8.1 Materialized View Definition Language

There is a trade-off between the expressive power of the view definition language and the efficiency (and even decidability) of the matching algorithms that enable answering a query using a materialized view. In practical terms, it is not very useful to have a very expressive view definition language if most of the time it would not be possible to determine whether a materialized view can be used to answer a given query. In this section we discuss a common view definition language that is handled by most current database management systems (DBMSs). A view is given by the following expression:

SELECT $S^1, S^2, \ldots$	– project columns (see below)
FROM $T^1, T^2, \ldots$	– tables in the database
WHERE J^1 AND J^2 AND $\ldots$	– equi-join predicates
R^1 AND R^2 AND $\ldots$	– range predicates (see below)
Z^1 AND Z^2 AND $\ldots$	– residual predicates (see below)
GROUP BY $G^1, G^2, \ldots$	– grouping columns

where:

- S^i are either base table columns, column expressions, or aggregates. If a group-by clause is present, then every S^i that is not an aggregate must be either equal to one of the grouping columns or an expression in terms of them.

- R^i are range predicates. The general form of a range predicate is a disjunction of open or closed intervals over the same column (point selections are special cases of intervals). An example of a range predicate is (1<a<10 OR 20<a<30).

- Z^i are residual predicates, that is, the set of predicates in the query definition that cannot be classified as either equi-join or range predicates (e.g., a+b<10).

In other words, we can express the class of SPJ queries with aggregation. The reason that predicates are split into three disjoint groups (join, range, and residual) is pragmatic. During query optimization, it is easier to perform subsumption tests for view matching if both the view and the candidate subquery are written in this structured way. Specifically, we can then perform simpler subsumption tests on each component and fail whenever any of the simple tests fail. For instance, we check that the join predicates in the query are a superset of the join predicates in the view, and the range predicates (column by column) in the query are subsumed by the corresponding ones in the view. The problem of determining whether two predicates are equivalent can be arbitrarily complex. For that reason, the matching procedure usually checks that every conjunct in the residual predicate of the view syntactically appears in the candidate query modulo column equivalences. Otherwise, although the view can still subsume the query, no match is produced.

We simplify the notation of a view as (S, T, J, R, Z, G), where S is the set of columns in the select clause, T is the set of tables, J, R, and Z are the sets of join, range, and residual predicates, respectively, and G is the set of grouping columns.

8.2 Search Space

Similar to the case of indexes (see Chapter 4), the search space for materialized views can be defined by first calculating a set of materialized views for each query in the workload and then obtaining the closure of such candidate set under view transformations. In this section we describe these two steps in detail.

8.2.1   Candidate Selection

The mechanisms used for candidate selection of indexes can naturally be extended to deal with views. However, the specific details are more complex due to the additional expressive power of views. The obvious approach of choosing a materialized view that exactly matches each query is not generally feasible. The reason is that the materialized view language is more restrictive than the query language. Instead, the idea is to obtain, for each query, the set of materialized views that covers the input query as much as possible.

8.2.1.1   Parsing-Based Approach

This approach requires understanding the structure of the query (or, as we discussed in Section 4.1.2 for the case of indexes, the corresponding execution plan). Once we gather information about the structure of the query, we can identify the maximum subexpressions that can be expressed in terms of the view definition language. Note that a single query might define several such subexpressions, *connected* by operators that are outside the view definition language (e.g., correlated subqueries, or UNION operators). Each subexpression can then be translated into a candidate materialized view, and the resulting views become the candidate set of each query in the workload.

8.2.1.2   Instrumentation Approach

The aforementioned approach does not require changes to the query optimizer but relies on a complex logic to determine subexpressions that are expressible in the view definition language. Moreover, since queries can be expressed in multiple equivalent ways, sometimes we can miss opportunities by focusing on a specific parsing tree. As a simple example, sometimes nested subqueries can be folded into the main query block. Unless the previous approach can leverage such transformations, it will miss the larger candidate view and obtain only the smaller candidate views that correspond to the inner and outer query blocks. At the same time, including all this specialized knowledge into the candidate selection module would duplicate much of the work done by the optimizer itself.

This discussion motivates an extension to the instrumentation approach described in Section 4.1.3 for the case of indexes. Specifically, we note that query optimizers have a specific view-matching component. This component takes as input a query subplan p and tries to match p with existing views (possibly using compensating actions) to explore plans that leverage materialized views. In doing so, the optimizer needs to analyze the input subquery and essentially to rewrite it in a way that can be better manipulated for doing view matching. We can then instrument the optimizer such that every time the view-matching-component is called with a subexpression p we store the *view request* at the root of the originating logical plan. At the end of optimization, we return, along with the execution plan and index requests, the set of all view requests generated during optimization. Each view request encodes the most specific materialized view that can be used to answer the generating logical subexpression.

> **Indexes on materialized views:** A materialized view is viewed by the optimizer as a regular table that can be used to evaluate queries. We can then define indexes on materialized views. We can combine the approaches in the previous sections with those in Chapter 4 to obtain a candidate set of materialized views and indexes (defined over either base tables or materialized views themselves). Once we obtain the initial candidate set of indexes and views for a workload using any of the previously described approaches, we extend it via transformations. We next describe the *merge* and *reduction* transformations that characterize the search space for the physical design problem, including both indexes and materialized views.

8.2.2   View Merging

Merging two materialized views V_1 and V_2 results in a new materialized view V_M that reduces the amount of redundancy between V_1 and V_2. The resulting view V_M is usually smaller than the combined sizes of V_1 and V_2 at the expense of longer execution times for queries that exploit V_M instead of the original ones. Consider the following two materialized views:

$$V_1 = \begin{array}{l} \text{SELECT a,b} \\ \text{FROM R} \\ \text{WHERE a < 10} \end{array} \qquad V_2 = \begin{array}{l} \text{SELECT b,c} \\ \text{FROM R} \\ \text{WHERE b < 10} \end{array}$$

Suppose that the space required to materialize both V_1 and V_2 is too large. In this case, we can replace both V_1 and V_2 by the alternative V_M, defined as

$$V_M = \begin{array}{l} \text{SELECT a,b,c} \\ \text{FROM R} \\ \text{WHERE a < 10 OR b < 10} \end{array}$$

The main property of this alternative view is that every query that can be answered using either V_1 or V_2 can also be answered by V_M. The reason is that we can rewrite both V_1 and V_2 in terms of V_M by adding appropriate filter predicates. If a significant fraction of the tuples in R satisfy both $R.a < 10$ and $R.b < 10$, the size of V_M might be much smaller than the sum of the sizes of the original views V_1 and V_2. In fact, V_M is the smallest view that can be used to generate both V_1 and V_2. It is also important to note that queries that are answered using V_1 or V_2 are less efficiently answered by V_M. The reason is that V_M is a generalization of both V_1 and V_2 and contains additional, nonrelevant tuples with respect to the original views. In other words, by merging V_1 and V_2 into V_M we are effectively trading space for efficiency. Given V_1 and V_2, we denote $V_M = V_1 \oplus V_2$ as the merging of V_1 and V_2 when the following properties hold:

1. $C_1(V_M) \equiv V_1$ and $C_2(V_M) \equiv V_2$ for some SQL fragments $C_1(V_M)$ and $C_2(V_M)$.

2. If the view-matching algorithm matches V_1 or V_2 for a subquery q, it also matches V_M for q (a view-matching algorithm matches a view V for a subquery q if q can be answered from V).

3. V_M cannot be further restricted with additional predicates and continue to satisfy the previous properties.

8.2.2.1   Case 1: No Grouping Columns

Consider merging $V_1 = (S_1, T, J_1, R_1, Z_1, \emptyset)$ and $V_2 = (S_2, T, J_2, R_2, Z_2, \emptyset)$. If the merging language were expressive enough, we could define $V_1 \oplus V_2$ as

```
SELECT  S₁ ∪ S₂
FROM T
WHERE (J₁ AND R₁ AND Z₁) OR (J₂ AND R₂ AND Z₂)
```

which satisfies properties 1 and 3. Since $V_1 \oplus V_2$ has to be defined in terms of the view definition language, we have no option but to consider the whole predicate in the WHERE clause as a single conjunctive residual predicate Z. The problem is that now the merged view would not be matched whenever V_1 or V_2 are matched (property 2) because of the simple procedures used during view matching with respect to residual predicates. Instead, we rewrite the "minimal" predicate as follows:

$$(J_1 \wedge R_1 \wedge Z_1) \vee (J_2 \wedge R_2 \wedge Z_2) \equiv (J_1 \vee J_2) \wedge (R_1 \vee R_2) \wedge (Z_1 \vee Z_2) \wedge C$$

where C is the conjunction of all crossed disjuncts $((J_1 \vee R_2) \wedge (R_1 \vee Z_2) \wedge \dots)$. The idea is to relax this expression until we obtain a predicate that can be written in the view definition language and matches any candidate query that is matched by the original views. Although this procedure seems to introduce a lot of redundancy and to result in larger views, in real-world scenarios this is not usually the case.

We first relax the previous expression by removing the conjunct C. The reason is that it leaves us with three conjuncts ($J_1 \vee J_2$, $R_1 \vee R_2$, and $Z_1 \vee Z_2$), which we next map into the three groups of predicates in the view definition language. First, consider $J_1 \vee J_2$ and recall that each J_i is a conjunct of equi-join predicates. We cannot simply use $J_1 \vee J_2$ in the resulting view because the language specifies that this must be a conjunction of simple equi-joins (i.e., no disjunctions are allowed). We rewrite

$$J_1 \vee J_2 \equiv (J_1^1 \wedge J_1^2 \wedge J_1^3 \wedge \dots) \vee (J_2^1 \wedge J_2^2 \wedge J_2^3 \wedge \dots) \equiv \bigwedge_{i,j}(J_1^i \vee J_2^j)$$

and relax this predicate as follows: we keep each (i, j) conjunct for which $J_1^i \equiv J_2^j$ and discard (i.e., relax) the remaining ones. We then obtain $\bigwedge_{J^k \in J_1 \cap J_2} J^k$ as the set of join predicates in the merged view. This predicate can be more general than the original $J_1 \vee J_2$, but the view-matching procedure would match V_m with respect to the join subsumption test in this case. We use the same idea for $Z_1 \vee Z_2$, and therefore the residual predicate for V_m is $\bigwedge_{Z^k \in Z_1 \cap Z_2} Z^k$.

It turns out that we can do better for range predicates $R_1 \vee R_2$ due to their specific structure. Using the same argument, we first rewrite $R_1 \vee R_2$ as $\bigwedge_{i,j} (R_1^i \vee R_2^j)$, where each R_1^i and R_2^j are disjunctions of open or closed intervals over some column. As before, if R_1^i and R_2^j are defined over different columns, we discard that conjunct. However, if they are defined over the same column, we keep the predicate even when R_1^i and R_2^j are not the same, by taking the union of the corresponding intervals (we denote this operation with the symbol $\bigsqcup$). To avoid missing some predicates, we first add conjuncts $-\infty < x < \infty$ to one of the range predicates if column x is present only in the other range predicate (it does not change the semantics of the input predicates but further restricts the result). If, after calculating the union of ranges, the predicate over some column x becomes $-\infty < x < \infty$, we discard this conjunct from the result. As an example, consider:

$$
\begin{array}{llll}
R_1= & (10 \leq a \leq 20 \vee 30 \leq a \leq 40) & \wedge\ 20 \leq b \leq 30 & \wedge\ c \leq 40 \\
R_2= & 15 \leq a \leq 35 & \wedge\ 10 \leq b \leq 25 \wedge c \geq 30 & \wedge\ 10 \leq d \leq 20 \\
\hline
R_1 \bigsqcup R_2= & 10 \leq a \leq 40 & \wedge\ 10 \leq b \leq 30 & \wedge\ 10 \leq d \leq 20
\end{array}
$$

After obtaining join, range, and residual predicates as described already, we assemble the set of columns in the merged view. At a minimum, this set must contain the union of columns present in both input views. However, this is not enough in general, as shown next:

$$
\begin{array}{ll}
V_1 = & \texttt{SELECT a} \\
& \texttt{FROM R} \\
& \texttt{WHERE 10<c<20}
\end{array}
\qquad
\begin{array}{ll}
V_2 = & \texttt{SELECT b} \\
& \texttt{FROM R} \\
& \texttt{WHERE 15<c<30}
\end{array}
$$

The candidate merged view $V=$`SELECT a,b FROM R WHERE 10<c<30` does not satisfy property 1 because V_1 and V_2 cannot be obtained from V. The reason is that we need to apply additional predicates to V (`c<20` to obtain V_1 and `15<c` to obtain V_2), but V does not expose column c. For that reason, we need to add to the set of columns in the merged view all the columns that are used in join, range, and residual predicates that are eliminated in the merged view. Similarly, if some range predicate changed from the input to the merged view, we need to add the range column as an output column, or otherwise we would not be able to reconstruct the original views. To summarize, the

merging of two views as described in this section is as follows:

$$
\begin{array}{rcccccccc}
V_1 =(& S_1 & , T & , J_1 & , R_1 & , Z_1 & , \emptyset \,) \\
\oplus\ V_2 =(& S_2 & , T & , J_2 & , R_2 & , Z_2 & , \emptyset \,) \\
\hline
V_1 \oplus V_2 =(& S_1 \cup S_2 \cup & , T & , J_1 \cap J_2 & , R_1 \bigsqcup R_2 & , Z_1 \cap Z_2 & , \emptyset \,) \\
& \{\text{required} \\
& \text{columns}\}
\end{array}
$$

We note that all the previous transformations take into account column equivalences. If both input views contain a join predicate R.x = S.y, then the range predicates R.x < 10 and S.y < 10 are considered to be the same.

The following example illustrates the ideas described in this section. If V_1 and V_2 are the following materialized views:

```
V₁ =  SELECT x, y              V₂ =  SELECT y, z
      FROM R, S                      FROM R, S
      WHERE R.x = S.y AND            WHERE R.x = S.y AND
            10 < R.a < 20 AND              15 < R.a < 50 AND
            R.b < 10 AND                  R.b > 5 AND R.c > 5 AND
            R.x + S.d < 8                 S.y + S.d < 8 AND
                                          R.d * R.d = 2
```

the merge of V_1 and V_2 is

```
V₁ ⊕ V₂ =  SELECT x, y, z, a, b, c, d
           FROM R, S
           WHERE R.x = S.y AND
                 10 < R.a < 50 AND
                 R.x + S.d < 8
```

8.2.2.2   Case 2: Grouping Columns

We now consider the case of merging views that involve group-by clauses. Grouping operators partition the input relation into disjoint subsets and return a representative tuple and some aggregates from each group. Conceptually, we see a GROUP BY operator as a postprocessing step after the evaluation of the SPJ subquery. Consider the merged view obtained when the grouping columns are eliminated from the input views. If the grouping columns in the input views are different, each view partitions the input relation in different ways. We then need to partition the merged view in the coarsest way that still allows us to recreate each input view. For that purpose, the set of grouping columns in the merged view must be the union of the grouping columns of the input views. Additionally, each column that is added to the select clause due to predicate relaxation in the input views must also be added as a grouping column. Note that we need to handle a special case properly. If one of the input views contains no group-by clause, the merged view should not contain any group-by clause either, or else we would compromise correctness (i.e., we implicitly define the union of a set of columns and the empty set as the empty set*). In these situations, we additionally unfold all original aggregates into base table columns so that the original aggregates can be computed from the resulting merged view. We therefore define $(S_1, T, J_1, R_1, Z_1, G_1) \oplus (S_2, T, J_2, R_2, Z_2, G_2)$ as $(S_M, T, J_1 \cap J_2, R_1 \bigsqcup R_2, Z_1 \cap Z_2, G_M)$, where:

- S_M is the set of columns obtained in the no group-by case, plus the grouping columns if they are not the same as the input views. If the resulting $G_M = \emptyset$, all aggregates are unfolded into base table columns.

- $G_M = (G_1 \cup G_2) \cup$ columns added to S_M (note that $G_1 = \emptyset \vee G_2 = \emptyset \Rightarrow G_M = \emptyset$).

The following example illustrates the ideas in this section:

```
V₁=  SELECT R.x, SUM(S.z)    V₂=  SELECT R.x, R.z
     FROM R, S                    FROM R, S
     WHERE R.x = S.y              WHERE R.x = S.y
       AND 10 < R.a < 20            AND 15 < R.a < 50
     GROUP BY R.x

V₃=  SELECT S.y, SUM(S.z)
     FROM R, S
     WHERE R.x = S.z
       AND 10 < R.a < 25
     GROUP BY S.y
```

```
V₁ ⊕ V₂=SELECT R.x, R.a, S.z, R.z   V₁ ⊕ V₃=SELECT R.x, S.y, R.a,
                                                   SUM(S.z)
        FROM R, S                           FROM R, S
        WHERE R.x = S.y                     WHERE R.x = S.y
          AND 10 < R.a < 50                   AND 10 < R.a < 25
                                            GROUP BY R.a, R.x, S.y
```

Note that in order to recreate the original views in the presence of general algebraic aggregates, we sometimes need to add additional columns in the merged view (e.g., `SUM(c)` and `COUNT(*)` for an original aggregate `AVG(c)`).

8.2.3 View Reduction

In the previous section we generalized index merging as a mechanism to decrease the amount of redundancy between a pair of materialized views. The

---

*For tables with unique constraints, we can define the set of grouping columns of a query without a group-by clause as the set of all columns in the table and thus keep the definition of union unchanged. However, this is not correct for tables with duplicate values, because a group-by clause with all columns eliminates duplicate rows and therefore is not equivalent to the query without the group-by clause.

idea was to merge them into a new view that might be smaller than the combined inputs but at the same time less efficient to answer queries. In this section we generalize the notion of index reduction to work over materialized views. Specifically, we exploit the fact that when a query optimizer attempts to match a query expression q, it will consider not only views that subsume q completely but also views that subsume some of the subexpressions of q. As a simple example suppose that the optimizer is matching the following query expression:

$$q = \Pi_{R.a,R.b,S.c}\left(\sigma_{R.a=15}(R \bowtie_{R.x=S.y} S)\right)$$

In this case, the view-matching engine would consider all available views V that subsume query expression q. If some view V matches q, the expression is rewritten using V and compensating actions (e.g., $q=\sigma_{R.a=15}(V)$ for $V=R \bowtie_{R.x=S.y} S$). However, query optimizers would also consider views that subsume subexpressions of q that omit table S but additionally project column $R.x$ so that a compensating join can be applied, as follows:

$$q' = \Pi_{R.a,R.b,R.x}\left(\sigma_{R.a=15}(R)\right)$$

Since $q = \Pi_{q'.a,q'.b,S.c}(q' \bowtie_{q'.x=S.y} S)$, we can recreate q from any view V' that matches q' by additionally performing a join with the primary index of S. In general, we can restrict an index over a view with some of its subexpressions and then apply compensating actions to recreate the original structure. Given V, we denote $V_R = \rho(V)$ as a reduction of V when the following properties hold:

1. $C(V_R) \equiv V$ for some SQL fragment $C(V_R)$.
2. If the view-matching algorithm matches V for a query expression q, it will attempt (and succeed) matching V_R for a subquery of q.

For efficiency purposes, query optimizers restrict the subqueries that are considered for view matching for a given query expression q. Most often, these optimizers consider only subexpressions q' with fewer joins than q but containing all applicable predicates in q that affect the tables in the subexpression q'. In these common scenarios, the reduction operation takes a view IV and a set of tables T' and returns a new view $\rho(V, T')$. For a view $V = (S, T, J, R, Z, G)$ and $T' \subseteq T$, we define $\rho(V, T') = (S', T', J', R', Z', G')$, where:

- $J' \subseteq J$, $R' \subseteq R$, and $Z' \subseteq Z$, where each base table column referenced in J', R', and Z' refers exclusively to tables in T'.
- S' contains the subset of columns in S that belong to tables in T' plus all columns in T' referenced in $J - J'$, $R - R'$, and $Z - Z'$.
- If $G \neq \emptyset$, G' contains all the columns in G that belong to tables in T' plus all columns in $S' - S$. Otherwise, $G'=G=\emptyset$.

To avoid irrelevant views, if the resulting $\rho(V, T')$ contains Cartesian products we consider the reduction invalid and stop (a cartesian product does not provide any efficiency advantage and it is almost always much larger than the input relations).

The following example illustrates the reduction operator:

```
V = SELECT R.c, S.c            ρ(V,{R}) = SELECT R.c, R.b, R.x
      FROM R, S                           FROM R
      WHERE R.x = S.y AND                 WHERE 10 < R.a < 50
            10 < R.a < 50 AND             GROUP BY R.c, R.b, R.x
            20 < S.a < 30 AND
            R.b + S.b < 10
      GROUP BY R.c, S.c
```

8.2.4 Indexes over Materialized Views

So far we have discussed the merging and reduction operations applied to materialized views without paying attention to indexes over those materialized views. In reality, each materialized view is associated with a set of indexes, and those indexes are used during query processing. To handle both structures in a unified manner, we consider all indexes as defined over some view (base tables are also trivial views, so this definition includes regular indexes as well). Specifically, an index with columns C defined over view V is denoted as $V(C)$ (when the view V is a base table, this notation agrees with that of indexes defined over base tables). For the special case $C = \emptyset$, we define $V(\emptyset)$ to be the unordered heap containing all the tuples in V (for simplicity, we use V and $V(\emptyset)$ interchangeably).

8.2.4.1 Unified Merging Operator

We now define the merging of two arbitrary indexes over views. In this section we overload the operator $\oplus$ to operate over indexes and materialized views (we explicitly state which case we are referring to when this is not clear from the context). Merging two indexes defined over the same view is the same operation that we defined in Section 4.2.2.1 for indexes over base tables. To address the general case, we need to first introduce the notion of *index promotion*. Consider an index $V(C)$ and suppose that $V_M = V \oplus V'$ for some view V'. Promoting $V(C)$ to V_M (denoted $V(C) \uparrow V_M$) results in an index over V_M that can be used (with some compensating action) whenever $V(C)$ is used. This promoted index contains, in addition to all columns in the original index, every column that was added to the select clause in V_M. For instance, consider:

```
V₁ = SELECT x,y      V₂= SELECT y,z      V₁ ⊕ V₂ = SELECT a,x,y,z
       FROM R                FROM R                  FROM R
       WHERE 10<a<20         WHERE 15<a<30           WHERE 10<a<30
```

Denoting $V_M = V_1 \oplus V_2$, we then have that $V_1(x) \uparrow V_M = V_M(x, a)$. Using index promotion, we now define the merging of two indexes over views as follows:

$$V_1(C_1) \oplus V_2(C_2) = (V_1(C_1) \uparrow V_M) \oplus (V_2(C_2) \uparrow V_M), \quad \text{where } V_M = V_1 \oplus V_2$$

That is, we first promote the original indexes to the merged view and then perform the original index merging operation.

8.2.4.2 Unified Reduction Operator

We similarly adapt the reduction operator so that it operates over indexes on materialized views. The extended reduction operator takes as inputs an index on a materialized view $V(C)$, a set of tables T', and a set of columns K' as inputs and returns a new index $\rho(V(C), T', K')$. For an index $V(C)$, where $V = (S, T, J, R, Z, G)$, we define $\rho(V(C), T', K')$ as follows:

1. If $\rho(V, T')$ is undefined, the reduction is ill-defined and we stop. Otherwise, we obtain the reduced version of V, $V' = \rho(V, T')$.

2. We obtain C' from C by first removing all columns that do not belong to tables in T' and then by adding all columns in S' of V' (this step is analogous to $I \uparrow V'$).

3. If $K' \not\subseteq C'$, the reduction is ill-defined and we stop. Otherwise, $\rho(V(C), T', K') = V'(K')$.

8.2.5 Characterizing the Search Space

We can characterize the extended search space of indexes and materialized views without *explicitly* considering materialized views by extending the approach in Section 4.3. Specifically, let $cand(Q)$ be the set of candidate indexes over base tables and materialized views for query Q, obtained by any of the techniques of Sections 4.1 and 8.2.1. Let C_i $(i \geq 0)$ be a family of indexes defined as follows:

- $VC_0 = \bigcup_{Q \in W} cand(Q)$
- $VC_{i+1} = VC_i \cup$

   $\{V_1(C_1) \oplus V_2(C_2) \text{ for each } V_1(I_1), V_2(I2) \in VC_i\} \cup$
   $\{\rho(V(C), T', K') \text{ for each } V(C) \in VC_i, K' \subseteq \text{keys}(V(C)), T' \subseteq$
      $\text{tables}(V)\} \cup$
   $\{V(C_1) \otimes V(C_2) \text{ for each } V(C_1), V(C_2) \in VC_i\} \cup$
   $\{\Gamma(V(C)) \text{ for each } V(C) \in VC_i\}$

That is, VC_{i+1} is obtained by considering all possible index merges, reductions, and promotions for indexes in VC_i, and index splits for indexes in VC_i defined over the same table or view. As discussed in Section 4.3, the search space for workload W is therefore defined as $closure(W) = VC_k$, where k is the smallest integer that satisfies $VC_k = VC_{k+1}$.

8.2.5.1 Discussion: Why Merge and Reduce?

We now explain why the merge and reduction operators in fact cover the set of relevant indexes over views for the physical design problem in the context of typical query optimizers.

Consider a subquery q_1 that exactly matches a view V_1 (i.e., q_1 and V_1 are semantically equivalent). Then, q_1 can be matched and answered by either V_1 or some generalization V' of V_1 (e.g., V' is obtained by adding to V_1 additional grouping columns or relaxing its selection predicates). By definition, V' is larger than V_1 and therefore less effective in answering subquery q_1. Why should we then consider V' in our search space, since it is both larger and less efficient for q_1 than the original V_1? The only reasonable answer is that q_1 is not the only query in the workload. Instead, there might be some other subquery q_2 (which is matched perfectly by V_2), for which V' can also be used. In this scenario, having V' instead of the original V_1 and V_2 might be beneficial, since the size of V' might be smaller than the combined sizes of V_1 and V_2 (albeit being less efficient for answering q_1 and q_2). We should then consider V' in our search space, noting that V' must be a generalization of both V_1 and V_2. Now, the merging of $V_1 \oplus V_2$ seems the most appropriate choice for V', since it results in the most specific view that generalizes both V_1 and V_2 (other generalizations are both larger and less efficient than $V_1 \oplus V_2$). The merge operation covers all the "interesting" views that can be used to answer expressions originally matched by the input set of views.

Let us now consider subexpressions. In fact, a view V_R that is not a generalization of a query q can still be used to rewrite and answer q. It would also make sense, then, to consider in our search space such subexpressions of q that can be used to speed up its processing. In general, the "reductions" that we look for are somewhat dependent on the view-matching engine itself. View-matching engines typically restrict the space of transformations and matching rules for efficiency purposes. Usually, the only subqueries that can be matched and compensated with a restricted view contain fewer joins. But this is how the reduction operator is defined (i.e., eliminating joins from the original view).* Thus, the reduction operator in its generality covers all the "interesting" views that can be used to rewrite queries originally matched

---

*In general, if the view-matching engine is capable of additional functionality (e.g., taking the union of several horizontal fragments of a single template expression to answer a given subquery), we should certainly extend the primitive operators accordingly (e.g., considering range partitioning over a column as a primitive operator).

by the input set of views (any generalization of a reduced view can also be used, but this is covered by the merge operator).

8.3   Cost Model

Extending the cost model so that it also handles materialized views requires modifying the optimizer to support what-if optimization on views. The changes require some nontrivial engineering effort but conceptually are similar to the extensions required for what-if optimizations using hypothetical indexes over base tables. One additional challenge is estimating the size of an index over a materialized view. Unlike indexes on base tables, we do not know the size of the materialized view unless we actually create it by executing its defining query. However, we can approximate the number of tuples in the materialized view by using the cardinality estimation module of the optimizer itself to estimate the number of tuples returned by the view definition. More accurate techniques can be used in special cases, such as using sampling for single-table views or those that use foreign-key joins.

8.3.1   Cost Upper Bounds

Some enumeration strategies rely on the capability of approximating the cost of a query under a hypothetical configuration *without* issuing optimization calls (e.g., see Section 6.2). This functionality was discussed in Chapter 5 in the context of indexes defined on base tables. Consider the execution plan p for query q obtained under configuration C, and suppose that we want to approximate an upper bound on the cost of q under C'. Analogous to the case of base table indexes, we identify all subplans of p that use index strategies over views and then obtain an upper bound on the cost of implementing such subplans using indexes in C'.

Consider a subplan that uses an index over view V. Further assume that C' contains some view V' that is obtained from V using merge or reduction operations. In that case, we know that the optimizer would match V' whenever it matched V and therefore can estimate the cost of answering the subquery using V' and corresponding compensating actions. While this idea is clear, a number of subtleties need to be taken into account. We illustrate some of these using views V_1, V_2, and $V_M = V_1 \oplus V_2$:

```
V₁=SELECT a, b            V₂=SELECT a, SUM(c)   Vₘ=SELECT a, b, c
     FROM R                    FROM R                 FROM R
     WHERE a<10 AND b<20       WHERE a<20             WHERE a<20
                               GROUP BY a
```

Let us assume that C includes both V_1 and V_2, and C' includes V_M instead. Suppose that query q under C seeks an index $I_1 = V_1(b, a)$ for some range predicate on column b. The corresponding index on V_M additionally contains tuples that satisfy $10 \leq R.a < 20$. When bounding the cost of evaluating the same subplan with the promoted index on V_M, the expected fraction of tuples retrieved from the index does not change since we assume independence, but we need to add the cost of a compensating filter for predicate $R.a < 10$. On the other hand, if the used index is originally $I_2 = V_1(a, b)$, the total number of tuples touched in the corresponding index on V_M stays the same (and therefore the fraction of tuples changes) since the leading key column in the index is precisely $R.a$. If q uses some index on V_2 under C, we need to add the cost of a final group-by operator after the subplan that uses V_M instead, because the merged view V_M removed the grouping clause on $R.a$.

In general, however, there might be no view in C' that is obtained via transformations from view V, which is used under C to evaluate query q. The problem in this case is that we do not know how to replace a subplan that uses V under C without calling the optimizer. An inexpensive approach to address this problem is as follows. Each time we consider a new view V during tuning, we optimize V with respect to the empty configuration and obtain C_V, the cost to evaluate V in the base configuration. The value C_V is an upper bound to the cost of "regenerating" the content of V from scratch, and we can use this value if no other view can be used. There are more expensive procedures to obtain tighter upper bounds, which duplicate some of the functionality in the optimizer (e.g., its view-matching component).

8.4   Enumeration Strategies

Enumeration strategies for the physical design problem that consider both indexes and materialized views are very similar to those described in Chapter 6 for the case of indexes over base tables only. The main difference is quantitative and arises from a much larger search space. In addition to indexes on base tables, there usually is a combinatorial explosion in the number of materialized views for a given workload. Moreover, indexes can be defined over such materialized views, further increasing the number of structures to consider. For top-down strategies that explore the enumeration space on demand, this is not a big problem. In fact, the technique discussed in Section 6.2 can be adapted with small changes to also handle materialized views. Specifically, we need to additionally consider view merging, reduction, and deletion as new operations to transform configurations and to use the extensions to the cost model discussed in the previous section to rank candidate configurations. Bottom-up strategies, in contrast, require the enumeration space to be generated eagerly (e.g., see *greedy(m,B)* and the knapsack-based strategies in Section 6.1). In such cases, it is crucial to restrict the enumeration space, or else the resulting techniques would simply not scale beyond trivial problem

instances. We next discuss an approach to limit the set of views to consider
in bottom-up enumeration strategies.

8.4.1   Restricting the Enumeration Space

An observation that motivates the following approach is that certain subsets
of tables are not particularly helpful to consider. Specifically, even if we were
to propose materialized views on those table subsets, the resulting configuration would be only slightly more efficient. This can happen because the
table subsets occur either infrequently in the workload or only in inexpensive
queries. For instance, consider a workload of 100 queries whose total cost is
10,000 units. Let T be a table subset that occurs in 25 queries whose combined
cost is 50 units. Even if we considered all syntactically relevant materialized
views on T, the maximum possible benefit of those materialized views for the
workload would be 0.5%. Furthermore, even among table subsets that occur
frequently or in expensive queries, not all table subsets are likely to be equally
useful. Materialized views proposed on subsets of *large* tables are more likely
to be useful than materialized views proposed on smaller ones. Based on these
observations, an approach to restrict the enumeration space can be described
as follows:

1. From the large space of all possible table subsets for the workload, we
   arrive at a smaller set of interesting table subsets. Based on the previous
   discussion, a metric that captures the relative importance of a table
   subset T is

$$TSW(T) = \sum_{q_i \in W \, \text{referencing} \, T} cost(q_i) \cdot \frac{\sum_{t \in T} size(t)}{\sum_{t \, \text{mentioned in} \, q_i} size(t)}$$

   That is, we sum over all queries that reference every table in T, the cost
   of the query under the current configuration multiplied by the fraction
   of the size between tables in T and all tables mentioned in the query.
   TSW is a simple function and can discriminate between table subsets
   even if they occur in exactly the same queries in the workload. However,
   it is not clear how to enumerate all interesting table subsets short of
   generating and evaluating every possible subset of tables. In practice,
   we can use a relaxed metric $TSC(T) = \sum_{q_i \in W \, referencing \, T} cost(q_i)$. In
   contrast to TSW, TSC satisfies the monotonicity property, in which
   $T_1 \subseteq T_2 \Rightarrow TSC(T1) \geq TSC(T2)$. This makes it possible to use efficient
   algorithms to identify all table subsets that exceed a certain threshold.
   Since $TSW(T) \leq TSC(T)$, we can postprocess the resulting list of the
   top-ranked tuples according to TSC and obtain all interesting table
   subsets according to the TSW ranking function.

2. We recommend candidate views that are defined over interesting table
   subsets only, by restricting the techniques discussed in Section 8.2.

3. Starting with the views obtained in the previous step, we generate an
   additional set of merged materialized views in a controlled manner. We

```
mergeViews (C:candidate views)
return merged views
1    R = C
2    while |R| > 1
3        M = { M1 ⊕ M2 : M1, M2 ∈ R and "M1 ⊕ M2 is not too large" }
         // V_m is too large if size(V_m) > α · Σ_{V∈ancestors(V_m)} size(V),
         for 1 ≤ α ≤ 2
4        if (M = ∅) break
5        R = R ∪ M
6        foreach view (M1 ⊕ M2) ∈ M
7            R = R - {M1, M2}
8    return R ∪ C
```

FIGURE 8.1 Generation of a controlled subset of merged views.

define the ancestors of a materialized view V to be all the views in the original candidate set that were merged together to produce V. The algorithm to produce a restricted set of merged views is given in Figure 8.1. The idea is to keep adding merged views to the subset as long as the increase in size is not large. Note that it is possible for a merged materialized view generated in line 3 to be merged again in a subsequent iteration of the outer loop (lines 2–7). This allows more than two views in M to be combined into one merged view even though the merging is done pairwise. Although the number of new merged views explored by this algorithm can be exponential in the size of C in the worst case, much fewer merged materialized views are explored in practice because of the size restriction in line 3. Note that the set of merged views returned by the algorithm does not depend on the exact sequence in which views are merged.

8.5 Summary

- After indexes, materialized views are the most common redundant data structure that is used in database systems to improve query performance.

- In addition to speeding up queries, materialized views use storage and need to be maintained for **UPDATE** statements.

- The traditional physical database design problem can be generalized to consider the space of indexes over base tables and materialized views. Although different components in techniques that handle indexes need to be extended to handle materialized views, the general architecture of existing solutions remains unchanged.

8.6   Additional Reading

Materialized views have been discussed in detail since 1985.[6] More recent work specifically discusses materialized view matching during query optimization,[4,5] gives a treatment of the merging and reduction operations on views in the context of physical design refinement,[3] and addresses the problem of recommending materialized views in detail.[1,2,7]

References

1. Sanjay Agrawal, Surajit Chaudhuri, and Vivek Narasayya. Automated selection of materialized views and indexes in SQL databases. In *Proceedings of the International Conference on Very Large Databases (VLDB)*, 2000.

2. Nicolas Bruno and Surajit Chaudhuri. Automatic physical database tuning: A relaxation-based approach. In *Proceedings of the ACM International Conference on Management of Data (SIGMOD)*, 2005.

3. Nicolas Bruno and Surajit Chaudhuri. Physical design refinement: The "merge-reduce" approach. *ACM Transactions on Database Systems*, 32(4), 2007.

4. Surajit Chaudhuri, Ravi Krishnamurthy, Spyros Potamianos, and Kyuseok Shim. Optimizing queries with materialized views. In *Proceedings of the International Conference on Data Engineering (ICDE)*, 1995.

5. Jonathan Goldstein and Per-Ake Larson. Optimizing queries using materialized views: A practical, scalable solution. In *Proceedings of the ACM International Conference on Management of Data (SIGMOD)*, 2001.

6. Paul Larson and H. Z. Yang. Computing queries from derived relations. In *Proceedings of the International Conference on Very Large Databases (VLDB)*, 1985.

7. Daniel Zilio, Calisto Zuzarte, Sam Lightstone, Wenbin Ma, Guy Lohman, Roberta Cochrane, Hamid Pirahesh, Latha Colby, Jarek Gryz, Eric Alton, Dongming Liang, and Gary Valentin. Recommending materialized views and indexes with IBM DB2 design advisor. In *International Conference on Autonomic Computing*, 2004.

Chapter 9

Incorporating Other Physical Structures

Over time, new releases of database management system (DBMS) products introduced additional types of access path methods to deal with scenarios that did not perform as efficiently as expected. Examples of such new features include various forms of data partitioning, materialized views, cubes, and hash, bitmap, partial, Extensible Markup Language (XML), columnar, spatial, and multidimensional indexes. Each new such structure comes along with its own benefits and overheads, and it is generally challenging to understand when and how to leverage its functionality. For that reason, after each new such structure is introduced, there are attempts to generalize the physical design problem to automatically recommend efficient configurations for input workloads. Analogous to the structure of Chapters 4 to 6, there are three main questions associated with recommending a new kind of physical design structure. First, we need to define what is the space of alternatives that we should consider and whether these would interact with other features in the DBMS. Second, we require a mechanism to evaluate the hypothetical benefit of a given configuration in the search space. Finally, we need efficient procedures to traverse the search space to quickly obtain the desired configuration. In this chapter we explore some recent work on automatically recommending some physical design structures that deal with scenarios involving large data sets and complex query workloads.

9.1 Data Partitioning

Data partitioning is an important aspect of physical design and can have a big impact on performance. Partitioning can additionally be used in parallel database systems, where partitions are stored in different autonomous servers and can even improve server manageability (if tables and indexes are partitioned in the same way, common operations such as backup/restore can be drastically simplified). In this section we summarize some work in the area of automated recommendation of partitioning under different scenarios.

9.1.1   Types of Data Partitioning

We identify the following variations of data partitioning:

Vertical partitioning: We vertically partition a table T by logically splitting it into two or more partitions, each one containing all rows of T for only a subset of columns. To be able to reconstruct the original table, each partition requires the same key of T to be part of its schema. For vertical partitioning to be complete, the union of all columns in the partitions must be the same as the set of columns in the original table. Figure 9.1b shows an example of a vertical partition of the original table R of Figure 9.1a. Since many queries access only a few columns in a table, vertical partitioning can reduce the amount of data that needs to be scanned during query processing (this is similar to the case of a secondary index but with the difference that vertical partitioning *replaces* the primary index of a table without redundancy). Queries that refer to columns in different partitions, however, incur an additional "reconstruction" cost in the form of a join (Figure 9.1b shows this mechanism for a simple query).

Horizontal partitioning: We horizontally partition a table T by dividing its tuples among multiple partitions that share the same schema of T. This division is specified using a partitioning function, which maps a given row in a table to a partition number. All rows of the table with the same partition number are stored in the same partition. Current DBMSs expose two main kinds of partitioning functions. A *hash-based* partitioning function is defined by a set of columns C and an integer value k. For each tuple in the original table, it maps the values of columns C into a pseudorandom partition number between 1 and k by using a system-defined hash function. A *range-based* partitioning function is defined by a set of columns C and an ordered sequence of disjoint ranges V that cover the domain of C. A tuple with value $C = C_0$ maps to the partition associated with the range in V that includes C_0. Figure 9.1c shows a range-based horizontal partitioning of the original table R in Figure 9.1a using column R.a and ranges R.a $< 4, 4 \leq$ R.a < 6, and $6 \leq$ R.a. Horizontal partitioning can help query processing in several ways. For instance, equality (respectively, range) predicates can leverage hash (respectively, range) partitioning to perform static partition elimination and process only the relevant partitions (see the sample query in Figure 9.1c). If both tables in a join are hash partitioned by the join columns, we can process the join as the union of partition joins (this is helpful if each partitioned join can be done in parallel). Grouping and aggregation can also take advantage of hash-based partitioning on the grouping columns to perform early aggregation.

Ra

id	a
1	2
2	4
3	8
4	5
5	2
6	1

Rb

id	b
1	10
2	20
3	20
4	30
5	40
6	10

R

id	a	b
1	2	10
2	4	20
3	8	20
4	5	30
5	2	40
6	1	10

$R1 = \sigma_{a<4}(R)$

id	a	b
1	2	10
5	2	40
6	1	10

$R2 = \sigma_{4 \leq a < 6}(R)$

id	a	b
2	4	20
4	5	30

$R3 = \sigma_{6 \leq a}(R)$

id	a	b
3	8	20

Q= SELECT b
   FROM R
   WHERE a < 5

(a) Original table.

Q= SELECT b
   FROM Ra, Rb
   WHERE Ra.id = Rb.id
   AND a < 5

(b) Vertical partitions.

Q= SELECT b FROM R1
   UNION ALL
   SELECT b FROM R2
   WHERE a < 5

(c) Horizontal partitions.

FIGURE 9.1 Vertical and horizontal table partitions.

9.1.2 Recommending Data Partitioning

The diversity of partitioning schemes supported in different DBMSs (e.g., vertical vs. horizontal, range vs. hash based) resulted in extensions to the physical design problem that handle specific scenarios. We next summarize two techniques for recommending data partitioning. For presentation purposes, we introduce both techniques in the context of the basic bottom-up scheme that we discussed in Chapters 4 and 6. Specifically, a candidate selection phase first picks partitioning candidates. A subsequent merging step identifies additional partitioning schemes that, while suboptimal for every query in the workload, might be part of the best configuration. Finally, an enumeration step traverses the resulting search space and identifies the best solution.

9.1.2.1 Hash-Based Partitioning in a Parallel DBMS

A parallel DBMS exploits fast and inexpensive processors to improve performance by connecting independent servers via high-speed networks. Each processor stores a portion of the database locally on disk, and query processing attempts to perform as much local work as possible, thus minimizing slower data transfer among servers. These systems thus partition data horizontally, and we are interested in recommending a partitioning scheme that maximizes workload performance. Subsequent index recommendations (if needed) can be done after the partitioning scheme has been decided. We now describe the steps involved in recommending hash-based partitioning in a parallel DBMS.

Candidate selection. We identify all candidate columns in the workload that are part of equality predicates or group-by clauses. As explained in Section 4.1, candidate selection can be done by either parsing the input queries or the output execution plans or instrumenting the optimizer. In addition to all candidate partitioning schemes identified in this manner, we also consider the option of *replicating* some tables across all servers, which can reduce communication overhead. Since replication incurs storage overhead, we consider replicating only tables whose sizes are below a threshold. Some optimizers extend the notion of interesting orders (see Section 2.3.1) to also generate interesting partitioning columns. Suboptimal plans that can exploit some interesting partitioning column are kept during optimization because they can be part of the optimal plan overall. Then, the optimizer is instrumented to simulate the availability of all partitioning and replication schemes simultaneously, so that after optimization we can obtain the optimal partitioning strategy for a given query.*

Merging. Consider a table T, and suppose that the best candidate partitioning for query q_1 is over $T(a, b)$ and that the best candidate partitioning for query q_2 is over $T(a, c)$. In this case, a hash-based partitioning over $T(a)$ could be the best partitioning overall, as it benefits both queries. In general, merging generates new partitioning candidates with columns that are a common subset of two or more candidates identified in the previous step. To avoid skewed distributions, we do not attempt to merge partitioning candidates if the resulting number of key values is under a given threshold.

Enumeration. Before enumeration starts, we compute a *benefit* value for each candidate partitioning. The benefit of a candidate partitioning P is obtained as the difference in cost, for all queries that picked P as a candidate partitioning, between the configuration that can leverage all possible partitioning candidates (including P) and the one for which no partitioning is available. Merged partitioning candidates inherit the sum of benefits of their respective parents. Note that this benefit value is just an approximation of the true reduction in cost for a given partitioning candidate, since it assigns the benefit of the whole query to all useful partitioning candidates equally. Using benefit values, we define the *initial* configuration as the one that uses, for each table, the

---

*We assume that the same table is not repeated in the query, and therefore the optimal plan contains a single partitioning scheme for each table. In the general case the technique needs to be extended, as discussed in Section 9.6.

partitioning scheme with the highest benefit. We additionally define the neighbors of a configuration C as all configurations that differ with C in exactly one partitioning function. The enumeration algorithm proceeds as follows. We keep a priority queue of unexplored configurations, which we first populate with the initial configuration already described. Then, until a time limit is reached, we (1) remove from the priority queue the highest-ranked configuration, (2) perform a *what-if* optimization to obtain the *true benefit value* of the configuration as described in Chapter 5, (3) keep the current configuration if it is the best so far, and (4) insert in the priority queue all unexplored configurations that are neighbors of the current one. While we can use the benefit of a configuration C as the ranking function in the priority queue, a refined formulation gives better empirical results. In addition to the benefit of a configuration, this refined rank of a configuration gives priority to partitions of large tables and penalizes small incremental changes. Section 9.6 discusses references that provide additional details on this ranking function as well as various optimizations to the basic scheme.

9.1.2.2   Integrated Recommendation of Partitioning

Recommending horizontal partitioning in isolation makes sense in a parallel DBMS, where the biggest performance overhead results from data movement across servers. In traditional centralized settings, however, it is much more important to integrate the recommendation of partitioning (both horizontal and vertical) with that of other physical structures, like indexes and materialized views. The reason is that different aspects of physical design can strongly interact. Experimental evaluation in the literature compares the best recommendation obtained by two alternative procedures. The first one selects the best (nonpartitioned) indexes and subsequently recommends how to best horizontally partition them. The second alternative considers indexes and horizontal partitioning together and returns the best recommendation overall. Even for simple TPC-H queries, it has been observed that the execution times under the recommendation produced by the integrated alternative can be significantly faster than those under the alternative that recommends physical structures in isolation. We next describe how we can recommend partitioning, indexes, and materialized views in an integrated way.

Candidate generation. Generating candidates for vertical partitions is complex because there are many different ways to divide the columns of each table. To avoid a combinatorial explosion of candidates, we apply a pruning technique similar to that in Section 8.4.1 in the context of materialized views. Specifically, the idea is to consider a subset of columns C for partitioning only if the fraction of the cost of all queries in the workload that reference C is above some threshold (and therefore C is deemed interesting). It has been shown experimentally that even a very conservative cost fraction of 2% results in a large fraction of column subsets being pruned (because many column subsets are not referenced often enough or are mentioned only in cheap queries). To further decrease the set of candidates we rank column subsets by some effectiveness metric. A possible definition of effectiveness for a column subset is given by the *VPC* metric, which captures the fraction of the scanned data in a partition that would be useful in answering queries (*VPC* is short for *vertical partitioning confidence*, and it is discussed in detail in the references provided in Section 9.6). We then take the top-*k* highest-ranked candidate subsets for each table in the workload and can generate a candidate vertical partitioning. Specifically, the candidate vertical partitioning based on column subset *C* contains *C* and the table key as one vertical partition and the remaining columns in the table (plus the key) as another vertical partition. Every vertical partitioning candidate therefore consists of exactly two partitions. We also consider the case where the table is not vertically partitioned. We next generate nonpartitioned candidate indexes and views as described in Chapters 4 and 8 and additionally consider horizontally partitioning each such candidate index and view. For range partitioning, we use the specific values from query range predicates as boundary points. For hash partitioning, we select number of partitions such that it is a multiple of the number of processors and each partition fits into memory. Finally, for each vertical partitioning candidate, we consider candidate indexes and views on such vertical partition candidates if they are well defined (i.e., if the set of columns of the index or view belongs to a single vertical partition).

Merging. To explore the space of merged structures, we iterate over the given set of candidates similarly to what we do in Section 8.4.1 in the context of materialized views. At each iteration, we generate all candidates that can be obtained by merging a pair of current candidates. We then pick the best merged structures, replace their parent candidates, and repeat this process. Thus, we return the *maximal* merged structures that can be obtained by repeatedly merging pairs of structures, which are added to the original set of candidates. We next describe how to merge a pair of physical design structures in the presence of vertical and horizontal partitioning. First, we generate interesting vertical partitioning candidates by merging vertical partitions that are the output of the candidate selection step. Merging two partitioning candidates involves manipulating two subsets of columns. There are different ways to generate merged partitioning candidates, which involve performing unions and intersections of the column subsets of the parent candidates. Then, for each single vertical partition (including the new merged ones), we merge all indexes and materialized views that are relevant for that vertical partition while taking horizontal partitioning into account. The inclusion of horizontal partitioning raises new challenges during merging. One reason is that partitioning and indexing columns can be interchangeably used. For instance, an index on columns (a, b) that is used to evaluate a predicate like (a=10 AND b=20) can be replaced by an index on (b) partitioned by column a. When merging two partitioned indexes, we need to consider rearranging index keys and partitioning columns in addition to the more standard index merging. If indexes on the same vertical partition are horizontally partitioned on the same columns, we merge the respective partitioning methods to arrive at a more generic partitioning method, similar to the case of merging range predicates in a view. More details on merging can be found in the references at the end of this chapter.

Enumeration. After we define the search space by candidate enumeration and merging of physical structures, we can use any of the strategies discussed in Section 6.1 to conduct the enumeration step. In fact, such strategies are sufficiently agnostic to the considered physical design structures that they can be adapted with minor changes. For instance, *greedy(m,B)* starts by evaluating all configurations with at most m structures (e.g., horizontally partitioned indexes) and then continues considering the remaining structures greedily. Certain problem formulations, however, require slightly different approaches. For instance, a common requirement when partitioning a database is that all indexes of a given table share the same partitioning function. This requirement simplifies database management, since database operations such as backup and restore become much easier to plan and execute. In this situation, unless we eagerly generate candidates with all combinations of partitioning for every candidate index, we might end up searching in an overconstrained space of physical structures. At the same time, generating all combinations of indexes and partitioning schemes can result in much larger search spaces. To overcome these difficulties, there are adaptations to the basic *greedy(m,B)* strategy that lazily generate useful horizontal partitions on demand and can efficiently traverse the full space of aligned configurations.

9.2 Data Cube Selection

Users of data warehouses typically need to manipulate and analyze data from multiple perspectives, and some environments handle this requirement by presenting data as a multidimensional *data cube*. Users can then explore two-, three-, or even higher-dimensional subcubes to discover interesting information, a task also known as *business intelligence*. In this section we introduce the concept of data cubes, explain how can they help query processing, and describe some challenges and algorithms to automatically materialize subcubes to improve performance.

9.2.1   Data and Query Models

A data cube can be seen as a higher-dimensional spreadsheet that allows users to analyze—typically financial—data from different perspectives. A data cube consists of numeric facts called *measures* that are categorized by attributes called *dimensions*. Data cubes are usually created directly from the schema of a relational database. Measures are then derived from records in the fact tables (e.g., `sales`) and dimensions from dimension tables (e.g., `suppliers` and `customers`).

As a simple example, consider a business that buys certain parts from suppliers and then sells them to customers at a sale price. A relational database has information about each transaction over a period of several years. In this case, three dimensions of interest are `part`, `supplier`, and `customer`. The measure of interest is the total amount of `sales`. This example results in a three-dimensional data cube. Each cell in this cube, given by specific values (`p`, `s`, `c`) for `part`, `supplier`, and `customer`, is associated with the total sales amount for part `p` bought from supplier `s` and sold to customer `c`.

Users are interested in both very specific information (e.g., the sales of a single cell in the data cube) and consolidated information (e.g., the total amount of sales of a given part `p` to a given customer `c`). Also, users can be interested in a single such cell or a set of results (e.g., the total amount of sales of each part to a given customer `c`). A common way to specify such queries is by a tuple that contains one value for each dimension in the cube. An additional value `ALL` is used to handle consolidated queries. For instance, we can ask for all sales of part `p` to customer `c` by using (`p`, `ALL`, `c`). When the result is not a single cell but instead a group of cells, we use the dimension name in the appropriate tuple position. For instance, we write the query that asks for the total sales to customer `c` of every part in the inventory as (`part`, `ALL`, `c`).

9.2.1.1   Standard Query Language (SQL) Representation of Data Cube Queries

We can write query (`part`, `ALL`, `c`) in terms of the raw relational data as follows:

```
SELECT part, customer, SUM(sales)
FROM Sales
WHERE customer = c
GROUP BY part, customer
```

In general, we can translate any such query to a SQL query like the previous one, which contains all dimensions except those marked as `ALL` as grouping columns and equality predicates for dimensions that have a specific value.

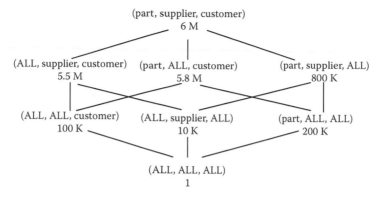

FIGURE 9.2 Lattice of subcubes.

9.2.1.2 Answering Data Cube Queries

Suppose that we materialize all cells in the result of query (part, supplier, customer) as a new table. This table might generally be different from the raw table because all duplicate values of part, supplier, and customer are aggregated in a single cell. We can answer any query by scanning this result and performing optional aggregation and filtering. For instance, consider again query (part, ALL, c). We can answer this query by scanning the materialized result of (part, supplier, customer), keeping only the tuples that satisfy customer=c and aggregating the resulting sales values grouped by part.

Suppose now that we materialize the result of query (part, ALL, customer). In this case, each cell in this materialized subcube contains the total amount of sales for each combination of part and customer over all possible suppliers. Answering the original query (part, ALL, c) can be done more efficiently over the result of (part, ALL, customer) because this table is potentially much smaller than (part, supplier, customer) due to preaggregation (additionally, since the table is already preaggregated, the query involves only a scan but no additional grouping and aggregation).

This example hints at the fact that we can use the result of some query (materialized as a subcube) to speed up the processing of other queries. For a cube with n dimensions, we can materialize 2^n different subcubes, by replacing each subset of attributes with the value ALL. Figure 9.2 shows an example of all subcubes for our running example, with the number of cells in each subcube. The subcubes are laid out as a lattice, showing which subcubes can be completely computed from others. For instance, consider (ALL, ALL, customer). We can compute this subcube by scanning either (ALL, supplier, customer) or (part, ALL, customer) and subsequently grouping on customer. Note that if both alternatives are available, it would be cheaper to do the processing over (ALL, supplier, customer) because it is smaller and therefore more efficient to process. When a subcube s_1 can be computed from another subcube s_2 (that is, when there is a path from s_1 down to s_2 in the lattice), we write $s_1 \preceq s_2$.

9.2.2 Recommending Data Subcubes

When fast interactive multidimensional data analysis is required, DBMSs frequently precompute some subset of subcubes. The following are some materialization strategies:

1. Materialize all subcubes. This approach results in the best performance for queries. At the same time, precomputing and storing every subcube is not a feasible alternative for large data cubes, because of the large amount of required storage (and also the time it would take to deploy such a configuration).

2. Materialize no subcube. In this case we need to go to the raw data and compute every query on request. While no additional space is required beyond that of the raw data, this approach does not generally result in efficient query processing.

3. Materialize some subcubes. This middle-ground approach materializes certain subcubes so that most queries can be efficiently executed with low storage overhead. As an example, consider (`part`, `ALL`, `customer`) in Figure 9.2, which contains 5.8 million cells. Now, assume that a query can be evaluated by relying on such subcube (e.g., (`p`, `ALL`, `ALL`)). On average, and in the absence of indexes, we would have to scan all 5.8 million cells to obtain the result. However, by scanning a slightly larger number of tuples (6 million), we can obtain the same result from the precomputed subcube (`part`, `supplier`, `customer`). By not materializing (`part`, `ALL`, `customer`) we can save almost 30% of storage without significantly compromising query performance.

We next discuss the problem of recommending subcubes to materialize under a storage constraint for a given workload, so that any query in the lattice can be answered from the materialized subcubes. We initially make some simplifying assumptions in our problem statement. Specifically:

- The input workload consists of all queries that are identical to some subcube definition (e.g., the eight queries in Figure 9.2).

- The cost of evaluating a query using an appropriate subcube is proportionate to the number of tuples in the cube (this assumes there are no indexes built on the subcubes and that aggregation and filtering are negligible compared with scanning the subcube).

- We are interested in minimizing the workload cost when materializing a fixed number of subcubes (rather than those satisfying a storage constraint).

The set of subcubes to materialize should always include the top subcube (see Figure 9.2), because there is no other subcube that can be used to answer the corresponding query without going to the raw data. Even under the simplifying assumptions previously discussed, the problem is shown to be NP-complete from a reduction from set cover. Interestingly enough, however, there is a greedy solution for this problem with good quality guarantees. Before introducing the greedy algorithm, we define the benefit of a subcube relative to a set of subcubes. Specifically, after selecting some set S of subcubes, the benefit of subcube s relative to S is defined as $B(s, S) = \sum_{v \preceq s} B_v$, where $B_v = \max(0, |s| - |u|)$, and u is the subcube of least cost in S such that $v \preceq u$ (since the top subcube is in S, there must be at least one such subcube in S). That is, we compute the benefit value B of a subcube s by considering how it can improve the cost of evaluating subcubes, including itself. Using this definition, Figure 9.3 shows the greedy algorithm to select a set of k subcubes to materialize, which selects, at each step, the subcube with the highest benefit with respect to the set of subcubes that were already selected. It can be shown that the greedy algorithm never has a benefit below 63% of that of the optimal solution. We next discuss some extensions to the basic greedy algorithm.

Workload. We assumed that all queries in the workload are equally likely. In general, we might want to associate a weight with each query proportional to the frequency that the query is evaluated. We can extend the greedy algorithm by multiplying each benefit value by the corresponding weight, which results in the same performance guarantee.

Storage bound. The greedy algorithm optimizes the workload cost under a constraint of a given number of subcubes. In reality, subcube sizes can vary by orders of magnitude (see Figure 9.2), and therefore we might want to optimize the cost of the workload for a given storage constraint instead. In this case, we need to consider benefit values per unit of storage in line 3 of Figure 9.3. In that way, if the largest aggregate view uses a fraction f of the storage constraint, the resulting greedy algorithm is guaranteed to result in a benefit of at least $(0.63 - f)$.

```
greedySC (T:Execution Plan)
1    S = { top sub-cube }
2    for i = 1 to k do
3        s = sub-cube not in S that maximizes B(s,S)
4        S = S ∪ { s }
5    return S
```

FIGURE 9.3 Greedy algorithm to recommend subcubes to materialize.

Several additional extensions to the basic problem formulation are discussed in the references found at the end of the chapter.

9.2.3   Relationship with Materialized View Selection

The ideas discussed in this section have similarities with the work on materialized view selection that we discussed in Chapter 8. In fact, each materialized subcube can be seen as a materialized view, and using a subcube to answer a query corresponds to the classical problem of answering queries using materialized views. However, the problem described in this section relies on additional restrictions compared with the generic problem of recommending views, and thus we are able to provide a greedy algorithm with quality guarantees. Specifically:

- Workload queries are templatized in a very specific way. There always are 2^n possible cubes to consider.

- The workload can be seen as composed of queries that exactly match one of the possible subcubes (modulo additional equality constraints).

- The cost model assumes that no indexes are available and that the cost of doing aggregation linearly depends on the size of the used subcube.

9.3   Multidimensional Clustering

Multidimensional clustering (MDC) is primarily motivated by the appearance of large repositories of relational data coupled with the need for complex data mining and business analytic processing. These workloads are characterized by multidimensional analysis of compiled enterprise data and typically include queries with group-by clauses, aggregation, and multidimensional range selections. Multidimensional clustering generalizes the idea of a clustered index with the ability to physically cluster a table on multiple dimensions at the same time. This is a powerful technique that offers significant performance benefits in several online analytical processing (OLAP) and decision support systems.

9.3.1   MDC Definition

An MDC table is created by specifying one or more columns as dimensions to cluster the table rows. Every unique combination of dimension values forms a logical *cell*, which is physically organized as a block of consecutive pages on disk. The set of blocks that contain pages with data having a certain value on a dimension column is called a *slice*. By definition, every page of

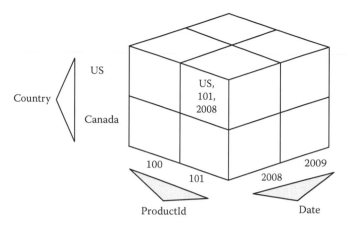

FIGURE 9.4 Example of multidimensional clustering on a **Sales** table.

the table is part of exactly one block, depending on the values of dimension columns. Additionally, each dimension column is associated with a *dimension index*, which is a single-column B^+-*tree* that has, at leaf nodes, pointers to appropriate blocks in the MDC. Consider a **Sales** table defined as follows:

```
CREATE TABLE Sales (
        date OrderDate,
        int StoreId,
        int ProductId,
        int Country,
        float Price )
```

Figure 9.4 illustrates an MDC table clustered along the dimensions **Country**, **ProductId**, and **Date=yearOf(OrderDate)**. Note that we can control the granularity of the clustering by defining computed columns for the case of **OrderDate** (which by itself might have resulted in a very sparse MDC). The figure shows a simple logical cube with only two values for each dimension column. Logical cells are represented by the subcubes in the figure (e.g., the cell that corresponds to the combination (**Canada, 100, 2008**)). A column or row in the cube represents a slice for a particular dimension. For example, all records containing the value **Canada** in the **Country** dimension are found in the blocks contained in the slice defined by the **Canada** column in the cube. Moreover, each block in this slice contains only records having **Canada** in the **Country** field. The figure also shows dimension indexes created on each dimension column, which could be used to find the blocks that contain tuples satisfying certain predicates over the dimension columns.

9.3.2 Query Processing

One of the goals of MDC is to facilitate efficient query processing for multidimensional range operations. Specifically, new processing techniques are introduced to take advantage of the block-oriented clustering and indexing techniques. Consider a query that calculates the total sales of product with ProductId = 100 over all dates and countries:

```
SELECT SUM(Price)
FROM Sales
WHERE ProductId = 100
```

This query can be efficiently answered as follows. First, we process the dimension index on ProductId to locate the slice (i.e., block ids) that corresponds to tuples satisfying ProductId = 100. Then, we process all records in the block. In this specific example, we can guarantee that each record in an accessed block satisfies the predicate on ProductId. In general, due to computed dimension columns such as Date in the example (or additional predicates on nondimension columns), we might need to do a postfiltering step to retrieve the valid tuples. This operation is most effective when all or most tuples in a block need to be processed for a given query. Note that the same MDC structure can efficiently answer a similar query with a predicate on Country, without the need to reorganize the data differently. A clustered index on ProductId might be comparable to the MDC in the figure for the query with a filter in ProductId but would result in a full sequential scan for a predicate on Country.

Consider a variation of the previous query, with an additional predicate on Country:

```
SELECT SUM(Price)
FROM Sales
WHERE ProductId = 100 AND Country = 'Canada'
```

In this case, we can consider traditional index intersection plans that operate on blocks rather than tuples. Thus, we can inspect the dimension index on ProductId obtaining the block ids that contain all tuples with ProductId = 100. We then do the same with the dimension index on Country for the block ids containing tuples that satisfy Country = Canada. We finally intersect those block ids and explore only the resulting ones that satisfy both predicates. Since dimension indexes are typically much smaller than the tuple-based ones, the intersection can be done efficiently by using bit-vector filtering techniques. In addition to index intersection, other, more sophisticated techniques (e.g., index union) are also possible.

9.3.3 Recommending MDCs

As we illustrated in the previous section, the performance of multidimensional queries is often improved through data clustering, which can significantly reduce input/output (I/O) cost. Yet the choice of clustering dimensions and the granularity of the clustering (i.e., which computed column to use) are nontrivial choices, and a bad design might even result in performance degradation. We first note that MDCs generally result in an increase in storage. The reason is that each cell in an MDC (which is composed of consecutive pages in disk) is bound to have some amount of free space in its last page. In the worst case, if each tuple in a table requires its own cell, the MDC would require one page per tuple, which can be much larger than the space required by the original table. For that reason, a common problem formulation requires that each recommended MDC satisfy a storage constraint. Specifically, it is common to ask that any valid MDC has at most 10% space overhead over the original table. Given this problem formulation, we next briefly discuss an automated technique to recommend a good MDC configuration for a given workload:

1. Approximate the best-case benefit for each candidate dimension column, which involves:

   a. Determine columns of interest, including those that are used for multidimensional predicates, grouping, and ordering clauses.

   b. Determine the minimum granularity for each interesting column that would result in at most 10% storage overhead. If we assume that there are k cells in the MDC and that the last page in each cell is on average $P\%$ full (50% is the expected value, but we can use a more conservative percentage like 65%), then the storage overhead is $k \cdot P\% \cdot pageSize$. This formula can be used to bound the maximum number of cells (k_{max}) in an MDC for a given storage constraint. In turn, k_{max} is also the maximum number of distinct values that we can consider for any dimension column (because the number of distinct values of a combination of columns is no smaller than the number of distinct values of each column in isolation). We can then determine the computed value for a dimension column as its position in an equi-width histogram with k_{max} buckets that covers the column domain. That is, if column a has values ranging from a_{min} to a_{max}, we define the computed column $a' = \lceil (a - a_{min})/(a_{max} - a_{min}) * k_{max} \rceil$ (if a has fewer than k_{max} distinct values, then $a' = a$). This constitutes the finest level of granularity for column a in the MDC that satisfies the storage constraint.

   c. Obtain a *benefit* value for each dimension column. We approximate the best-case benefit for a given dimension column by optimizing each query in the workload assuming the finest granularity obtained as already explained and also by assuming that every tuple in the dimension column maps to a unique cell (which should be the worst-case granularity for the column). The benefit is then calculated as relative reduction in query costs between these two extremes.

2. Model the benefit of candidate dimensions for varying granularities. So far we have obtained the benefit of each query in the workload under the finest and coarsest granularities. In practice we might want to cluster our data at some intermediate granularity to arrive at a better configuration.

The finest and coarsest granularities give us two points of reference on performance vs. number of distinct values. The exact shape of this curve cannot be easily determined but in practice can be modeled as a smooth logarithmic relationship. We can then perform a curve-fitting procedure that gives as a formula to obtain, for a given number of distinct values, the expected benefit of using such granularity for the corresponding dimension column.

3. Define candidate granularities for each dimension column. Once we have identified the finest granularity value, 4 to 10 progressively coarser granularities are usually useful. For instance, while considering a date column, we can imagine having granularity values on days, months, quarters, and years. Similarly, for an integer column, we can increase the finest granularity by using an exponential scale (i.e., dividing the corresponding computed column by 2, 4, 8, and so on).

4. The previous steps allows us to (1) identify candidate dimensions, (2) estimate the benefit of a candidate dimension at the finest granularity, and (3) model the benefit of a candidate dimension at intermediate granularity values. The search procedure aims to pick the best possible MDC from such a list of candidate dimensions and granularities. One way to carry the search involves relying on a weighted randomized procedure. Specifically, we select several combinations of dimensions at various granularity levels in proportion to their relative benefit for the input workload. Each such combination forms a candidate solution. We then rank all candidate solutions by aggregated benefit. Since the candidate dimensions and granularities have been picked randomly, chances are that the combined number of distinct values (and therefore the overhead of the MDC) is larger than the storage budget. We then traverse the list of candidates in decreasing order of benefit and pick the first one that satisfies the storage budget. To efficiently approximate the number of distinct values of a candidate MDC, we rely on a precomputed sample of the table and distinct value estimators.

The previous (simplified) technique can be extended in different ways, such as by improving the granularity model and storage estimates in the presence of data skew or by adaptively choosing the storage budget on a per-table basis. More details can be found in the references at the end of this chapter.

9.4   Extensible Physical Design

In this chapter (and also in Chapter 8) we have discussed several extensions to the original physical design problem, which address different physical structures (e.g., materialized views and partitioning). Specifically, we have discussed either how to recommend these new structures in isolation or how to integrate them in a combined search space. This is an important design point whenever we include a new type of structure into the physical design problem. We next comment on some general approaches to address this issue.

Iterative approach: A simple iterative approach begins by dividing the available space among all available types of physical structures (e.g., 75% of the budget for indexes and the remaining 25% for materialized views) and then iteratively processing one structure type at a time. This alternative is the easiest to engineer since it requires independent tuners for each physical structure (these components can be treated as black boxes, as we do not need to know the details inside of a specific tuner to implement another one). The main problem with the approach, however, is one of interdependence (i.e., physical structures influence one another). For instance, the choice of a single index might remove the need of a materialized view. At the same time, indexes can be defined over materialized views, but only after these have been recommended. Several studies in the literature show that recommending physical structures in isolation can be significantly suboptimal. A secondary but important problem is that of defining a good allocation of resources to each physical structure.

Combined approach: Since in the worst case all types of structures depend on each other, a combined approach simply defines the search space as the joint set of all possible structures. In this approach, the search is conducted directly on the combined space, and heuristics are applied to limit the candidates being enumerated. While this approach is suitable to select a few types of physical structures and results in the best quality of recommendations, it might not scale very well with the addition of new features. The reason is that the search space grows combinatorially with respect to the number of new design structures, and also a large portion of the algorithms might need to be adapted to support such joint enumeration.

Hybrid approach: Some studies suggest that the degree of dependency among different physical structures can be better understood and lever-

	Index	Materialized View	Partitioning	MDC
Index	—	Strong	Weak	Weak
Materialized view	Strong	—	Strong	Strong
Partitioning	Weak	Strong	—	Weak
MDC	Weak	Strong	Weak	—

FIGURE 9.5 Dependence analysis for various physical structures.

aged. We say that a structure class *A* strongly depends on another structure class *B* if a change in selection of *B* often results in a change in that of *A*. Otherwise, we say that *A* "weakly" depends on *B*. It can be argued that weak dependencies are likely to exist because a new physical structure is normally introduced to help areas in which existing structures do not apply or do not perform well. Figure 9.5 summarizes a dependency table for various types of physical design structures. Mutual strong dependencies are difficult to *break* and thus are better handled by using a combined approach. If only *B* strongly depends on *A*, we can iteratively search *A* followed by *B*, so that *B* is properly influenced by *A*. Weakly coupled components can be scheduled separately in any order. In principle, it is even possible to go through a series of iterations of all physical structures until some convergence condition is met. In this way, the hybrid approach can break the implementation of different physical structures into smaller components while capturing the most important interdependencies among them.

9.5   Summary

Each physical design structure added to a DBMS requires new algorithms to automatically recommend configurations that leverage the new functionality. In this chapter we discussed techniques that can be used to automatically recommend:

- Horizontal and vertical partitioning
- Data cubes
- Multidimensional clustering

9.6   Additional Reading

We next provide some references that can be used as a starting point to obtain more detailed information on the different techniques and algorithms discussed in this chapter. Rao et al. describe in detail different techniques to recommend hash-based horizontal partitioning on parallel DBMSs.[7] Agrawal et al. focus on integrated recommendation of indexes, materialized views, and horizontal and vertical partitioning.[2] In this chapter we briefly commented on a basic approach to select subcubes to materialize. More details on this approach can be found in the work of Shukla et al.[8] We note, however, that several subsequent techniques improve and extend the original approach in different ways (e.g., considering indexing[3] and multicube systems[4]).

Padmanabhan et al. introduce the concept of multidimensional clustering and provide additional details on the automated procedure to recommend clustering dimensions and granularity levels.[5,6] Some experimental results[1,2] point to the fact that an iterative selection of indexes and materialized views or partitioning can result in suboptimal recommendations and thus advocate a combined approach to physical database design. Subsequent work in the area[9] refines this concept by introducing the idea of strong and weak dependencies and the iterative and hybrid approaches to the physical design problem.

References

1. Sanjay Agrawal, Surajit Chaudhuri, and Vivek Narasayya. Automated selection of materialized views and indexes in SQL databases. In *Proceedings of the International Conference on Very Large Databases (VLDB)*, 2000.

2. Sanjay Agrawal, Vivek Narasayya, and Beverly Yang. Integrating vertical and horizontal partitioning into automated physical database design. In *Proceedings of the ACM International Conference on Management of Data (SIGMOD)*, 2004.

3. Himanshu Gupta, Venky Harinarayan, Anand Rajaraman, and Jeffrey D. Ullman. Index selection for OLAP. In *Proceedings of the International Conference on Data Engineering (ICDE)*, 1997.

4. Venky Harinarayan, Anand Rajaraman, and Jeffrey D. Ullman. Implementing data cubes efficiently. In *Proceedings of the ACM International Conference on Management of Data (SIGMOD)*, 1996.

5. Sam Lightstone and Bishwaranjan Bhattacharjee. Automating the design of multi-dimensional clustering tables in relational databases. In *Proceedings of the International Conference on Very Large Databases (VLDB)*, 2004.

6. Sriram Padmanabhan, Bishwaranjan Bhattacharjee, Tim Malkemus, Leslie Cranston, and Matthew Huras. Multi-dimensional clustering: A new data layout scheme in DB2. In *Proceedings of the ACM International Conference on Management of Data (SIGMOD)*, 2003.

7. Jun Rao, Chun Zhang, Nimrod Megiddo, and Guy M. Lohman. Automating physical database design in a parallel database. In *Proceedings of the ACM International Conference on Management of Data (SIGMOD)*, 2002.

8. Amit Shukla, Prasad Deshpande, and Jeffrey F. Naughton. Materialized view selection for multi-cube data models. In *Proceedings of the International Conference on Extending Database Technology (EDBT)*, 2000.

9. Daniel Zilio et al. DB2 design advisor: Integrated automatic physical database design. In *Proceedings of the International Conference on Very Large Databases (VLDB)*, 2004.

Chapter 10

Continuous Physical Database Design

The techniques discussed in Part II are sophisticated and useful in many common scenarios. However, they take an *offline* approach to the physical design problem and still leave significant decisions to database applications (DBAs). Specifically, DBAs need to explicitly identify representative workloads and feed them to tuning tools. DBAs are also expected to *guess* when a tuning session is needed and when to deploy recommendations. Naturally, this is not a one-time process, but instead DBAs continuously monitor, diagnose, and tune database installations.

These manual tasks become even more problematic in current complex scenarios. Consider, as an increasingly common example, large installations that support the database-as-a-service paradigm. Database applications hosted in such services may come and go and usually exhibit unexpected spikes in their loads. At the same time, the hosting infrastructure might have some additional amount of resources to globally tune the physical design, and all applications would compete for these valuable resources. As another motivating example, some applications exhibit periodic, sometimes unexpected changes in the mix of SELECT and UPDATE queries in the workload. Consider, for instance, a bug-tracking system. Most days the system is queried and browsed (SELECT load), but a few days—sometimes called bug-bash days—are used to primarily identify and insert large numbers of bugs (UPDATE load). If we gather a representative workload over, say, a month, chances are that no index is globally useful, as the gains in query processing are outweighed by the update costs during bug-bash periods. It is very difficult to explicitly model the workload in these scenarios and equally difficult to decide *when* to tune the database and deploy the resulting recommendations (tuning too frequently results in wasted resources, but tuning too sporadically misses critical opportunities to improve performance).

With increasingly common database management system (DBMS) features like *online indexes* (which allows query processing to continue in parallel with indexes that are built in the background), it is appealing to explore more automated solutions to the physical design problem. There are, however, new and significant challenges to address. Such fully automated solutions should be *always on*, continuously monitoring changes in both the workload and the database state and refining the physical design as needed. It is therefore critical that such solutions have very low overhead and do not interfere with the normal functioning of the DBMS. Additionally, in contrast to current offline approaches, fully automated solutions must also balance the cost to transition between physical design configurations and the potential benefits of such design changes for the future workload. Although we would like to react quickly to changes in the workload, reacting too quickly can result in unwanted oscillations, in which the same indexes are continuously created and dropped. A fully automated solution must do no harm for stable workloads but also react in a timely manner to significant workload changes.

In this chapter we discuss *online* techniques to tune indexes in a DBMS. The main difference from the techniques discussed so far is that the input is often considered a *sequence* of queries rather than a set, and the output is not a single configuration but instead a continuous reorganization of the physical design that adapts to changes in the workload.

10.1   An Alerting Mechanism

A simple way to extend existing solutions so that they handle evolving workloads is to include the physical design problem as part of a continuous cycle that works as follows:

1. As queries are executed, we save their Standard Query Language (SQL) definitions in a workload repository using profiling tools as described in Section 7.1.

2. Every certain amount of time (e.g., an hour or a day), we run a traditional physical design tool over the workload captured during the current iteration.

3. If the tool returns a configuration whose improvement is beyond a certain threshold, we implement the recommendation at the end of the current iteration.

This approach does not require any intervention by DBAs, since the workload gathering, tuning, and deployment are done automatically. At the same time, however, it suffers from significant drawbacks. First, the time interval between iterations needs to be carefully calculated. On one hand, changes in workloads and data distributions *might* result in the current configuration becoming suboptimal. DBAs therefore would like to frequently run a tuning tool that recommends changes (if any) to the current configuration. On the other hand, unless the current configuration *is* suboptimal, no changes would be necessary and the significant load on the server due to the tuning session is wasted. Worse still, the only way to determine whether a tuning session would be worthwhile is to actually run it! A second problem with this approach is that the tuning tool does not take into account the resources needed to implement a new configuration. While this is not a problem in the traditional physical design problem, where a configuration is obtained and deployed only once it might be very inadequate to spend considerable resources in deploying a configuration that only marginally improves performance of subsequent queries.

An alternative approach that can address problem 1 is to determine whether the current configuration is suboptimal a priori (i.e., *before* running an expensive tuning tool). We next describe a technique, which we henceforth call *alerter*, that analyzes a workload and quickly determines whether a tuning session would result in a configuration significantly better than the current one. It has the following characteristics:

- *Low-overhead diagnostics:* The alerter can be called repeatedly whenever the DBA suspects that changes might be necessary or at fixed time intervals. The alerter works only with the information that was gathered when the workload was originally optimized and does not rely on additional optimizer calls.

- *Reliable lower-bound improvement:* When the alerter reports that certain improvement is possible, we can be certain that the improvement achieved by a comprehensive tuning tool would indeed be at least as large. This is crucial since false positives would defeat the purpose of the alerting mechanism and are therefore unacceptable.

Figure 10.1 illustrates how the alerter fits into a physical database design solution. As new queries are optimized and executed, the DBMS maintains information about the workload that would later be consumed by the alerter. After a triggering condition happens (e.g., a fixed amount of time), the alerter is automatically launched, and it quickly diagnoses the current situation. After the lightweight diagnostics, if the alerter determines that running a comprehensive tuning tool would result in an improvement beyond a certain prespecified threshold, the DBA is alerted to run such a comprehensive alternative.

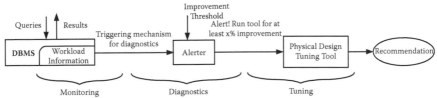

FIGURE 10.1 Architecture for a physical design alerter. (Used with permission from Bruno, N. & Chaudhuri, S. In *Proceedings of the International Conference on Very Large Databases [VLDB]*, 2006.)

10.1.1 Instrumenting the Optimizer

The alerter leverages information gathered during regular query optimization by reusing the instrumentation-based approach of Section 4.1.3. Figure 10.2a illustrates some access path requests intercepted for a three-way join query. Request ρ_1 is associated with the selection condition on table T_1 and specifies that (1) there is one equality predicate on column $T_1.a$ returning 2,500 tuples, (2) the additional required columns are $T_1.a$, $T_1.w$, and $T_1.x$, and (3) the subplan would be executed once at runtime. Similarly, request ρ_2 was generated when the optimizer considered an index-based join alternative with T_1 and T_2 as the outer and inner relations, respectively. It specifies that $T_2.y$ is part of an equality-based predicate that would be executed 2,500 times (once per outer row) and produce 500 rows overall. There is no request for the join at the top right of Figure 10.2a because an index-based implementation requires the inner relation to be a base table.

Rather than gathering all possible requests for a given query, we keep only those that are associated with an operator in the final execution plan. For the plan in Figure 10.2b, such requests are $\{\rho_1, \rho_2, \rho_3, \rho_5\}$. The reason for this restriction is twofold. First, returning requests for all subplans enumerated by the optimizer imposes a larger overhead on top of regular optimization. Second, requests associated with the final plan are sufficient to reason in terms of local plan transformations (see Section 5.2.2.1) and thus infer plan costs without performing additional optimizer calls (we discuss this issue in the next section).

It is important to note that some requests might conflict with others. For instance, requests ρ_3 and ρ_5 in Figure 10.2b are mutually exclusive. In other words, if a plan implements ρ_3 (that is, contains an index-based join with T_3 as the inner table), it could not simultaneously implement ρ_5. As another example, request ρ_5 in Figure 10.2b would conflict with a request $\rho_6 = (T_3, E = \emptyset, R = \emptyset, P = \emptyset, O = \emptyset, A = \{b, z\})$ rooted at the Scan(T_3) operator (we do not show ρ_6 in Figure 10.2 for simplicity). The reason is that any execution plan uses one access path for each table. We can implement either ρ_6 (by scanning an index on T_3 and filtering $T_3.b= 8$ on the fly) or ρ_5 (by directly seeking valid tuples in T_3).

To explicitly represent these relationships, we encode the requests in an AND/OR tree,* where internal nodes indicate whether the respective subtrees can be satisfied simultaneously (AND) or are mutually exclusive (OR). The AND/OR tree is built by traversing the execution plan in postorder. Figure 10.3 illustrates how to generate the AND/OR tree for an input execution plan P. Intuitively, if P is a single node, we return a simple AND/OR tree with the request (if any) of such node (case 1 in Figure 10.3). Otherwise, if P's root

---

*The AND/OR tree can be seen as a restriction of the CMEMO structure of Chapter 5 considering only the final execution plan.

node has no requests, we **AND** together the trees generated for each of *P*'s execution subplans, since these are orthogonal (case 2). Otherwise, if the root of *P* has a request, the answer depends on the type of node. If it is a join, its request ρ corresponds to an attempted index-based join alternative. We know that ρ and the requests on *P*'s right subplan are mutually exclusive (see ρ_3 and

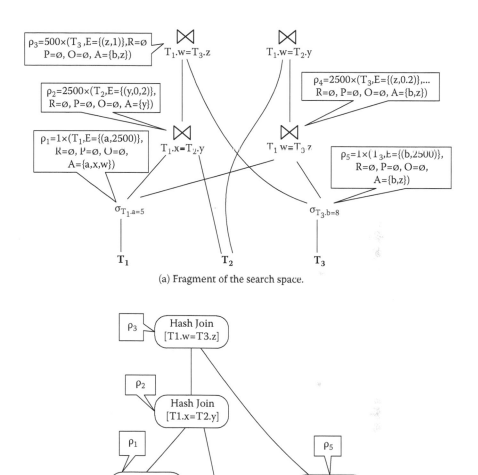

(a) Fragment of the search space.

(b) Final execution plan.

FIGURE 10.2 Gathering information during optimization. (Used with permission from Bruno, N. & Chaudhuri, S. In *Proceedings of the International Conference on Very Large Databases [VLDB]*, 2006.)

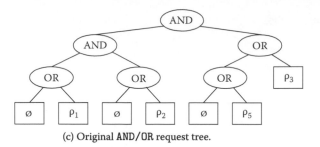

(c) Original **AND/OR** request tree.

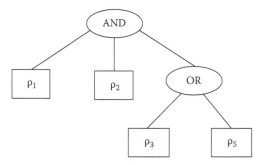

(d) Normalized **AND/OR** request tree.

FIGURE 10.2   (Continued)

ρ_5 in Figure 10.2b). However, these requests are orthogonal to the requests in P's left subplan, and thus we return the AND/OR tree of case 3. Finally, if the root P is not a join node, the request ρ conflicts with any request in a subplan of P (we cannot implement both alternatives), and therefore we return the AND/OR tree of case 4.

```
buildAOT (P:Execution Plan)
return AND/OR tree for P
1    if (P.isLeaf) // Case 1
2        return P.request
3    else if (P.request is null) // Case 2
4        return AND(buildAOT(P.child₁), ..., buildAOT(P.childₙ) )
5    else if (P.isJoin) // Case 3
6        return AND(buildAOT(P.leftChild),
                    OR(P.request,
                        buildAOT(P.rightChild)))
7    else // Case 4
8        return OR(P.request, buildAOT(P.child))
```

FIGURE 10.3   Building the AND/OR request tree. (Used with permission from Bruno, N. & Chaudhuri, S. In *Proceedings of the International Conference on Very Large Databases [VLDB]*, 2006.)

Figure 10.2c shows the resulting `AND/OR` tree for the requests of Figure 10.2b. As a final step, we normalize the `AND/OR` tree so that it contains no empty requests or unary intermediate nodes and strictly interleaves `AND` and `OR` nodes. In our example (see Figure 10.2d), the normalized tree consists of an `AND` root node whose children are either base requests or simple `OR` nodes. Due to the specific nature of execution plans and requests, this is true in general. In fact, we can prove by structural induction that the normalized `AND/OR` request tree for an input query is either (1) a single request, (2) a simple `OR` root whose children are requests, or (3) an `AND` root whose children are either requests or simple `OR` nodes. Since requests for different queries are orthogonal and can be satisfied simultaneously, we can combine the `AND/OR` request trees for the current workload by using an `AND` root node. Normalizing this combined tree, we obtain, for an arbitrary input workload, an `AND/OR` request tree that satisfies the previous property. This normalized tree can be used to make inferences about the workload in the presence of physical design changes *without issuing additional optimization calls.*

10.1.2 Upper Bounds Using `AND/OR` Trees

The idea of the alerter is to quickly identify whether the current configuration is suboptimal. For doing so, we try a small number of variations in the physical design and determine whether any of the alternatives can substantially improve the cost of the workload under the current configuration. For efficiency purposes, however, we cannot perform additional optimization calls. For that reason, a crucial component in the alerter is the ability to calculate, without making an optimization call, upper bounds on the workload cost for different configurations. Suppose that we want to calculate the cost of an alternative subplan that uses indexes I to implement ρ. For that purpose, we use the cost upper-bound techniques discussed in Section 5.2.2 (let us denote this cost as $Cost_I^\rho$). If the original cost of the subplan associated with the request ρ is $Cost_{orig}^\rho$, we define $\Delta_I^\rho = Cost_{orig}^\rho - Cost_I^\rho$. Then, Δ_I^ρ is a *lower bound* on the local cost difference that we would gain by using I to implement ρ rather than the index used originally by the optimizer. Δ_I^ρ values need not be positive; a bad choice of I can result in a subplan that is more expensive than the current one.

A configuration contains multiple indexes defined over request tables. We then calculate the difference in cost by implementing a request ρ with the best index strategy from a configuration C as $\Delta_C^\rho = \min_{I \subseteq C} \Delta_I^\rho$. In general, the workload is encoded as an `AND/OR` request tree, and `OR` nodes rule out multiple simultaneous requests in a query plan. The difference in cost for an `AND/OR` request tree T and a configuration C is defined as

$$
\Delta_C^T = \begin{cases}
\Delta_C^{T.\rho} & \text{if } T \text{ is a leaf node with request T.}\rho \\
\sum_i \Delta_C^{T.child_i} & \text{if } T \text{ is an AND node} \\
\min_i \Delta_C^{T.child_i} & \text{if } T \text{ is an OR node}
\end{cases}
$$

```
Alerter (T:AND/OR request tree,
          B_min, B_max:storage constraints,
          P:minimum percentage improvement)
1    R = ∅;
2    Obtain locally optimal configuration C
3    while (size(C)>B_min and 100% · Δ_C^T/cost_current > P)
4       if (size(C)<B_max)
5          R = R∪ C
6          Pick transformation TR that minimizes penalty(C, TR(C))
7          C = TR(C)
8    if (R ≠ ∅) ALERT(R)
```

FIGURE 10.4 Alerting main algorithm. (Used with permission from Bruno, N. & Chaudhuri, S. In *Proceedings of the International Conference on Very Large Databases [VLDB]*, 2006.)

The value Δ_C^T is therefore a lower bound on the difference in the workload cost between C and the original configuration (Δ_C^T values are lower bounds on such difference, since we obtain feasible—but perhaps suboptimal—plans that the optimizer would find for C).

10.1.3 Alerting Technique

Recall from Figure 10.1 that during normal operation, the DBMS gathers relevant information about the execution plans that are processed. This information is consolidated in the form of an AND/OR request tree. When a prespecified triggering event happens, the alerter main algorithm is launched (see Figure 10.4). The inputs to the alerter are the AND/OR request tree, space bounds B_{min} and B_{max} that are acceptable for a new configuration, and the minimum percentage improvement P that we consider important enough to issue an alert.

The alerter efficiently searches a space of configurations for one (or some) that fits in the available space and is as efficient as possible. Similarly to the approaches in Section 6.2, we start with an optimal configuration and relax it into smaller and less efficient ones. We first obtain in line 2 the locally optimal configuration C as the union of the indexes that implement the best strategy for each request in the AND/OR request tree. Note that the best we can do by following this approach is to obtain a *locally* optimal execution plan. That is, we replace the physical subplans associated to each request in the original plan with alternatives that are as efficient as possible. We would not be able to, say, obtain a plan with a different join order or other complex transformation that optimizers apply during plan generation. In that sense, we are giving up some opportunities to obtain the globally optimal execution plan but avoid expensive optimization calls that would prevent low overhead. The cost of the plan that we obtain by local changes is therefore an upper bound of that of the global optimal plan that the optimizer would find under the new configuration.

Once we obtain the initial, locally optimal configuration, we gradually relax it to obtain alternative ones that might be more attractive from a cost-benefit point of view. Specifically, we transform each configuration into another one that is smaller but less efficient (lines 3–7). Since the alerter needs to be very fast, we use *index deletion* and *index merging* as the only transformations and perform a greedy search in which we move from one configuration to the next using the most promising transformation (this technique is a simplification of the top-down approach discussed in Section 6.2). In general, there are many alternatives to transform a given configuration C. We can delete each index in C, or we can merge any pair of indexes defined over the same table. To rank the transformations, we use the *penalty* of transforming a configuration C into C' by an index deletion or index merge as defined in Section 6.2.1.4. Penalty values measure the increase in execution cost per unit of storage that we save in C' compared with C. For an AND/OR request tree T, $penalty(C, C') = (\Delta_C^T - \Delta_{C'}^T)/(size(C) - size(C'))$. At each iteration of lines 3–7, we choose the transformation TR with the smallest penalty value and create a new configuration (lines 6–7). After we exit the main loop, in line 8 we check whether some configuration satisfies all the constraints, and in such a case we issue an alert. The alert contains the list of all configurations that fit in the available space (i.e., $B_{min} \leq size(C) \leq B_{max}$) and are estimated to have at least P improvement. The DBA can then analyze the alert and proceed as appropriate (e.g., by explicitly performing a full physical database design session).

If implemented appropriately, a physical design alerter can diagnose hundreds of queries in the order of seconds, and the overhead imposed to the query optimizer during normal operation for generating the AND/OR tree is below 1%.

10.2 Continuous Physical Design Tuning

Although the alerting mechanism described earlier can identify when a tuning session is necessary, the subsequent physical design tuning process is unchanged. Therefore, each tuning session assumes that any change in the physical design is useful, independent of the cost of creating and dropping indexes. This might not be adequate in general, because indexes that only marginally improve performance but are expensive to create can cause unacceptable overhead on a production server. We next discuss an alternative approach to the physical design problem. Specifically, we present algorithms that are always-on and continuously modify the current physical design, reacting to changes in the workload. The techniques have low overhead and take into account both storage constraints and the cost to create temporary indexes. To simplify the presentation, in the rest of this section we abstract the functionality related to access path requests and local transformations using the following functions:

- `getRequests(q:query)`: Gets the AND/OR request tree for q encoding the requirements of each index strategy (see Section 10.1.1).

- `getBestIndex($\rho$:request)`: Gets the index that results in the cheapest alternative implementing ρ (see Section 4.1.3.3).

- `getCost($\rho$:request, $\{I_j\}$:indexes)`: Approximates the cost of the best locally transformed plan implementing ρ when $\{I_j\}$ are available (see Section 5.2.2).

We next introduce the continuous physical design tuning problem. A *configuration* is defined as the set of indexes available at some point in time. For a configuration C, we denote the cost of creating an index I as b_I^C (note that b_I^C depends on the indexes in C). Let a workload $W=(q_1, q_2, \ldots, q_n)$ be a sequence of queries and updates. As usual, we define $cost(q_i, C)$ as the estimated cost of q_i when optimized under configuration C. A *configuration schedule* $\mathcal{C}$ is a sequence of configurations $\mathcal{C}=(C_0, C_1, \ldots, C_n)$, such that q_i is executed when the DBMS is in configuration C_i. The cost of W under $\mathcal{C}$ is

$$cost(W, \mathcal{C}) = \sum_{i=1}^{n} \Big(cost(q_i, C_i) + transition(C_{i-1}, C_i) \Big)$$

where $transition(C_0, C_1) = \sum_{I \in (C_1 - C_0)} b_I^{C_0}$. Therefore, $cost(W, \mathcal{C})$ is the sum of each query cost in W under the corresponding configuration, plus the total cost to transition between configurations in $\mathcal{C}$. The optimal configuration schedule $\mathcal{C}^*$ is the one with minimum cost, so $\mathcal{C}^* = minarg_{\mathcal{C}}(cost(W, \mathcal{C}))$. An online algorithm that solves this problem must progressively determine $\mathcal{C}=(C_0, \ldots, C_n)$ *without seeing* the complete workload $W=(q_1, \ldots, q_n)$. Specifically, to determine each C_i we have knowledge only about the prefix $(q_1, \ldots, q_i)$.

10.2.1   Single-Index Scenario

To simplify the presentation, we first address the case of a single-index I. In this scenario, a configuration C is denoted as either 1 (when the given index I is present) or 0 (when it is absent). We only create I can from $C=0$, so we denote I's creation cost simply as b_I. The transition cost between configurations is given by

$$transition(C_0, C_1) = \begin{cases} b_I & \text{if } C_0 = 0 \text{ and } C_1 = 1 \\ 0 & \text{otherwise} \end{cases}$$

```
Opt-SI (W=(q₁, ... , qₙ):workload, C₀:configuration)
01   i=0
02   while (i<n)
03       if (Cᵢ=0)  // see Cases A1, A2, A3 in Figure 10.6
04           if (Case A1) Cₖ=0 for i+1 ≤ k ≤ j; i=j
05           else if (Case A2) Cₖ=1 for i+1 ≤ k ≤ j; i=j
06           else (Case A3) Cₖ=0 for i+1 ≤ k ≤ n; i=n
07       else   // Cᵢ=1, see Cases B1, B2, B3 in Figure 10.6
08           if (Case B1) Cₖ=1 for i+1 ≤ k ≤ j; i=j
09           else if (Case B2) Cₖ=0 for i+1 ≤ k ≤ j; i=j
10           else (Case B3) Cₖ=0 for i+1 ≤ k ≤ n; i=n
```

FIGURE 10.5 Optimal algorithm for single-index case. (Used with permission from Bruno, N. & Chaudhuri, S. In *Proceedings of the International Conference on Data Engineering [ICDE]*, 2007.)

We now explain how to obtain the optimal schedule C^* for a given workload W when we have information about the whole workload in advance. For that purpose, given a workload W and integers i_0, i_1, we define $\Delta(W, i_0, i_1) = \sum_{i=i_0}^{i_1} (cost(q_i, 0) - cost(q_i, 1))$. If W is clear from the context, we simply write Δ_{i_0,i_1}. Intuitively, Δ_{i_0,i_1} measures, for a subsequence of the workload, the cumulative difference in cost between the configuration that does not contain index I ($C=0$) and the one that does contain it ($C=1$). That is, executing queries $(q_{i_0}, \ldots, q_{i_1})$ without the index ($C=0$) is Δ_{i_0,i_1} units more expensive than doing it with the index ($C=1$). Therefore, we can see Δ values as the aggregated benefit (or penalty, for negative Δ values) of having the index in the configuration for a given workload subsequence.

Figure 10.5 shows how to obtain the optimal schedule using Δ values. The idea is to progressively calculate the optimal schedule C^* for longer workload prefixes by using a case-by-case analysis on the subsequent behavior of Δ. Each new partial schedule is appended to the optimal prefix after determining whether a physical change would be beneficial. Consider case $A2$ in Figure 10.6. If the benefit of the index I at a point in the future is larger than its creation cost (and is never negative), it makes sense to create I for such a period of time.

We next show that algorithm Opt-SI determines the optimal configuration schedule for an input workload W. From Figure 10.6 it follows that any instance of Δ satisfies one and only one among $\{A1, A2, A3, B1, B2, B3\}$. Algorithm Opt-SI therefore always advances i at each iteration and in doing so determines longer prefixes of the optimal schedule. Eventually, it reaches $i=n$ and terminates. We need to show that each determination in lines 4–6 and 8–10 leads to an optimal schedule. For instance, consider case $A2$ and suppose that $C_i=0$. Algorithm Opt-SI appends the subschedule $C_O=(1, 1, \ldots, 1)$ from positions $i+1$ to j. Suppose there is an alternative schedule C_A that contains at least one index deletion. C_A starts with a block of zero or more configurations

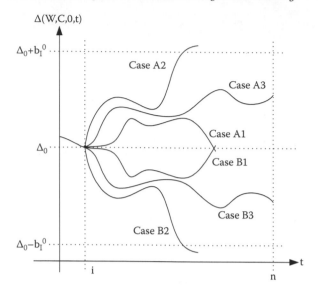

$$
\begin{array}{ll}
\text{Case A1:} & \exists j > i \text{ such that } \Delta_{i,j} \le 0 \text{ and } \forall j' < j,\, 0 < \Delta_{i,j'} < b_I \\
\text{Case A2:} & \exists j > i \text{ such that } \Delta_{i,j} \ge b_I \text{ and } \forall j' < j,\, 0 < \Delta_{i,j'} < b_I \\
\text{Case A3:} & \forall i < j \le n,\, 0 < \Delta_{i,j} < b_I \\
\hline
\text{Case B1:} & \exists j > i \text{ such that } \Delta_{i,j} \ge 0 \text{ and } \forall j' < j,\, -b_I < \Delta_{i,j'} < 0 \\
\text{Case B2:} & \exists j > i \text{ such that } \Delta_{i,j} \le -b_I \text{ and } \forall j' < j,\, -b_I < \Delta_{i,j'} < 0 \\
\text{Case B3:} & \forall i < j \le n,\, -b_I < \Delta_{i,j} < 0
\end{array}
$$

FIGURE 10.6 Possible behavior of $\Delta_{i,n}$. (Used with permission from Bruno, N. & Chaudhuri, S. In *Proceedings of the International Conference on Data Engineering [ICDE]*, 2007.)

with no index $(C=0)$, continues with a strict alternation between blocks of configurations with the index $(C=1)$ and without it $(C=0)$, and optionally ends with a block of configurations with the index $(C=1)$. Let us obtain the difference in cost between subschedules $\mathcal{C}_A$ and $\mathcal{C}_O$:

$\mathcal{C}_A$		C_1^0	b_I	C_2^1	C_3^0	b_I	C_4^1	$\ldots$	C_n^0	[	b_I	C_{n+1}^1	]
$\mathcal{C}_O$	b_I	C_1^1		C_2^1	C_3^1		C_4^1	$\ldots$	C_n^1	[		C_{n+1}^1	]
$\mathcal{C}_A{-}\mathcal{C}_O$		δ_1			δ_3	b_I		$\ldots$	δ_n	[	b_I		]

where C_i^0 and C_i^1 denote the partial cost of the blocks with configuration $C=0$ and $C=1$, respectively. Before switching from $C=0$ to $C=1$ in $\mathcal{C}_A$, we add b_I, the cost of creating I. Also, the final costs between brackets represent the optional block with $C=1$. Consider now δ_1. According to its definition, $\delta_1=\Delta_{i,i'}$ for some $i < i' \le j$. By definition of case A_2, we know that $\delta_1 > 0$. Similarly, it can be shown that $\delta_n=\Delta_{j',j} > 0$, and for each $1 < k < n$, $|\delta_k| \le b_I$ (see Figure 10.6 for additional intuition). Putting it all together,

$cost(W, C_A, i+1, j) > cost(W, C_O, i+1, j)$. (Note that if C_A contains no index creations or deletions, $C_A - C_O = C_n^0 - C_n^1 = \Delta_n > 0$ as well.) Now consider line 5 (case $A2$). Algorithm Opt-SI generates a subschedule $C_O = (1, 1, \ldots, 1)$ from $i+1$ to j. Suppose there is an alternative schedule C_A that contains at least one index deletion. Then:

C_A		C_1^0	b_I	C_2^1	C_3^0	b_I	C_4^1	$\ldots$	C_n^0	[	b_I	C_{n+1}^1	]
C_O	b_I	C_1^1		C_2^1	C_3^1		C_4^1	$\ldots$	C_n^1	[		C_{n+1}^1	]
$C_A - C_O$		δ_1			δ_3	b_I		$\ldots$	δ_n	[	b_I		]

Similar to the analysis for case $A1$, we can show that $\delta_1 > 0$, $\delta_n > 0$, and $|\delta_i| < b_I$ for the remaining cases. If C_A contains no index creations or deletions, $C_A - C_O = C_n^0 - C_n^1 = \Delta_n > 0$ as well. Putting it all together, we again have that $cost(W, C_A, i+1, j) > cost(W, C_O, i+1, j)$. We can prove case $A3$ with the same argument as for case $A1$, and cases $B1$ through $B3$ can be proved analogously to cases $A1$ through $A3$.

10.2.1.1   Online Algorithm

A careful look at algorithm Opt-SI in Figure 10.5 reveals the following property. Suppose that at some iteration we add a configuration block of $C_i = 0$. Algorithm Opt-SI will then transition to $C = 1$ if $\Lambda_{i,j} > b_I$ for the smallest $j > i$, and $\Delta_{i,j'}$ does not goes below zero for $i < j' < j$. Another way of obtaining this behavior is to maintain the minimum value of $\Delta_{0,i}$ since Opt-SI lastly transitioned to $C = 0$ (let us call it Δ_{min}) and to transition to $C = 1$ if there is $j > i$ such that $\Delta_{0,j} > \Delta_{min} + b_I$ and no $j' < j$ satisfies $\Delta_{0,j'} < \Delta_{min}$. Similarly, if $C = 1$, we maintain the maximum value of $\Delta_{0,i}$ since Opt-SI lastly transitioned to $C = 1$ (let us call it Δ_{max}), and transition to $C = 0$ if there is a $j > i$ such that $\Delta_{0,j} < \Delta_{max} - b_I$ and no $j' < j$ satisfies $\Delta_{0,j'} > \Delta_{max}$.

This alternative formulation of Opt-SI suggests an online algorithm. We maintain Δ_{min} and Δ_{max} as explained already, but instead of looking into the (unknown) future we transition configurations *after* gathering the information that proves that the optimal strategy would have done so at a past point in time. Algorithm Online-SI is shown in Figure 10.7. We note that in line 1 we need to obtain the expected cost of the input query under the "opposite" configuration. We do that without issuing an additional optimization call by using the getCost function (introduced at the beginning of this section) over the request that used (or could have used) index I. Note that we store a constant amount of information per index (i.e., Δ, Δ_{min}, and Δ_{max}). Also, every time we execute a query we update only Δ values, whose cost is negligible compared with that of executing the actual queries.

Competitive analysis: Conceptually, algorithm Online-SI lags behind Opt-SI and modifies physical designs only after the evidence that

```
Online-SI (qᵢ:query, C:current configuration)
// Initially, Δ=Δ_min=Δ_max = 0
1    δ = cost(qᵢ,0) − cost(qᵢ,1)
2    Δ = Δ + δ
3    Δ_min = MIN(Δ_min, Δ)
4    Δ_max = MAX(Δ_max, Δ)
5    if (C=0 and Δ−Δ_min ≥ b_I) Δ_max=Δ; C=1    // create index
6    if (C=1 and Δ_max−Δ ≥ b_I) Δ_min=Δ; C=0    // drop index
```

FIGURE 10.7   Online algorithm for single-index case. (Used with permission from Bruno, N. & Chaudhuri, S. In *Proceedings of the International Conference on Data Engineering [ICDE]*, 2007.)

Opt-SI would have gathered "from the future" has already passed. We now bound the suboptimality of Online-SI by presenting a worst-case scenario for which Online-SI keeps creating and dropping index I as often as possible without ever exploiting it. Consider workload $W=(q_1, q_2, q_1, q_2, \dots)$, where $cost(q_1, 0)=\epsilon+b_I$, $cost(q_1, 1)=\epsilon$, $cost(q_2, 0)=\epsilon$, and $cost(q_2, 1) = \epsilon + b_I$. The optimal schedule $\mathcal{C}^*$ for W is $(C_0=0, 1, 0, 1, 0, \dots)$. In other words, index I is built before each instance of q_1 and dropped before each instance of q_2. The cost of such a schedule is $(b_I + 2\epsilon)$ for every pair (q_1, q_2) in W. The schedule produced by Online-SI is $\mathcal{C}_{online}=(C_0=0, 0, 1, 0, 1, 0, \dots)$. The cost of such a schedule is $(\epsilon + b_I) + b_I + (\epsilon + b_I)$, or $(3b_I + 2\epsilon)$ for every pair (q_1, q_2) in W. Then, the ratio $cost(W, \mathcal{C}_{online})/cost(W, \mathcal{C}^*)$ is $\frac{3b_I+2\epsilon}{b_I+2\epsilon} < 3$ since $\epsilon > 0$. Therefore, algorithm Online-SI is three competitive (i.e., no worse than three times the optimal algorithm Opt-SI).

10.2.2   Multiple-Index Scenario

We now extend the ideas of the previous section to multiple indexes. For that purpose, we first revise the definition of Δ values to reflect this scenario. For a workload W, a configuration C, an index I, and integers i_0, i_1, we define

$$\Delta(W, C, I, i_0, i_1) = \sum_{i=i_0}^{i_1} cost(q_i, C - \{I\}) - cost(q_i, C \cup \{I\})$$

If W, C, and I are clear from the context, we simply write Δ_{i_0, i_1}. Using Δ values, we can generalize Online-SI. For each query q_i we execute Online-SI in parallel for each index $I \in \{\text{getBestIndex}(\rho): \rho \in \text{getRequests}(q_i)\}$. This is a reasonable generalization for the case of multiple indexes but suffers from some deficiencies.

10.2.2.1 Index Interactions

Consider indexes $I_1=(a, b, c)$ and $I_2=(a, b, c, d)$. If we do not consider the inherent *index interaction* between I_1 and I_2, we risk (1) underestimating Δ values for I_2 by ignoring suboptimal—but better than existing—plans that use I_2 for requests served optimally by I_1, (2) overestimating Δ values for I_1 after creating I_2 because I_2 can be a better alternative than the original one if I_1 is not present, and similarly, (3) underestimating Δ values for I_2 if I_1 is removed from the current configuration. Since `Online-SI` relies on Δ values to create and drop indexes, this problem can unexpectedly affect the resulting physical design.

Recall that, for each index I that we consider in configuration C, we need to accumulate the value $\Delta_{i_0,i_{now}} = \sum_{i=i_0}^{i_{now}} cost(q_i, C - \{I\}) - cost(q_i, C \cup \{I\})$. To simplify the notation, we use O_i instead of $cost(q_i, C - \{I\})$ and N_i instead of $cost(q_i, C \cup \{I\})$. For each incoming query q_i, we obtain O_i (original cost for q_i when I is not present) and N_i (new cost of q_i when I is present) by using `getCost` as described earlier in this section. Instead of maintaining $\Delta=\sum(O_i - N_i)$, we exploit the equality $\sum_i(O_i - N_i)=(\sum_i O_i)-(\sum_i N_i)$ and maintain these two aggregates separately. Additionally, we decompose each aggregate into four terms, $\sum_i O_i=O^0+O^1+O^2+O^U$ and $\sum_i N_i=N^0+N^1+N^2+N^U$, and modify these values depending on *how* index I is used for each request coming from the workload:

- If I's columns are required in no particular order, we add O_i to O^0 and N_i to N^0.

- If I's key column is required (e.g., for an index seek), we add O_i to O^1 and N_i to N^1.

- If more than one key column in I is required (e.g., for a multicolumn index seek or sort request), we add O_i to O^2 and N_i to N^2.

- If I is updated by the query, we add O_i and N_i from the update shell to O^U and N^U.

Since we now have more granular information about each index usage, we can handle index interactions more accurately (although still in an approximate sense). For that purpose, we define the *usefulness level* of I_1 with respect to I_2 by the following table:

Level	Condition
-1	I_1 columns do not include I_2 columns.
0	I_1 columns include I_2 columns.
1	Additionally, I_2's leading column agrees with I_1's.
2	Additionally, I_2 is a prefix of I_1.

Informally, if the usefulness level of I_1 with respect to I_2 is $l \geq 0$, then I_1 can (suboptimally) implement requests whose costs were stored in O^m and N^m components of Δ for I_2 (for $m \leq l$). Note that this is an approximation and that some indexes can help implement additional requests, but we consider these cases only to keep the overhead low. As an example, consider $I_1 = R(a, b, c)$ and $I_2 = R(a, c)$. The usefulness level of I_1 with respect to I_2 is 1, and the usefulness level of I_2 with respect to I_1 is -1. This means that all the requests whose costs were stored in (O^0, N^0) or (O^1, N^1) for I_2 can also take advantage of I_1.

Suppose that we create index I in the current configuration. We need to update the Δ values for the remaining indexes that we consider to reflect that the current configuration contains I. Then, for each index I_j, we:

1. Find l_j, the usefulness level of I with respect to I_j.

2. For each level $l \leq l_j$, set O^l to $\min(O^l, \alpha_j \cdot N^l)$, where $\alpha_j = size(I_j)/size(I)$. The rationale is that if I is created, the original cost O^l in I_j for all $l \leq l_j$ might be reduced due to I. We thus refine O^l for I_j as the minimum between the original value and a factor α_j of N^l (we linearly extrapolate the cost of index usages as a function of the index sizes). Since I_j was optimal for the requests it served, N^l values remain unchanged. The net effect is that we potentially reduce the value of Δ for index I_j as a result of creating I.

3. Adjust Δ_{min} and Δ_{max} as appropriate.

Similarly, if we drop index I in the current configuration, we update Δ values of each remaining indexes I_j as follows:

1. Find l_j, the usefulness level of I with respect to I_j.

2. For each level $l \leq l_j$, multiply O^l by β^l, where $\beta^l = O^l/N^l$ from index I. The rationale is that if I is dropped, the original cost O^l in I_j for all $l \leq l_j$ might be increased if I was originally used in the corresponding requests. We multiply the original O^l values by β^l, the average increase in cost for level l when I is not present in the configuration. Since I_j was optimal for the requests it served, the values of N^l remain unchanged. The net effect is that we might increase the value of Δ for index I_j as a result of dropping I.

3. Adjust Δ_{min} and Δ_{max} as appropriate.

When we update Δ values for index I, it is because I can optimally serve some request in the workload. Suboptimal usages are not recorded explicitly but can be approximated as follows:

1. For each index I_j under consideration, find l_j, the usefulness level of I with respect to I_j. For each level $l \leq l_j$, add to Δ for I the value $O^l - \alpha_j \cdot N^l$ from I_j, where $\alpha_j = size(I)/size(I_j)$.

2. If I is a newly considered index, find I', the most similar index to I among the considered ones using the distance function $|I \cap I'|/|I \cup I'|$. Then, subtract from I's Δ the value $(O^U - N^U)$ from I' (i.e., approximate update costs for I' from the most similar index).

FIGURE 10.8 *Residual(I, C)* and *benefit(I, C)* values. (Used with permission from Bruno, N. & Chaudhuri, S. In *Proceedings of the International Conference on Data Engineering [ICDE]*, 2007.)

Finally, note that an additional kind of index interaction results from OR nodes in the AND/OR request tree. In fact, only one of the multiple requests with an OR parent node can be implemented in an execution plan. For this reason, every time we create an index, the Δ values of the remaining indexes that were optimal for requests that shared an OR parent node need to be updated. To address this issue, we maintain an additional value per index that captures the fraction of $(\sum_i N_i)$ generated from "shared-OR nodes" and update Δ values appropriately.

Note that the techniques discussed in this section are heuristics designed to efficiently address the most common types of index interactions. Section 10.4 points to recent work that extends this approach by handling index interactions in a more principled way.

10.2.2.2 Storage Constraints

After executing an input query, there might be indexes I that should be created (i.e., indexes for which $\Delta - \Delta_{min} > b_I^C$) but no available space and no existing indexes to drop (i.e., indexes $I' \in C$ for which $\Delta_{max} - \Delta > b_{I'}^C$). To handle this common scenario, we define the *residual cost* of an index I under configuration C as $residual(I, C) = b_I^C - (\Delta_{max} - \Delta)$. If $residual(I, C) < 0$, I should be dropped from C. Otherwise, $residual(I, C)$ indicates how much slack I has before being deemed a "dropping candidate." Also, we define the *benefit* for an index $I \notin C$ as $benefit(I, C) = (\Delta - \Delta_{min}) - b_I^C$. Thus, if $benefit(I, C) > 0$, index I should be added. Also, positive values of $benefit(I, C)$ indicate the "excess in confidence" for adding I to C (see Figure 10.8 for an illustration).

Suppose that $benefit(I, C) > 0$ for some $I \notin C$, but no space is available for creating I and, for all indexes $I' \in C$, $residual(I', C) > 0$ (i.e., we cannot drop any existing index). Now, if we find a subset of indexes $C' \subseteq C$ such that $\sum_{I' \in C'} residual(I', C) < benefit(I, C)$, we know that the benefit of creating I exceeds the combined slack of indexes in C'. We can then update $C = C - C' \cup \{I\}$. There might be many choices for I and C' at any time. We next explain how we can choose among these alternatives.

Addressing the oscillation problem. Suppose that we identify a set of indexes that are useful but do not fit in the available space. We know that, by definition, $residual(I, C)$ is upper bounded by b_I^C for indexes

$I \in C$. At the same time, $benefit(I, C)$ keeps growing for $I \notin C$ as new queries arrive. Therefore, eventually indexes that are not in C would replace indexes in C. But now, the indexes we just dropped would start increasing their *benefit* values, while the ones we just created would have a bounded *residual* value. We are caught in an endless oscillation, although the relative benefit of all indexes is similar. To address this oscillation problem, we proceed as follows. Suppose that we are updating the Δ value of some index $I \in C$ with an additional δ but $residual(I, C) = b_I^C$. After updating Δ to $\Delta + \delta$, $\Delta_{\max}$ would also be updated appropriately, and $residual(I, C)$ would stay unchanged at b_I^s. To make I's benefit explicit, in these situations we proportionally decrease Δ values of all indexes $I' \notin C$ so that the new value of $benefit(I', C)$ becomes $\max(0, benefit(I', C) - \delta)$. In other words, as current indexes $I \in C$ keep being helpful, we adjust down the benefit of the remaining indexes $I' \notin C$, thus avoiding the previously described oscillations.

10.2.3   Putting It All Together

Figure 10.9 shows an online algorithm for physical design tuning. Each time a query is optimized, we generate its AND/OR request tree T and obtain the best index to implement each request. When a query is executed, we retrieve its AND/OR request tree T and update Δ values for the indexes that are not in C but optimally implement some request in T (lines 3 and 4). (We maintain in H the set of candidate indexes that were optimal for some request in the workload.) We also update Δ values for the indexes in C that were used to implement some request in T (lines 5 and 6). If the input query was an update, we refine Δ values in lines 7 and 8. Lines 1–8 are very efficient because they manipulate only in-memory values. In line 9 we drop all indexes $I \in C$ for which $\Delta_{max} - \Delta > b_I^C$. In lines 10–18 we analyze the current candidate indexes and determine if we can create (and optionally drop) indexes in C. For that purpose, we initialize $ITC = H$ and process each index in ITC. We first obtain accurate Δ values (line 13) and optionally find a subset of elements from C that, if dropped, would make enough space for I to be created. For efficiency, we periodically sort the existing indexes by $residual(I, C)/size(I)$ so that indexes that are either large or are almost dropping candidates are chosen first. In lines 15–17 we adjust the benefit of I by subtracting the combined *residual* values from C'. If the resulting benefit is the largest seen so far, we keep I as the best candidate. Finally, we lazily generate merged indexes and include them in ITC for later analysis (line 18). After all indexes in ITC are processed, we implement the best design change (if any) in lines 19–21.

We conclude this section by discussing some refinements and technical details of OnlinePT.

Impact of online index creation. There is a period of time between the asynchronous online index creation (line 21) and the time the index

```
OnlinePT (q_i:query, C:current configuration)
// Initially, H=∅ (no candidate indexes to create)
01  AOT = getRequests(q_i)
    // Update Δ values
02  foreach request ρ in AOT
03      I = getBestIndex(ρ)
04      if (I ∉ C) H=H ∪{I}; update Δ for I
05      I_used = index in C used to implement ρ
06      update Δ for I_used
07  if q_i is UPDATE on table T
08      add O^U, N^U to Δ for each index over T
    // Remove bad indexes
09  drop I ∈ C if residual(I,C) ≤ 0
    // Analyze candidate indexes to create
10  ITC = { I ∈ H such that benefit(I,C) > 0}   // candidates
11  bestI = NULL; bestB = 0; bestC'=∅
12  foreach index I in ITC
13      B_I = Δ - b_I^s
14      get prefix C' of C in residual(I',C)/size(I') order such
            that size(C-C'∪{I}) fits in the available storage
15      B_I = B_I - ∑_{I'∈C'} residual(I',C)
16      if (B_I ≥ bestB)
17          bestI = I; bestB = B_I; bestC'= C'
18      ITC= ITC ∪ { merge(I, I'): I' ∈ C ∪ ITC }
    // Create indexes (optionally removing others)
19  if (bestI is not NULL)
20      drop I' ∈ C' from C
21      create bestI in C; H= H-{bestI}
```

FIGURE 10.9 Online physical design tuning algorithm. (Used with permission from Bruno, N. & Chaudhuri, S. In *Proceedings of the International Conference on Data Engineering [ICDE]*, 2007.)

is ready to be used. During this time, queries cannot use the index, but `OnlinePT` must "understand" that the index is being created and not consider it again for creation. We achieve this by removing the index from H as soon as the creation begins, so it is not considered again in ITC at the next iteration. However, we keep updating its Δ value as new queries arrive. If the *benefit* value of the index being created drops more than b_I^s due to updates, we abort the index creation.

Supporting statistics. The cost inference in the algorithms would certainly benefit from statistics on the relevant columns. However, we cannot greedily create statistics due to the additional overhead that this would impose on the DBMS. As a middle ground, we can trigger asynchronous statistics creation tasks on the key columns of a candidate index in H whenever $\Delta - \Delta_{min}$ is larger than a fraction of b_I^S (e.g., $0.8 \cdot b_I^S$).

Thus, after we gather enough evidence about the usefulness of a given candidate index, we create supporting statistics to have more accurate information in the near future.

10.3   Summary

Motivated by complex applications with unexpected workload characteristics, new approaches to the physical database design problem are required. To address such scenarios, we showed progressively more dynamic solutions:

- Simple adaptations of offline tools that periodically tune workloads and automatically deploy the resulting configurations

- Alerting mechanisms that very efficiently can determine whether a tuning session would be worthwhile and therefore would avoid wasting resources in unneeded but expensive tuning sessions

- Continuous tuning, which incrementally maintains the physical design of a database reacting to changes in workload patterns and takes into account the cost to transition between physical design configurations.

10.4   Additional Reading

Bruno and Chaudhuri introduce the alerting mechanism described in Section 10.1 and give more details on how to handle UPDATE queries and views and how to obtain upper bounds on improvement (this effectively reduces the chances of false negatives, by bounding the best possible outcome of a comprehensive tuning tool).[3,4] Most of the content of Section 10.2 on continuous physical design tuning is taken from the work of Bruno and Chaudhuri. Some recent work in the literature describes prototypes that address online physical design tuning,[2,5,6] and discusses how to benchmark different proposals.[7] A very recent thesis discusses online tuning in great detail, and presents a principled approach based on index interactions that refines the approach described in this chapter.[8] A slightly different but related approach is an offline technique that finds the optimal physical schedule considering the workload as a sequence,[1] which helps developers writing code that takes into account physical design changes.

References

1. Sanjay Agrawal, Eric Chu, and Vivek Narasayya. Automatic physical design tuning: Workload as a sequence. In *Proceedings of the ACM International Conference on Management of Data (SIGMOD)*, 2006.

2. Nicolas Bruno and Pablo Castro. Towards declarative queries on adaptive data structures. In *Proceedings of the International Conference on Data Engineering (ICDE)*, 2008.

3. Nicolas Bruno and Surajit Chaudhuri. To tune or not to tune? A lightweight physical design alerter. In *Proceedings of the International Conference on Very Large Databases (VLDB)*, 2006.

4. Nicolas Bruno and Surajit Chaudhuri. An online approach to physical design tuning. In *Proceedings of the International Conference on Data Engineering (ICDE)*, 2007.

5. Kai-Uwe Sattler, Ingolf Geist, and Eike Schallehn. Quiet: Continuous query-driven index tuning. In *Proceedings of the International Conference on Very Large Databases (VLDB)*, 2003.

6. Karl Schnaitter, Serge Abiteboul, Tova Milo, and Neoklis Polyzotis. Colt: Continuous on-line tuning. In *Proceedings of the ACM International Conference on Management of Data (SIGMOD)*, 2006.

7. Karl Schnaitter and Neoklis Polyzotis. A benchmark for online index selection. In *Proceedings of the International Conference on Data Engineering (ICDE)*, 2009.

8. Karl Schnaitter. On-line index selection for physical database tuning. Ph.D. dissertation. University of California Santa Cruz, 2010.

Chapter 11

Constrained Physical Database Design

In this chapter we discuss some important real-world scenarios that are not adequately addressed by the physical design problem as defined in Part II. We then explain how to generalize both the problem formulation and corresponding techniques to address these limitations. Consider, as a motivating example, the following query:

```
SELECT a, b, c, d, e
FROM R
WHERE a = 10
```

and suppose that a single tuple from R satisfies a=10. If the space budget allows it, a covering index $I_C = R(a, b, c, d, e)$ would be the best alternative for the query, requiring a single input/output (I/O) to locate the qualifying row and all the required columns. Now consider a narrow single-column index $I_N = R(a)$. In this case, we would require two I/Os to answer the query (one to locate the record id (RID) of the qualifying tuple from the secondary index I_N and another to fetch the relevant tuple from the primary index). In absolute terms, I_C results in a better execution plan than I_N. However, the execution plan that uses I_N is only slightly less efficient than the one that uses I_C (especially compared with the simple alternative that performs a sequential scan over table R), and at the same time it looks simpler. If updates on columns b, c, d, or e are possible, it might make sense to penalize wide indexes such as I_C from appearing in the final configuration. However, current techniques cannot explicitly model this requirement without resorting to artificial changes. For instance, we could simulate this behavior by introducing UPDATE statements in the workload. This mechanism, however, is not general enough to capture other important scenarios that we discuss below. In any case, the previous example does not lend itself to a new "golden rule" of tuning. There are situations for which the covering index is the superior alternative (e.g., there could be no updates on table R by design). In fact, an application that repeatedly and almost exclusively executes the aforementioned query can result in a 50% improvement when using the covering index I_C instead of the narrow alternative I_N.

In general, there are several scenarios for which the traditional physical design problem statement is not adequate. In many cases we would like to incorporate additional information into the tuning process. Unfortunately, it is often not possible to do so by manipulating only either the input workload or the storage constraint. For instance, we might want to tune a given workload for maximum performance under a storage constraint, but ensuring that no query degrades by more than 10% with respect to the original configuration. Or we might want to enforce that the clustered index on a table T cannot be defined over certain columns of T that would introduce hot spots (without specifying which of the remaining columns should be chosen). Or, to decrease contention during query processing, we might want to avoid any single column from appearing in more than, say, three indexes (the more indexes defined on a column, the more contention due to exclusive locks during updates).

These examples show that a single storage constraint does not model some important scenarios in current database management system (DBMS) installations. To overcome this limitation, we need instead a generalized version of the physical design problem statement that can handle complex constraints in the solution space and that effectively restricts the search strategy to admissible solutions. In this chapter we introduce a framework that addresses this challenge.

11.1   Constraint Language

We next describe a simple constraint language that can express all the motivating scenarios discussed earlier. The constraint language understands simple types such as numbers and strings and also domain-specific ones, such as database tables, columns, indexes, and queries. It also supports a rich set of functions over these data types. As an example, we can obtain the columns of table T using `cols(T)`, the expected size of index I using `size(I)`, and the expected cost of query q under configuration C using `cost(q, C)`. We use W to denote the input workload and the following constants to specify certain commonly used configurations:

- C: Denotes the desired configuration, on top of which constraints are typically specified.

- COrig: This is the configuration that is currently deployed in the database system.

- CBase: The base configuration contains only those indexes originating from integrity constraints. Any physical design must contain such indexes, because their purpose is not improving performance but instead guaranteeing correctness. CBase contains only mandatory indexes and is therefore the worst possible valid configuration for SELECT queries in the workload and the one with the lowest UPDATE overhead.

- **CSelectBest:** This configuration is the best possible one for SELECT queries in the workload. Specifically, CSelectBest contains the best indexes that implement each access path request generated while optimizing the workload (see Section 4.1.3.3).

11.1.1 Constraint Language by Example

We next illustrate the different features of the constraint language by using examples.

Simple constraints: To specify the storage constraint that is used in virtually all physical design tuning tools we use:

$$\text{ASSERT size(C)} \leq \text{200M}$$

where size(C) returns the combined size of the final configuration. Constraints begin with the keyword ASSERT and follow the *function-comparison-constant* pattern. As another example, the following constraint ensures that the cost of the second query in the workload under the final configuration is not worse than twice its cost under the currently deployed configuration:

$$\text{ASSERT cost(W[2], C)} \leq 2 * \text{cost(W[2], COrig)}$$

For a fixed Q, the value cost(Q, COrig) is constant, so the ASSERT clause is valid.

Generators: Generators allow us to apply a template constraint over each element in a given collection. For instance, the following constraint generalizes the previous one by ensuring that the cost of *each query* under the final configuration is not worse than twice its cost under the currently deployed configuration:

```
FOR Q IN W
ASSERT cost(Q, C) ≤ 2 * cost(Q, COrig)
```

In turn, the following constraint ensures that every index has at most four columns:

```
FOR I in C
ASSERT numCols(I) ≤ 4
```

Filters: Filters allow us to choose a subset of a generator. For instance, if we want to enforce the previous constraint only for indexes that have leading column col3, we can extend the original constraint as follows:

```
FOR I in C
WHERE I LIKE "col3,*"    // LIKE does "pattern matching"
                         // on index columns
ASSERT numCols(I) ≤ 4
```

Aggregation: Generators allow us to duplicate a constraint multiple times by replacing a free variable in the `ASSERT` clause with a range of values given by the generator. In many situations, we want a constraint acting on an *aggregate* value calculated over the elements in a generator. As a simple example, we can rewrite the original storage constraint used in physical design tools using generators and aggregates as follows:

```
FOR I in C
ASSERT sum(size(I)) ≤ 200M
```

As a more complex example, the following constraint ensures that the combined size of all indexes defined over table `T` is not larger than four times the size of the table itself:

```
FOR I in C
WHERE table(I) = TABLES["T"]
ASSERT sum(size(I)) ≤ 4 * size(TABLES["T"])
```

where `TABLES` is the collection of all the tables in the database, and function `size` on a table returns the size of its primary index.

Nested constraints: Constraints can have free variables that are bound by outer generators, effectively resulting in nested constraints. The net effect of the outer generator is to duplicate the inner constraint by binding each generated value to the free variable in the inner constraint. The following constraint generalizes the previous one over all tables:

```
FOR T in TABLES
  FOR I in C
  WHERE table(I) = T
  ASSERT sum(size(I)) ≤ 4 * size(T)
```

Soft constraints: The implicit meaning of the language defined so far is that a configuration has to satisfy all constraints to be valid. Among those valid configurations, we keep the one with the minimum expected cost for the input workload. There are situations, however, in which we would prefer a relaxed notion of constraint. For instance, consider a constraint that enforces that every non-`UPDATE` query results in at least 10% improvement over the currently deployed configuration. In general, no configuration may satisfy this constraint, especially in conjunction with a storage constraint. In these situations, a better alternative is to specify a *soft constraint*, which states that the final configuration should get as close as possible to a 10% improvement (a configuration with, say, 8% improvement would still be considered valid). We specify such *soft* constraints by adding a SOFT keyword in the ASSERT clause. The resulting constraint thus becomes

```
FOR Q in W
WHERE type(Q) = SELECT
SOFT ASSERT cost(Q, C) ≤ cost(Q, COrig) / 1.1
```

Note that the traditional optimization function (i.e., minimizing the cost of the input workload) can be then specified as follows:

```
FOR Q in W
SOFT ASSERT sum(cost(Q, C)) = 0
```

If no soft constraints are present in a problem specification, we implicitly add the previous soft constraint and therefore optimize for the expected cost of the input workload. In general, however, soft constraints allow significantly more flexibility while specifying a physical design problem. For instance, suppose that we are interested in the smallest configuration for which the cost of the workload is at most 20% worse than that for the currently deployed configuration (this problem statement is useful to eliminate redundant indexes without significantly degrading the expected cost of the workload). We can specify this scenario using soft constraints as follows:

```
FOR Q in W
ASSERT sum(cost(Q, C)) ≤ 1.2 * sum(cost(Q, COrig))

SOFT ASSERT size(C) = 0
```

11.1.2   Motivating Examples Revisited

We next show that although this simple language is able to specify all the motivating examples in the previous section, the following constraint ensures that no column appears in more than three indexes to decrease the chance of contention:

```
FOR T in TABLES
    FOR col in cols(T)
        FOR I in C WHERE I LIKE "*,col,*"
        ASSERT count(I) ≤ 3
```

The next constraint enforces that the clustered index on T must start with a, b, or c:

```
FOR I in C
WHERE clustered(I)
ASSERT I LIKE "(a,*)|(b,*)|(c,*)"
```

Note that the ASSERT clause is a predicate and does not follow the pattern *function-comparison-constant* introduced earlier. We thus implicitly replace a predicate ρ with $\delta(\rho)=1$, where δ is the characteristic function (i.e., $\delta(true)=1$ and $\delta(false)=0$).

The following constraint enforces that no **SELECT** query degrades by more than 10% compared with the currently deployed configuration:

```
FOR Q in W
WHERE type(Q) = SELECT
ASSERT cost(Q, C) ≤ 1.1 * cost(Q, COrig)
```

The last constraint enforces that no index can be replaced by the corresponding *narrow* alternative without at least doubling the cost of some query:

```
FOR I in C
    FOR Q in W
    ASSERT cost(Q, C - I + narrow(I))/cost(Q, C) ≤ 2
```

where **narrow(I)** results in a single-column index with I's leading column. For instance, we have that **narrow(**$R(a, b, c)$**)** = $R(a)$.

11.1.3   Language Semantics

Constrained physical design is a multiconstraint, multiobjective optimization problem (soft constraints naturally lead to multiple optimization functions). A common approach to handling such problems is to transform constraints into objective functions (also called *c-objectives*) and then to solve a multiobjective optimization problem. We next explore this approach.

11.1.3.1   From Constraints to *C-Objectives*

Note that the *function-comparison-constant* pattern for **ASSERT** clauses enables us to assign a nonnegative real value to each constraint with respect to a given configuration. It is in fact straightforward to create a *c-objective* that returns zero if the constraint is satisfied and positive values when it is not (and moreover, the higher the *c-objective* value, the more distant is the configuration to one that satisfies the corresponding constraint). Figure 11.1 shows this mapping, where $F(C)$ denotes the constraint function over the current configuration, and K denotes the constant in the **ASSERT** clause. For constraints that iterate over multiple **ASSERT** clauses, we sum the values of the individual **ASSERT** clauses.

By proceeding in this way, each configuration is now associated with $n_s + n_h$ values for n_s soft constraints and n_h hard (i.e., nonsoft) constraints. Minimizing the n_h *c-objectives* down to zero results in a valid configuration that

Constraint	*C-Objective*
$F(C) \leq K$	$\max(0, F(C) - K)$
$F(C) = K$	$|F(C) - K|$
$F(C) \geq K$	$\max(0, K - F(C))$

FIGURE 11.1   Converting constraints into *c-objectives*.

satisfies all hard constraints while minimizing the n_s *c-objectives* results in the most attractive configuration (which might not satisfy some hard constraint). Usually, the n_h *c-objectives* are in opposition to the n_s *c-objectives* and also to each other, and therefore the search problem is challenging.

To solve this multiobjective problem, we can in principle combine all *c-objectives* together into a new single-objective function:

$$single\,Objective(C) = \sum_{i=1}^{n} w_i \cdot c\text{-}objective_i(C)$$

where w_i is a user-defined weight for the *i-th* c-objective. While this approach is universally applicable, it suffers from a series of problems. The choice of weights is typically a subtle matter, and the quality of the solution obtained (or even the likelihood of finding a solution whatsoever) is often sensitive to the values chosen. A deeper problem arises from the fact that usually *c-objectives* are *noncommensurate*, and therefore trade-offs between them range from arbitrary to meaningless.

Therefore, it is not generally a good idea to reduce the original problem to a single-objective optimization instance. A better choice is to rely on the concept of *Pareto optimality*, which looks for the set of solutions with the "best possible trade-offs."

11.1.3.2 Pareto Optimality for Configurations

The concept of Pareto optimality can be explained by using the notion of *dominance*. We say that vector $x = (x_1, \ldots, x_n)$ dominates vector $y = (y_1, \ldots, y_n)$ if the value of x along each dimension is at least as good as that of y and strictly better for at least one dimension. Therefore, assuming that smaller values are better:

$$x \text{ dominates } y \iff \forall i : x_i \le y_i \wedge \exists j : x_j < y_j$$

An element x is *Pareto optimal* in a set Y if it is not dominated by any other element $y \in Y$.

In our scenario, each configuration is associated with a vector of size $n_s + n_h$ for n_s soft constraints and n_h hard constraints, and thus we can talk about dominance of configurations. If there is a single soft constraint and all hard constraints are satisfiable, there must be a unique *Pareto optimal* solution. In fact, for a configuration to be valid, each of the n_h *c-objectives* must be zero, and thus the valid configuration with the smallest *c-objective* value for the soft constraint dominates every other configuration. For multiple soft constraints, the *Pareto optimal* solutions might not be unique but instead may show the best trade-offs among soft constraints for the set of valid configurations.

So far we have reduced a specification in the constraint language into a multiobjective optimization problem without giving an explicit mechanism to do the optimization. We next adapt the top-down framework of Section 6.2 to solve the constrained version of the problem.

11.2 Search Framework

Figure 11.2 shows a high-level architectural overview of the search framework, which is very slightly adapted from the top-down enumeration strategy of Figure 6.6. An important component of the framework is the global cache of explored configurations, shown at the bottom of Figure 11.2. This global cache contains both the set of nondominated configurations (which can be multiple in case of more than a single soft constraint) and the remaining suboptimal configurations that were explored.

Similar to the original top-down approach of Section 6.2, the search begins from the initial configuration (step 1 in the figure), which becomes the current configuration. Unless a specific initial configuration is given, the default starting point is CSelectBest, which contains the most specific indexes that can be used anywhere by the query optimizer for the input workload and thus should be appropriate to handle all but nonstandard constraints.* After choosing the initial configuration, we progressively explore the search space until a stopping condition is satisfied (typically a time bound). Each exploration iteration consists of the following steps. First, we evaluate the current configuration and store it in the global cache (step 2 in the figure). Evaluating a configuration involves obtaining the values of each *c-objective* defined in the constraint specification. Then, we perform a pruning check on the current configuration. If we decide to prune the current configuration, we retrieve from the global cache a previously explored configuration that is not pruned. At this point, we consider transforming the current configuration to generate new candidates (step 3 in the figure). The transformations that we consider are the same as for the traditional physical design problem (e.g., merging and reduction). We rank candidate configurations based on their expected promise and pick the best candidate configuration that is not already in the global cache, which becomes the current configuration. This cycle repeats until the stopping condition is met, when the database application (DBA) picks the best configuration among those that are nondominated (step 4 in the figure). The search framework eventually considers any configuration that is a subset of the closure of the initial configuration under the set of transformations. Thus, if no subset of the *closure* of the initial configuration satisfies all the constraints, the problem is unfeasible. As we can see, the search strategy is very similar to that of the traditional physical design problem. The main difference is the manner in which we rank and prune configurations, which we discuss in the rest of this section.

---

*An example of a nonstandard constraint requires that some index not useful for any query in the workload be present in the final configuration.

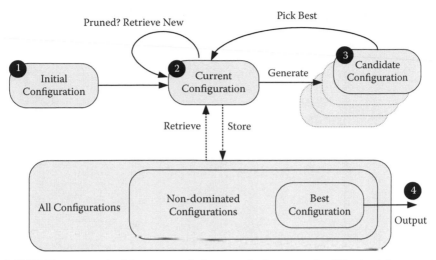

FIGURE 11.2 Architecture of the search framework. (Used with permission from Bruno, N. & Chaudhuri, S. In *Proceedings of the VLDB Journal*, 19, 1, 2010.)

11.2.1 Configuration Ranking

Using the notion of dominance, we can obtain a total ranking of configurations in two steps (similar to what is done in the context of constrained evolutionary algorithms). First, we assign to each configuration a "rank" equal to the number of solutions that dominate it. As an example, Figure 11.3b shows the rankings of all the two-dimensional vectors shown in Figure 11.3a. This ranking induces a partial order, where each vector with ranking i belongs to an equivalence class L_i, and every element in L_i goes before every element in L_j for $i < j$ (see Figure 11.3c for an illustration). Note that equivalence classes L_i are not the same as "sky-bands," where each class L_i is the skyline of the subset that does not contain any L_j ($j < i$). The final

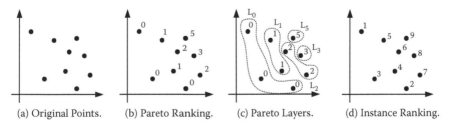

(a) Original Points.   (b) Pareto Ranking.   (c) Pareto Layers.   (d) Instance Ranking.

FIGURE 11.3 Inducing a partial order from the dominance relationship. (Used with permission from Bruno, N. & Chaudhuri, S. In *Proceedings of the VLDB Journal*, 19, 1, 2010.)

```
RankConfigurations (C=C₁, C₂, ..., Cₙ:configurations)
returns ranked list of configurations
1    foreach Cᵢ ∈ C
2        rank(Cᵢ) = |{ Cⱼ ∈ C : Cⱼ dominates Cᵢ}|
3    for i = 1 to n
4        Lᵢ = { C ∈ C : rank(C) = i }
5    R = random permutation of L
6    return R
```

FIGURE 11.4   Ranking configurations. (Used with permission from Bruno, N. & Chaudhuri, S. In *Proceedings of the VLDB Journal*, 19, 1, 2010.)

ranking is then obtained by probabilistically choosing a total order consistent with the partial order given by equivalence classes L_i (see Figure 11.3d). We shuffle elements in each equivalence class to avoid local minima due to some arbitrary ordering scheme. This step can be implemented as shown in Figure 11.4. The search strategy relies on the ability to rank configurations at two specific points. First, in step 3 in Figure 11.2, we pick the transformation that would result in the most promising configuration. Second, after pruning the current configuration in step 2 in Figure 11.2, we backtrack to the most promising configuration that can still be further transformed.

11.2.2   Search Space Pruning

The idea of pruning relies on identifying when future transformations would not be able to improve the current configuration. To handle multiple constraints, we introduce a function D that takes a configuration and the left-hand-side function F of an **ASSERT** clause and returns one of four possible values (which intuitively represent the "direction" on which F moves after applying transformations to the input configuration). Thus,

$$D : configuration \times function \rightarrow \{\uparrow, \downarrow, \leftrightarrow, ?\}$$

Recall that for any given configuration C^*, we evaluate the value $F(C^*)$ by binding the free variable C in F (i.e., the objective configuration) with C^*. The semantics of $D(C, F)$ are

$$D(C, F) = \begin{cases} \uparrow & \text{if } F(C') \geq F(C) \text{ for all } C' \in closure(C) \\ \downarrow & \text{if } F(C') \leq F(C) \text{ for all } C' \in closure(C) \\ \leftrightarrow & \text{if } F(C') = F(C) \text{ for all } C' \in closure(C) \\ ? & \text{otherwise} \end{cases}$$

As an example, consider the following constraint:

```
ASSERT size(C) - size(COrig) ≤ 200M
```

In this situation, $\mathcal{D}(C, F) = \downarrow$ for any C because any sequence of transformations starting with C will result in a smaller configuration, and therefore the value of F always decreases. Although the definition of $\mathcal{D}$ is precise, in practice it might be unfeasible to evaluate $\mathcal{D}$ for arbitrary values of F. If we cannot prove that $\mathcal{D}(C, F) \in \{\uparrow, \downarrow, \leftrightarrow\}$ we return the unknown value "?". Operationally, we evaluate $\mathcal{D}$ in a bottom-up manner. We first assign $\mathcal{D}$ values for the primitive function calls:

$$\mathcal{D}(C, size(\texttt{C})) = \downarrow$$

$$\mathcal{D}(C, size(Tables[\text{"}R\text{"}])) = \leftrightarrow$$

$$\mathcal{D}(C, cost(Q, \texttt{C})) = \text{if type}(Q) \text{ is \textsf{SELECT} then } \uparrow \text{ else ?}$$

and then propagate results through operators using rules, such as (1) $\uparrow + \uparrow = \uparrow$, (2) $\uparrow + \downarrow = ?$, and (3) $\max(\uparrow, \leftrightarrow) = \uparrow$. Consider the following example:

```
ASSERT cost(W[1], C) / cost(W, COrig) ≤ 0.1
```

In this case, if `W[1]` is a **SELECT** query, then $\mathcal{D}(C, F) = \uparrow$. In fact, $\mathcal{D}(C, \texttt{cost(W[1],C)}) = \uparrow$, $\mathcal{D}(C, \texttt{cost(W,COrig)}) = \leftrightarrow$, and $\uparrow / \leftrightarrow = \uparrow$. Constraints with generators and aggregations are handled similarly, but the inference mechanism is generally less accurate. For a constraint of the form **FOR x IN X ASSERT F(x) ≤ K** we need to check both $\mathcal{D}(C, F(x))$ for each x and $\mathcal{D}(C, |X|)$. For instance, consider a generalization of the previous constraint:

```
FOR Q in W ASSERT cost(Q, C) / cost(W, COrig) ≤ 0.1
```

If all queries in the workload are **SELECT** queries, we would obtain, as before, that $\mathcal{D}(C, F(Q)) = \uparrow$ for each Q in W. Also, since transformations do not change the workload, we have that $\mathcal{D}(C, |W|) = \leftrightarrow$. Combining these facts, we can infer that $\mathcal{D} = \uparrow$ overall (recall from Section 11.1.3.1 that in presence of generators we sum the values of each **ASSERT** clause).

Using the definition of $\mathcal{D}$, Figure 11.5 specifies sufficient conditions to prune the current configuration for a given hard constraint. Consider again the constraint

```
ASSERT cost(W[1], C) / cost(W, COrig) ≤ 0.1
```

and suppose that the current configuration C satisfies $F(C) > 0.1$ (i.e., C violates the constraint). We can then guarantee that no element in closure(C) obtained by transforming C would ever be feasible, because values of $F(C')$ are always larger than $F(C)$ for any C' transformed from C. Therefore, pruning C is safe (see Figure 11.6 for an illustration of this reasoning). For a single storage

Constraint template	Instance	$\mathcal{D}(C, F)$
$F \leq K,\ F \neq K$	$F(C) > K$	$\uparrow$ or $\leftrightarrow$
$F \geq K,\ F \neq K$	$F(C) < K$	$\downarrow$ or $\leftrightarrow$

FIGURE 11.5 Sufficient pruning conditions for hard constraints.

constraint `ASSERT size(C)` $\leq$ B, the pruning condition reduces to that of the traditional physical design problem (i.e., if the current configuration is smaller than the storage constraint, prune it and backtrack to a previous configuration).

Soft constraints: In addition to the conditions stated in Figure 11.5, pruning a configuration C based on a soft constraint additionally requires that C satisfy all the hard constraints (since any value of the *c-objective* associated with the soft constraint is acceptable, we might otherwise miss overall valid solutions).

11.2.3 Additional Search Guidance

We next show how we can alter the default search procedure by modifying the way we deal with constraints and thus obtain new functionality.

11.2.3.1 Additional Pruning Guidance

Although the technique described previously safely prunes configurations guaranteed to be invalid, certain situations require additional support.

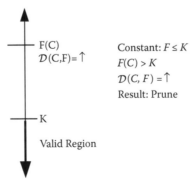

FIGURE 11.6 Sample pruning condition. (Used with permission from Bruno, N. & Chaudhuri, S. In *Proceedings of the VLDB Journal*, 19, 1, 2010.)

Suppose that we want to minimize the cost of a workload with updates using the following constraint:

$$\text{SOFT ASSERT cost(W, C)} \leq 0$$

Since the workload has updates, $\mathcal{D}(C, cost(W, C))$=?. However, suppose that the initial configuration does not contain any index on table R and that all update queries refer exclusively to table R. In this situation we *know* that the cost of the workload would always increase as we apply transformations, but the inference system might not reach the same conclusion. To address such scenarios, we augment the constraint language with annotations that override the default pruning behavior. Specifically, by adding the keyword MONOTONIC_UP (respectively, MONOTONIC_DOWN) before the **ASSERT** clause, we specify that the respective constraint function F satisfies $\mathcal{D}(C, F) = \uparrow$ (respectively, $\mathcal{D}(C, F) = \downarrow$). Of course, the framework has no way to verify whether the annotation is correct (otherwise it would have used this knowledge up front!) and implicitly trusts the annotation as being correct. The previous example can then be augmented as follows:

$$\text{SOFT MONOTONIC\_UP ASSERT cost(W,C)} \leq 0$$

11.2.3.2 Heuristic Pruning

To allow for additional flexibility in defining the search strategy, there are annotations that heuristically restrict the search space. In contrast to the previous section, these annotations result in a trade-off between search space coverage and the efficiency of the search procedure and are interesting when at least one constraint satisfies $\mathcal{D}(C, F) =$?. The search strategy keeps applying transformation rules to the current configuration with the objective to obtain the best configuration that satisfies all constraints. Since *c-objectives* are usually conflicting, a configuration that improves some objectives might move away from others. However, if the transformed configuration does not improve any objective, there might be no incentive to continue exploring beyond that point (of course, this is a heuristic and as such might prune valid solutions). We might then consider such a configuration a dead end and backtrack to a previously seen configuration. This pruning condition can be succinctly expressed using the notion of dominance. Suppose that the current configuration, C, was obtained by using some transformation over configuration C_p. Then, whenever C_p dominates C, we prune C.

Two additional annotations alter how pruning is handled for individual constraints that satisfy $\mathcal{D}(C, F) =$?. We can specify the following behaviors:

HILL_CLIMB: If a constraint is marked as HILL_CLIMB, any transformation from C_p to C that results in a value of the constraint in C that is worse than that of C_p gets pruned, even though C_p does not dominate C.

KEEP_VALID: Values of a constraint marked KEEP_VALID can go up or down from C_p to C. However, if C_p satisfies the constraint and C does not, we prune C.

The previously discussed annotations effectively change the search strategy and can be very useful. At the same time, however, they require a nontrivial understanding of the search space, its relationship with constraints, and even internals of the framework itself.

11.2.3.3 Transformation Guidance

Suppose that we want an existing index *goodI* to appear in the final configuration. We can achieve this with

```
FOR I in C
WHERE name(I) = "goodI"
ASSERT count(I) = 1
```

An alternative, more direct approach to achieve the same goal for this common scenario is

```
AVOID delete(I) WHERE name(I) = "goodI"
```

which ignores transformations that match the predicate. In general we can write

```
AVOID transformations [WHERE predicate]
```

As a less trivial example, to avoid merging large indexes we can use the following fragment:

```
AVOID merge(I1,I2)
WHERE size(I1) ≥ 100M OR size(I2) ≥ 100M
```

As with other heuristic annotations discussed in this section, the usage of these alternatives should be guided by special knowledge about the search space and its impact on the input constraints.

11.2.3.4 Handling Constraint Priorities

By manipulating the pruning conditions, we can enable a prioritized way of dealing with constraints. In this special modality, constraints are sorted in the order in which they appear in the specification, and we must satisfy them in such order. For concreteness, let the ordered constraints be $\mathcal{X}_1, \ldots, \mathcal{X}_n$, and suppose that we transform C_{before} into C_{after}. Let $\mathcal{X}_i^{\text{before}}$ and $\mathcal{X}_i^{\text{after}}$ be the score of $\mathcal{X}_i$ under C_{before} and C_{after}, respectively. We can implement prioritized constraints by pruning C_{after} whenever the following condition holds:

$$\exists\, i \le n : \mathcal{X}_i^{\text{after}} > \mathcal{X}_i^{\text{before}} \text{ and } \forall j < i : \mathcal{X}_j^{\text{before}} = 0$$

11.3   Examples of Tuning Sessions with Constraints

In this section we illustrate the constrained physical design problem with some examples based on a 1 GB TPC-H database and a 22-query workload. Suppose that we want to find a good configuration under 2 GB for which no query executes slower than 70% of the time under the currently deployed configuration (we denote that constraint, *S70*, next). The specification looks as follows:

```
FOR I IN C ASSERT sum(size(I)) ≤ 2G
FOR Q IN W ASSERT cost(Q, C) ≤ 0.7 * cost(Q, COrig)
```

After running a tool for 5 minutes, we obtained no feasible solution for this specification. Instead, the search procedure returned the nondominated configurations in Figure 11.7. We then infer that constraints are too strict. Specifically, the tight storage constraint is preventing simultaneously satisfying the *S70* constraint.

To relax the problem and obtain a solution, we can replace the hard storage constraint by the following one:

```
FOR I IN C SOFT ASSERT sum(size(I)) ≤ 2G
```

Essentially, we transform the problem into a multiobjective problem (reducing both execution time and storage) with a single *S70* constraint. As there are multiple *soft constraints*, the search strategy is not guaranteed to return a single solution. Instead, it returns the set of nondominated configurations shown in Figure 11.8. These are the configurations satisfying *S70* with the best trade-offs between size and execution cost. The figure also shows that

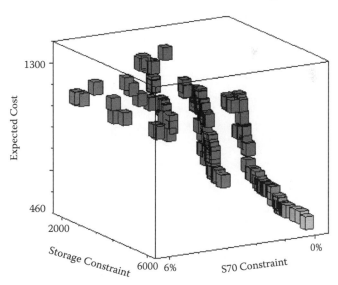

FIGURE 11.7   Nondominated configurations for *S70*.

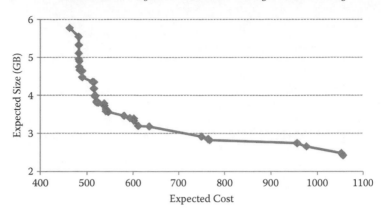

FIGURE 11.8   Nondominated configurations for relaxed *S70*.

the reason for the original specification resulting in no solutions is that the smallest such configuration requires 2.4 GB.

Suppose that we pick this *smallest* configuration in Figure 11.8 (after all, our initial hard constraint limited the storage to 2 GB). Figure 11.9 contrasts the execution cost of the queries in the workload under both this configuration and the one obtained when optimizing only for storage (i.e., when dropping the *S70* constraint) but giving the 2.4 GB storage bound that the *S70* configuration required. Each query in the figure is associated with a light bar that represents 70% of the cost of the query under the base configuration (i.e., the baseline under the *S70* constraint). Additionally, each query in the figure is associated with a narrower black/white bar, whose extremes mark the cost of the query under the configuration obtained with just a storage constraint and the configuration obtained by additionally enforcing *S70*. If the configuration obtained with *S70* is the cheaper one, the bar is painted black; otherwise, it

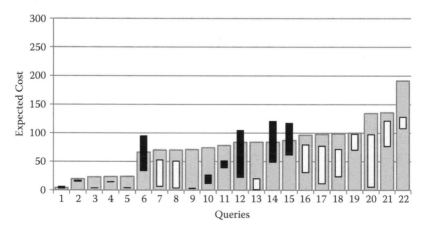

FIGURE 11.9   Expected query costs for *S70*.

is painted white. We can clearly see that the configuration satisfying $S70$ is always under the baseline (as expected). The figure also helps understand the trade-offs in cost for queries when the $S70$ constraint is additionally enforced. As with the previous example, the $S70$ constraint is worse than the storage-only constraint overall (901 vs. 1,058 units) because the search space is more restricted. However, some queries in the "no-$S70$" configuration fail to enforce the 70% bound that is required.

11.4   Summary

- As DBMS applications become increasingly complex and varied, the constrained physical design problem is an important addition to the tool set of advanced DBAs.

- A simple constraint language can express several real-world constraints easily.

- Extensions to traditional top-down solutions are able to handle multiple, possibly conflicting constraints.

11.5   Additional Reading

The field of constrained optimization has been extensively studied in the past, and the approaches vary depending on the nature of both the constraints and the optimization function. More specifically, combinatorial optimization is concerned with problems where the set of feasible solutions is discrete. A clear and rigorous book by Papadimitriou and Steiglitz describes several combinatorial optimization techniques in detail.[2] In the context of physical database design, Bruno and Chaudhuri present additional implementation details and an experimental evaluation of the approach described in this chapter.[1]

References

1. Nicolas Bruno and Surajit Chaudhuri. Constrained physical design tuning. In *Proceedings of the VLDB Journal*, 19, 1, 2010.

2. Christos Papadimitriou and Kenneth Steiglitz. *Combinatorial Optimization: Algorithms and Complexity*. Prentice-Hall, 1998.

Chapter 12

New Challenges in Physical Database Design

In this chapter we discuss some future directions and challenges in the area of physical database design. Some of the problems we introduce in the following sections have been partially addressed in the recent literature, while others remain fairly open-ended. Figure 12.1 depicts a high-level architecture of a traditional physical design tool and introduces the four challenges that we cover in subsequent sections. Specifically, we discuss the ability to (1) handle richer workloads, (2) make additional recommendations related to physical design, (3) interact with physical design tools in different ways, and (4) evaluate competing physical design algorithms in a principled manner.

12.1 Leveraging Richer Workloads

Different formulations of the physical design problem assume that the workload consists of a set (or sequence) of Standard Query Language (SQL) statements. While this is actually the case in the majority of scenarios, there are still some special cases and extensions that deserve further analysis. In this section we discuss some challenges in workload modeling.

12.1.1 Parametric Workloads

Some common workloads contain queries that repeat over time with slight variations. For instance, the following query attempts to obtain the total U.S. sales that were made in the (current) month of March 2010:

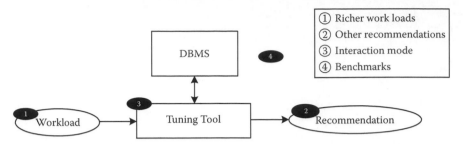

FIGURE 12.1 Some open-ended challenges in physical database design.

```
SELECT SUM(price)
FROM sales
WHERE country = 'USA'
    AND 03/01/2010 <= date < 04/01/2010
```

If the input workload was gathered over a couple of months, there might be multiple variations of this query, each one with a different country and date ranges. Techniques such as index merging can take advantage of such workloads by combining multiple range predicates into larger ones (e.g., if the workload spans 3 months' worth of reports, a recommended materialized view can contain a predicate on **date** that covers the full period). This example, however, introduces the following challenges:

Constants vs. parameters: Not all constants in a query should be treated in the same way. For instance, if the company always requires a report of all the sales in the U.S., the constant in predicate `country = 'USA'` can be included in a predicate of a materialized view. Other constants are just instances of parameter for templatized queries. For instance, in the previous query, it is likely that date ranges always vary across reports. Therefore, including any specific date range (or even a merged range) as a predicate in a materialized view might not be beneficial in general, since future queries are likely to be defined on different ranges.

Temporal workloads: Consider again the previous reporting query, and suppose that it is part of a workload gathered over a month. It is very likely that this and other similar queries refer to the same month of March (probably because it is the current—or past—month). In that case, it is highly likely that in the following month, the workload shifts **date** ranges to the month of April. Although implicit, there is a hint that queries referring to current periods of time are evolving temporal queries. These situations might not always be simple to detect automatically and can have a big influence in both static and continuous physical design tuning.

```
DECLARE @a int = 1, @b int = 0

WHILE (@b < 1000) BEGIN
    SELECT @b = @b + MIN(colB)
    FROM R
    WHERE colId < @a

    IF (@b % 2 = 0)
        SELECT @a = @a + 1
    ELSE
        SELECT @a = @a + COUNT(*)
        FROM S
        WHERE colId < @b
END
```

FIGURE 12.2 Example of an SQL script that uses control-flow statements.

12.1.2 Beyond Single-Statement SQL

Although SQL queries are the most common way of interacting with a database management system (DBMS), there are extensions that provide more flexibility and expressive power. It is common for SQL-based languages to support flow control constructs, local variables, and many other features that increase the complexity of plain SQL. Figure 12.2 shows a fragment written in T-SQL, which is Microsoft and Sybase's extension to SQL. The code fragment shows SQL statements that are executed inside WHILE loops and others that execute (or not) depending on specific values of temporary values. Specifically, we first initialize two local variables @a and @b. We then execute iteratively a sequence of statements in a loop, until the value of @b exceeds the value 1,000. During each loop iteration, we execute a query over table R, which returns the smallest value of colB that satisfies colId < @a. This result is added to the local variable @b and then, depending on whether @b is odd or even, updates the value of @a by either incrementing it by one or adding the number of tuples from S for which colId is smaller than the current value of @b. Although the example is not necessarily realistic, it illustrates features in T-SQL that lie outside pure SQL. Suppose that we want to tune the previous fragment. Just by analyzing the script, it is not clear to understand (1) how many times (if any) each SQL statement would be executed, and (2) which would be the values of @a and @b at each execution. To tune this workload, we can follow various approaches:

- We can consider each valid SQL statement in the fragment as a different query that would be executed once and can tune the resulting workload. We can also instantiate local variables by using default values.
- We can perform some form of static analysis to infer better multiplicity values for each query in the script. We might be able to infer that the

IF clause is true half of the time on average, and thus the SQL query over table R would execute twice as often as the SQL query over table S.

- We can rely on actual execution profiles to capture the actual number of executions of each SQL query. This alternative is the most accurate one but requires executing workloads, which might not be feasible in all scenarios.

These alternatives introduce an explicit tradeoff between the overhead of the estimation procedures and the quality of the resulting recommendations.

12.2　Other Aspects of Physical Database Design

The different techniques discussed in this book are mainly concerned with recommending a set of physical design structures. In a real system, there are additional issues to address in fully tuning the physical design of a database. We next summarize some of these challenges.

12.2.1　Fragmentation

Complex decision support queries usually require scanning large portions of tables (via their corresponding indexes). When data are updated, indexes can get fragmented due to B^+-*tree* page splits or simply as a consequence of re-ordering data within pages. There are two kinds of index fragmentation, both of which can have a significant impact on input/output (I/O) performance of a query. Internal fragmentation occurs when a leaf page of an index is only partially filled, thus increasing the number of pages that need to be scanned. External fragmentation occurs when the logical order of leaf pages in the B^+-*tree* differs from the physical order in which the pages occur in the data file, therefore increasing the number of random seeks required to traverse the index in order. Thus, compared with an index that is not fragmented, both internal and external fragmentation can result in more I/Os for scan-based queries.

As anecdotal evidence, during an experimental evaluation of a tuning tool, we noticed that the actual execution cost of a plan under the base configuration was twice as fast as the corresponding plan under a recommended configuration. This was odd because the recommended configuration contained a strict superset of the indexes in the base configuration, and the query did not do any updates. Even more puzzling, a closer inspection of both plans revealed that they were indeed identical (the plan under the recommended configuration used only indexes that were present in the base configuration as well). After a long debugging session, we realized that the root cause of the problem was index fragmentation. In fact, the query required a sequential scan over a large index. Since the index under the base configuration was not fragmented, the execution engine could go through the index using sequential I/O, which is very fast. In contrast, under the recommended configuration the execution engine had to do one random I/O every five disk blocks on average due to fragmentation in the index, which resulted in a larger execution time overall.

Current DBMSs expose mechanisms to defragment indexes, which compact data in pages to reduce internal fragmentation and reorder pages themselves to reduce external fragmentation. Index defragmentation, however, is a heavy-weight operation that can result in significant I/O cost and must therefore be invoked with care. Since it is usually not feasible to defragment all indexes within a typical batch window, database applications (DBAs) today use rules of thumb to select which indexes to defragment.

The granularity at which index defragmentation is supported is the full B^+-*tree*, which can be very expensive for large indexes. In many cases, however, the impact of fragmentation may not be uniformly distributed throughout the B^+-*tree*. For example, consider a clustered index on the `date` column of a large fact table that stores order information. As new data are inserted into the fact table, the B^+-*tree* gets fragmented. Often, many of the queries reference only recent data (e.g., last month or last quarter). Also, the benefit from defragmenting the index is effective only for ranges scanned by queries. Thus, the ability to perform index defragmentation for a specific range on the key column of a B^+-*tree* (e.g., `date > 06/30/2010`) can provide most of the benefits of defragmenting the full index at a lower cost. Additionally, while data-driven approaches to index defragmentation are easy to understand and implement, a purely data-driven approach can suggest defragmenting indexes that have little or no impact on query performance. This is because they ignore potentially valuable workload information (i.e., information about queries that scan the index).

Using workload information can be crucial in large data warehouses consisting of hundreds of indexes, which is typical in enterprise applications. While leveraging workload information can be important, a couple of key challenges make it difficult for DBAs to exploit workload information for index defragmentation. First, it is difficult to estimate the impact of defragmenting an index on the I/O performance of a query that scans that index. Such *what-if* analysis of the impact of defragmentation on query performance is an essential component to enable a workload-driven approach to index defragmentation. Second, even if the *what-if* analysis functionality is available, selecting which indexes to defragment for large databases and workloads is in general a non-trivial task.

12.2.2 Compression

Data compression is commonly used in modern DBMSs for different reasons, including reducing storage/archival costs (which is particularly important for large data warehouses), improving query workload performance by reducing the I/O costs, and reducing manageability costs by decreasing the time and storage needed by applications like backup/restore.

While data compression yields significant benefits in the form of reduced storage costs and reduced I/O, there is a substantial central processing unit (CPU) cost to be paid in decompressing the data during query processing. Thus, the decision on when to use compression needs to be made carefully. Given that compression increases the space of physical design options, there is a natural motivation to extend automated physical design tools to handle compression. In order to meet the storage bound as well as to reason with I/O costs during query execution, it is necessary to perform a quantitative analysis of the effects of compression. Specifically, given an index, we need to understand how much space will be saved by compressing it and how the work-load performance is impacted by compressing it. One of the key challenges in answering these questions is to estimate the size of an index if it were to be compressed. With that functionality, we can reuse the what-if approach of Chapter 5 by appropriately modifying the hypothetical index metadata. Since the space of physical design options is large, it is important to be able to perform this estimation accurately and efficiently. The naïve method of actually building and compressing the index in order to estimate its size is obviously not feasible. Thus, an important challenge to incorporate compression as another physical design dimension is to accurately estimate the compressed size of an index without incurring the cost of actually compressing it. This problem is challenging because the size of the compressed index significantly depends on both the data distribution and the specific compression algorithm. This is in contrast to the size estimation of an uncompressed index, which can be derived from the schema and table cardinality.

12.2.3   Layout

In addition to the question of which indexes to materialize, an important decision is to determine how the resulting indexes would be assigned to the available disk drives (i.e., designing the *database layout*). A good layout should result in balanced loads in the storage subsystem, or otherwise the most loaded disk would quickly become the bottleneck while others might be underutilized. Traditionally, DBMSs rely on solutions that spread out tables and indexes uniformly over all available disk drives (e.g., by relying on redundant arrays of inexpensive disks, or RAID configurations). Such alternatives are relatively easy to manage because DBAs do not need to be concerned about specific object placement. At the same time, when multiple large indexes are accessed concurrently during execution (e.g., in complex decision support queries), these solutions may perform suboptimally. The reason is interference between requests for different objects that are laid on the same disk. For instance, if two indexes are laid out in the same disk and need to be read sequentially at the same time (e.g., by a merge-based join operator), interference among I/O requests would prevent the underlying disk from exploiting sequentiality, increasing overall I/O times due to additional random seeks.

Some of the challenges involved in automatic layout recommendation include defining cost models that appropriately approximate the performance of alternative data layouts, incorporating manageability and availability requirements, reflecting the different characteristics of the underlying storage subsystems, and reacting to interference, not only from a single query but also due to concurrent execution of workloads.

12.3 Interactive Physical Design Tuning

Previous chapters discussed various extensions to the traditional physical database design problem, regarding both the kinds of physical structures to consider (Chapters 8 and 9) and generalizations to the optimizing function and constraints (Chapters 10 and 11). These extensions result in significant flexibility and provide additional control to database administrators that routinely tune physical database designs. At the same time, current physical design tools are monolithic, expose tuning options that are set at the beginning, and generate a final configuration to deploy into a production system without much further user feedback. These architectural decisions in physical design tools force users to specify the whole problem up front and prevent even experienced DBAs from making changes a posteriori or in general interacting with the system. We believe that a paradigm shift might be required to take physical database design to the next level. Specifically, physical design sessions should be highly interactive and allow DBAs to quickly experiment and validate design choices. We next discuss a possible architecture that might be more suitable for such interactive sessions.

12.3.1 An Architecture for Interactive Physical Design Tuning

Figure 12.3 shows a layered architecture for interactive physical design tools that can result in better and richer interaction with DBAs. While the two lowest layers are already implemented in commercial systems, the remaining ones differ considerably from current implementations. We next describe this architecture in more detail.

Core DBMS: The lowest layer resides within the database system and provides native support for operations such as what-if optimization (see Chapter 5) and access path request interception (see Chapter 4).

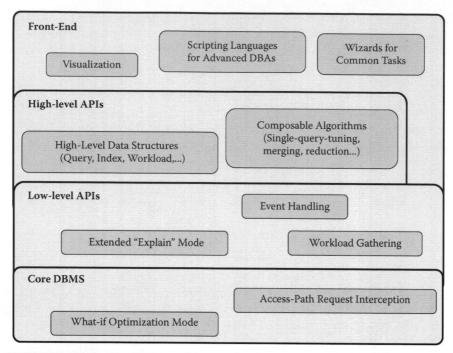

FIGURE 12.3 Architectural layers for interactive physical design tuning tools. (Used with permission from Bruno, N. & Chaudhuri, S. In *Proceedings of the International Conference on Data Engineering [ICDE]*, 2010.)

Low-level application programming interfaces (APIs): The low-level APIs expose, in formats that are simple to consume (e.g., Extensible Markup Language [XML]), the functionality related to physical design of both the core DBMS layer and the DBMS itself. As an example, this layer exposes primitives to leverage what-if functionality, and also richer explain modes after optimizing queries. These APIs also encapsulate existing DBMS functionality, such as the ability to monitor and gather workloads.

High-level APIs: The previous two layers are, in some form or another, already present in current commercial DBMSs. Physical design tools are typically built on top of the low-level APIs and expose only a rigid functionality (e.g., point to a workload, set the storage bound, and tune). A high-level API layer exposes the internal representations and mechanisms used by current physical design tools in a modular way. Basic concepts such as queries, tables, indexes, and access path requests are exposed and can be used in different ways. In addition to these data structures, the high-level API layer exposes composable and simple algorithms that are used by current tuning tools. For instance, this layer exposes mechanisms to merge two indexes or to obtain the best set of indexes for a single query. These primitive data structures and algorithms are not necessarily meant to be consumed by DBAs but instead provide a foundational abstraction for building new applications. Using these data structures and algorithms, we can rather easily build functionality similar to existing physical design tools and can package it in yet another monolithic tool. However, a more interesting alternative is to expose all data structures and algorithms in a library that can be leveraged and extended by experienced DBAs.

Front Ends: Front ends are based on both the low- and high-level APIs and deliver functionality to end users. A very powerful interaction model is a scripting platform to interact with the physical database design. The scripting language understands the data structures and algorithms exposed by the underlying layers and allows users to write small interactive scripts to tune the physical design of a database. Common tasks, such as minimizing cost for a single storage constraint, obtaining the best configuration for a given query, or other functionality provided by current physical design tools, can be implemented as scripts accessed using graphical user interfaces by relatively inexperienced DBAs.

12.3.2   A Sample Tuning Session

We next illustrate an interactive tuning session using a prototype built on top of Windows PowerShell, an interactive scripting language that integrates with the Microsoft .NET Framework. Windows PowerShell provides an environment to perform administrative tasks by execution of cmdlets (which are basic operations), scripts (which are compositions of cmdlets), or stand-alone applications or by directly instantiating regular .NET classes. The example leverages a PowerShell provider that exposes all the information about a tuning session in a hierarchical and intuitive object model (analogous to a file system). By using this provider, we can navigate and manipulate the state of a tuning session easily. Additionally, we exploit several scripts that are built by leveraging the high-level APIs discussed earlier. Figure 12.4 illustrates how an interactive approach can benefit DBAs by providing flexibility and control during physical database design. We expect that advanced DBAs could create their own scripts to further customize the physical design tuning experience. Interactive sessions have the potential to change the way DBAs think about physical database design.

12.4   Physical Database Design Benchmarks

Although there has been considerable research in techniques to address the physical design problem, much less attention has been paid to systematic methodologies to evaluate the quality of different approaches. Instead, each

```
> # create a new physical design provider
> New-PDTDrive -Name P -Database tpch1g

> # set the current location at the root of the provider
> cd P:

> # load the TPC-H workload
> $w = Get-Query -Path D:/workloads/tpch-all.sql
Reading queries from D:/workloads/tpch-all.sql...

> # get the cost of all queries in the base configuration in decreasing order of cost
> $c = Get-Configuration base
> $w | Optimize-Query -Configuration $c | sort -desc cost | out-chart -values Cost
```

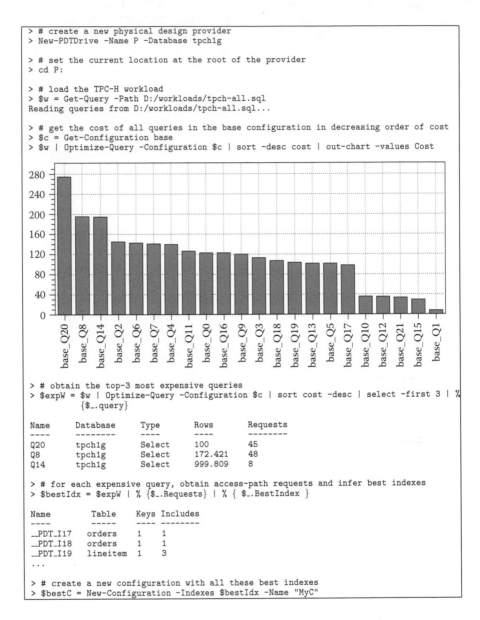

```
> # obtain the top-3 most expensive queries
> $expW = $w | Optimize-Query -Configuration $c | sort cost -desc | select -first 3 | %
          {$_.query}

Name      Database      Type      Rows      Requests
----      --------      ----      ----      --------
Q20       tpch1g        Select    100       45
Q8        tpch1g        Select    172.421   48
Q14       tpch1g        Select    999.809   8

> # for each expensive query, obtain access-path requests and infer best indexes
> $bestIdx = $expW | % {$_.Requests} | % { $_.BestIndex }

Name      Table      Keys Includes
----      -----      ---- --------
__PDT_I17 orders     1    1
__PDT_I18 orders     1    1
__PDT_I19 lineitem   1    3
...

> # create a new configuration with all these best indexes
> $bestC = New-Configuration -Indexes $bestIdx -Name "MyC"
```

FIGURE 12.4   Interactive physical design tuning example. (Used with permission from Bruno, N. & Chaudhuri, S. In *Proceedings of the International Conference on Data Engineering* [*ICDE*], 2010.)

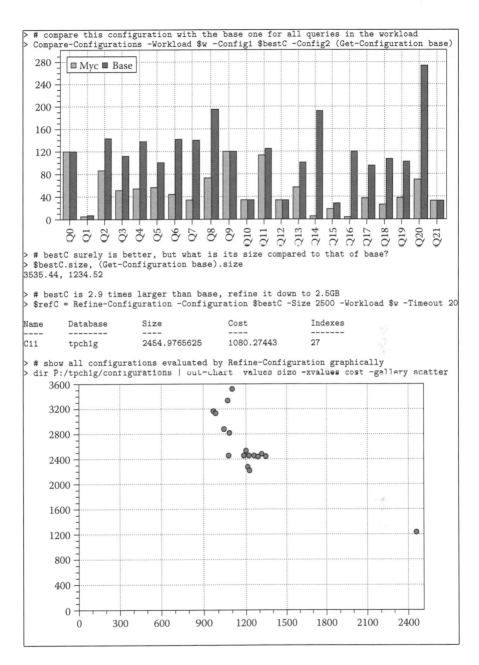

FIGURE 12.4 (Continued).

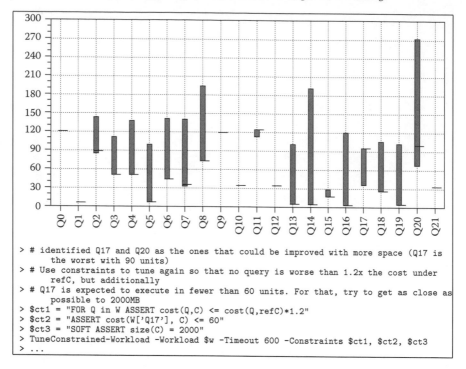

```
> # identified Q17 and Q20 as the ones that could be improved with more space (Q17 is
    the worst with 90 units)
> # Use constraints to tune again so that no query is worse than 1.2x the cost under
    refC, but additionally
> # Q17 is expected to execute in fewer than 60 units. For that, try to get as close as
    possible to 2000MB
> $ct1 = "FOR Q in W ASSERT cost(Q,C) <= cost(Q,refC)*1.2"
> $ct2 = "ASSERT cost(W['Q17'], C) <= 60"
> $ct3 = "SOFT ASSERT size(C) = 2000"
> TuneConstrained-Workload -Workload $w -Timeout 600 -Constraints $ct1, $ct2, $ct3
> ...
```

FIGURE 12.4   (Continued)

new solution is associated with a custom, ad hoc set of experiments that validate the approach. An important challenge is to devise a principled way to generate databases and workloads to compare competing tools that might be based on different approaches. Some work in the area assumes that the underlying database system does not change across alternative physical design tuners. If this assumption does not hold, it is not even clear how the different tuners could (or should) be compared. This is a rather deep problem that might have profound implications in future research on physical database design. We next comment on three components of a physical design benchmark: the set of databases and workloads to tune, a baseline configuration to compare against recommendations, and the evaluation metrics themselves.

12.4.1   Database/Workloads

A very important component of a benchmark is the actual databases and workloads over which the physical design would be tuned. Numerous examples in the literature show how careful we need to be when designing benchmarks: a poorly designed benchmark can give unfair advantage to certain approaches or can open the door to specific ways of "gaming the benchmark." Database and workload generation for the purposes of physical design benchmarking is an open area of research. Useful benchmarks should contain databases and workloads taken from at least the following three sources:

Micro-benchmarks: These are very specific databases and workloads that evaluate the different DBMS capabilities and for which optimal configurations can be manually derived.

Synthetic benchmarks: These involve complex workloads that exercise the full capabilities of the underlying query processor and cannot be manually analyzed. An example of a synthetic benchmark in the broader context of query processing is the TPC-H benchmark.

Real benchmarks: These involve databases and workloads taken (or adapted) from real-world scenarios, which can address subtle issues overlooked by the previous two approaches.

12.4.2   Baseline Configuration

Baseline configurations can be useful for standardizing results. Different alternatives are compared against a baseline, which in turn allows us to easily compare different approaches. We next discuss some ways to define baseline configurations.

Base configuration: The base configuration is the one that contains no indexes except for those required by constraints (e.g., uniqueness or foreign keys). This configuration is the worst possible one for select statements (since no indexes are available other than those that must always exist) and the best possible one for update shells (since the minimum number of indexes needs to be updated). The base configuration is also the one that has the smallest space overhead and can always be generated, as it is independent of the workload instance.

Standard indexes: A slightly more complex baseline involves considering index templates. For instance, we can consider configurations that have all possible single-column indexes available. These configurations still have the advantage that they are independent of the workload and therefore can be programmatically generated for arbitrary benchmark instances. Except for heavy-update workloads, these configurations generally result in a more reasonable baseline than the base configuration.

Manually tuned configuration: An interesting baseline results from manually tuning the database for the given workload by an expert DBA. In contrast to previous alternatives, this baseline depends on the specific database and workload and therefore cannot be generated programmatically. It is, however, a more realistic alternative to compare different approaches.

12.4.3 Evaluation Metrics

The metric used to evaluate a given physical design tool is a crucial component of a benchmark. Usually, the existing literature uses a single number to measure the quality of recommendations, called *percentage improvement*. Given a baseline configuration C_0, the percentage improvement of a recommended configuration C_R for a workload W is given by $100 \cdot (1 - cost(C_0, W)/cost(C_R, W))$. Improvement values can be negative (when the recommended configuration is less efficient than the initial one due to stricter space constraints), but always are smaller than 100%. In general, however, a single value like the percentage improvement might not provide enough detail to thoroughly evaluate and compare physical design tuners, and more detailed metrics might be necessary.

We next discuss a metric $\mathcal{M}$ that shows more detailed information about the quality of physical design solutions. Consider a workload W over a database D, and suppose that a tuner recommends configuration C for W. The quality of C using $\mathcal{M}_{C,W}$ returns, for an input time t, the number of queries in W that executed faster than t:

$$\mathcal{M}_{C,W}(t) = \frac{|\{q \in W : cost(q, C) \leq t\}|}{|W|}$$

where $cost(q, C)$ is the actual execution time of query q under configuration C. For pragmatic purposes, sometimes a time-out T_{max} is chosen and $cost(q, C)$ is capped by T_{max}. Therefore, it is always the case that $\mathcal{M}_{C,W}(T_{max}) = 1$.

Figure 12.5a shows a graphical representation of the $\mathcal{M}$ metric for three different configurations and a 22-query TPC-H workload. We can see in the figure that 90% of the queries ran in less than 500 seconds under $C1$, where only 30 and 22% of the queries did the same under either $C2$ or $C3$, respectively. The $\mathcal{M}$ metric can be used to compare multiple tuners simultaneously and makes possible some amount of goal-oriented evaluation (e.g., 30% of the queries should execute in subsecond time).

A drawback of the $\mathcal{M}$ metric is that it does not report per-query comparisons because the individual queries are sorted in different orders. It is not possible, just by looking at Figure 12.5a, to draw conclusions about the performance of specific queries. For instance, although some queries were better under $C2$ than under $C1$, Figure 12.5a does not show this fact. A complementary metric, called $\mathcal{I}$, focuses on query-by-query performance. Consider configurations C_1 and C_2 produced by two tuning tools. We then compute, for each query q_i in the workload, the value $v_i = cost(q_i, C_1) - cost(q_i, C_2)$. Clearly, positive v_i values correspond to queries that were better under C_1 than under C_2, and negative v_i values correspond to the opposite situation. We then sort v_i values and plot the results. Figure 12.5b shows the $\mathcal{I}$ metric for the same workload described earlier. We can see that at least one query results in better cost in $C2$ than in $C1$, even though $C1$ looks much better overall (as was also the case in Figure 12.5a). Although the $\mathcal{I}$ metric gives additional information on a per-query basis, it cannot be used to compare more

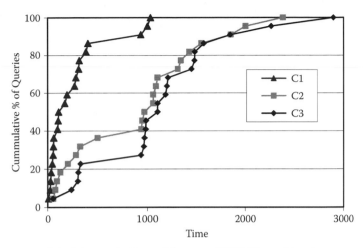

(a) $\mathcal{M}$ metric for a 22-query TPC-H workload

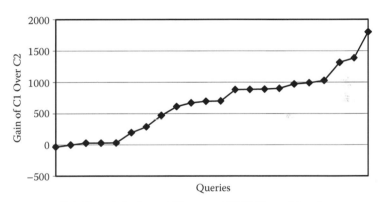

(b) $\mathcal{I}$ metric for a 22-query TPC-H workload.

FIGURE 12.5 Metrics to compare physical design tuners. (Used with permission from Bruno, N. *SIGMOD Record*, 36(4), 2007).

than two configurations. $\mathcal{M}$ and $\mathcal{I}$ are complementary metrics that provide different insights when comparing physical design tuners.

In the rest of this section we comment on some important aspects that should be considered while designing an evaluation metric.

Actual vs. estimated cost. An important question is whether to use the actual cost of executing queries in the workload or the estimated cost by the optimizer. In the context of evaluating a full system (i.e., not only the tuning tool but also the query optimizer, query processor, and even the underlying operating system), the actual query cost is clearly the best, most unbiased choice. However, if the purpose of the benchmark is an isolated evaluation of different physical design tools, execution costs are, although important, less relevant. The reason is that using execution costs potentially introduces additional variables that are outside the scope of the evaluated tool. When purely evaluating the *quality of a physical design tuner*, we should be careful to freeze any external variables. It is therefore reasonable to assume that the optimizer is correct and the physical design tool exploits accurate information. Using the optimizer's expected cost rather that the actual execution cost of queries has precisely that effect, provided that the optimizer is operating under the same statistical model for all configurations.

It is important to note the we can execute only what the optimizer considers is the best plan for a given query. Consider the following example:

```
SELECT R.*
FROM R, S
WHERE predicate(R) AND R.x=S.y
```

and suppose that the optimizer estimates that only a handful of tuples from R satisfy `predicate(R)`. If an index on $S.y$ is available, the optimizer would find that an index-based join that first gets all valid tuples from R and then looks up the matches from S might be a better alternative than, say, a hash join. Now suppose that the estimate is not right due to limitations in the optimizer's cost model and in reality that almost all tuples in R satisfy `predicate(R)`. In this case, the index-based join plan, although it is costed the lowest by the optimizer and therefore chosen if possible, would execute much slower than the suboptimal (to the eyes of the optimizer) hash-based join alternative. Now the problem is clear. Consider the previous query under the base configuration (denoted C_0) and the one that includes all single-column indexes (denoted C_1). The optimizer would pick the hash-based join-based alternative under C_0 (because there is no index on $S.y$ in C_0) and the index-based join alternative under C_1 (because the index is present). The net effect is that the execution cost under C_1 would be significantly worse than that under C_0, and we would tend to rank the tuner that produced C_0 higher than the one that produced C_1. However, note that under C_1 the optimizer *considered* the hash-based join alternative but discarded it in favor of the index-based join plan! In fact, within the optimizer's cost model, the index-based join alternative is better than the hash-based join alternative in both C_1 and C_0 (although the former plan is not implementable under C_0).

Consequences of "tweaking" metrics: It is sometimes tempting to introduce small tweaks to the evaluation metric to address special corner cases. This, however, has to be done with much care to avoid unintended consequences. We illustrate this issue with an example taken from the $\mathcal{M}$ metric. As explained earlier, the $\mathcal{M}$ metric optionally relies on a time-out value T_{max} that caps the maximum execution time of a query. Although this is a practical issue to avoid very long-running queries, it introduces some problems in the benchmark methodology. Specifically, it changes a posteriori the optimization function that has been agreed upon and leveraged in tuning tools. Consider the following extreme scenario, with a two-query workload that contains a light query q_1 that executes in 5 seconds under the base configuration C_0 and a heavy query q_2 that executes in 3,600 seconds under C_0. Suppose that a tuner T_1 optimizes q_2 as much as possible at the expense of not fully optimizing q_1, and assume that the resulting times are $(q_1=4, q_2=1,900)$, with an overall execution time of 1,905 seconds, or a 47% improvement. A second tuning tool, T_2, knowing *in advance* a given 1,800 second time-out value, might optimize q_1 without considering q_2, obtaining the following times $(q_1=1, q_2=3,600)$, with an overall execution time of 3,601 seconds, or just 0.1% improvement. Considering time-outs, the results are $(q_1=4, q_2=T_{max})$ for T_1 vs. $(q_1=1, q_2=T_{max})$ for T_2, harshly underestimating T_1's quality.

12.5 Summary

Although much work has been done in the context of the physical design problem, there are still significant challenges that need to be addressed:

- Extensions that go beyond pure SQL workloads
- Other related aspects in physical design, such as defragmentation or compression
- Interactive physical design tuning sessions for advanced DBAs
- Robust benchmarks of physical database design tools

12.6 Additional Reading

In this chapter we discussed several challenges in the space of physical database design. We now complement our presentation with some references that address some of the problems presented in the preceding sections. Our examples in Section 12.1.2 used several domain-specific extensions to SQL, which are part of the T-SQL specification.[8] In this chapter we mentioned other aspects of physical database design, such as the automatic defragmentation problem,[10] different challenges for recommending compressed indexes and estimating their sizes,[2,9] and automated layout of database objects.[1,11] Bruno and Chaudhuri[4] discuss some ideas on interactive physical design sessions and comment on the architecture that we discussed in this chapter, including the use of Windows PowerShell[7,12] as the scripting engine.[6] Some recent work discusses challenges and pitfalls in benchmarking physical design tools.[3,5,13]

References

1. Sanjay Agrawal, Surajit Chaudhuri, Abhinandan Das, and Vivek Narasayya. Automating layout of relational databases. In *Proceedings of the International Conference on Data Engineering (ICDE)*, 2003.

2. Bishwaranjan Bhattacharjee, Lipyeow Lim, Timothy Malkemus, George Mihaila, Kenneth Ross, Sherman Lau, Cathy McArthur, Zoltan Toth, and Reza Sherkat. Efficient index compression in DB2 LUW. In *Proceedings of the International Conference on Very Large Databases (VLDB)*, 2(2), 2009.

3. Nicolas Bruno. A critical look at the TAB benchmark for physical design tools. *SIGMOD Record*, 36(4), 2007.

4. Nicolas Bruno and Surajit Chaudhuri. Interactive physical design tuning. In *Proceedings of the International Conference on Data Engineering (ICDE)*, 2010.

5. Mariano P. Consens, Denilson Barbosa, Adrian M. Teisanu, and Laurent Mignet. Goals and benchmarks for autonomic configuration recommenders. In *Proceedings of the ACM International Conference on Management of Data (SIGMOD)*, 2005.

6. Microsoft Corporation. Interactive physical design tuner, 2010. Accessible at http://research.microsoft.com/en-us/downloads/f97b957c-38fb-445a-ba9e-7ebde5f2e0cf.

7. Microsoft Corporation. Scripting with Windows PowerShell, 2006. Accessible at http://technet.microsoft.com/en-us/scriptcenter/dd742419.aspx.

8. Microsoft Corporation. Transact-SQL reference, 2008. Accessible at http://msdn.microsoft.com/en-us/library/ms189826(SQL.90).aspx.

9. Stratos Idreos, Raghav Kaushik, Vivek Narasayya, and Ravishankar Ramamurthy. Estimating the compression fraction of an index using sampling. In *Proceedings of the International Conference on Data Engineering (ICDE)*, 2010.

10. Vivek Narasayya and Manoj Syamala. Workload driven index defragmentation. In *Proceedings of the International Conference on Data Engineering (ICDE)*, 2010.

11. Oguzhan Ozmen, Kenneth Salem, Jiri Schindler, and Steve Daniel. Workload-aware storage layout for database systems. In *Proceedings of the ACM International Conference on Management of Data (SIGMOD)*, 2010.

12. Bruce Payette. *Windows PowerShell in Action.* Manning Publications, 2007.

13. Karl Schnaitter and Neoklis Polyzotis. A benchmark for online index selection. In *Proceedings of the International Conference on Data Engineering (ICDE)*, 2009.

Index